Emigr...
in Australia

The Irish Emigrant Experience in Australia

Edited by
John O'Brien & Pauric Travers

POOLBEG

A Paperback Original
First Published 1991 by
Poolbeg Press Ltd.,
Knocksedan House,
Swords, Co. Dublin, Ireland

© Introduction John O Brien and Pauric Travers
© Individual articles by the authors

ISBN 1 85371 129 2

Cover design by Pomphrey Associates
Typeset by Seton Music Graphics, Bantry
Printed by The Guernsey Press Ltd.,
Vale, Guernsey, Channel Islands

Contents

Introduction

JOHN O BRIEN and PAURIC TRAVERS

Irish emigrants to Australia were not a homogeneous group; some were rich, others poor; some Protestant, most Catholic, while they came from nearly all parts of the country. Similarly, in Australia their experiences differed depending on the date of their arrival, the region in which they settled, the amount of money they brought with them or later made in Australia, chance encounters, tragedies or even just luck. All this might suggest a heterogeneity too daunting for historical generalisation, the only common thread being the fact that they all came from Ireland and went to Australia. However, for most, that memory of Ireland, reinforced by correspondence and by new arrivals, often distorted by distance and time, nevertheless affected their responses in Australia and so helped distinguish Irish from other immigrants.

The following collection of essays deals with all these aspects of the Irish emigrant experience in Australia. In the first two chapters the origins of some of the migrants are examined. Then the pattern of Irish settlement in Queensland and South Australia is investigated and finally an attempt is made to assess the influence which their Irish precedents had on selected Irish immigrants drawn from university, the legal profession, and the Church.

A true understanding of the Irish migrant experience in Australia requires an emphasis both on its Irish origins and its Australian outcomes. Trevor Parkhill traces the development of emigration from Ulster to Australia from 1790 to 1860. The real take–off in Ulster emigration to Australia dates from the last two decades of the nineteenth century but the pattern had been well established by the 1860s. The

1

pattern is broadly similar to that for the country as a whole. The departure of the first Irish convict ship from Cork in 1791 inaugurated a half century of forced emigration. The political, social and mostly ordinary criminals who filled the holds of the convict ships quickly adjusted to their new environment. By the 1820s and 1830s, more and more emancipated convicts were writing to their families in Ireland asking them to join them in their new home. From being a penal colony, Australia quickly became an attractive destination for those unhappy with their lot or eager to try their luck elsewhere. Economic depression at home pushed and the attractions of the new colonies pulled the Irish towards Australia. The relative expense of the passage to Australia compared to America limited the volume and type of emigration, at least until the advent of the various assisted passage schemes from the 1830s. Parkhill follows this transition through the stories of individual Ulster emigrants whose backgrounds and experiences illustrate the diversity of the migrant army. Convicts, tradesmen and orphans figured largely but so did businessmen and prosperous farmers' sons.

The way in which emigration responded to circumstances at both ends of the chain is graphically illustrated by the controversial scheme introduced in 1848 for the emigration to Australia of female workhouse orphans. Irish workhouses were overflowing with destitute children who were a burden on the rates while the colonies badly needed young single girls for domestic service and as wives for the predominantly male population. Joseph Robins examines the genesis of the proposal to solve both problems at once. He shows clearly how the appalling social conditions in Ireland in the 1840s made such a scheme attractive. Judy Collingwood looks at the same scheme from the other end and follows the orphans in Australia. The mixed reception they received reveals as much about prejudices in the colonies as about the girls themselves.

Eric Richards, in his study of Irish settlement in South Australia, questions the hypothesis that because the Irish were the original settlers in most of the Australian colonies, this made a great difference to them later on. He argues that in South Australia the Irish were not only latecomers but also fewer in number than elsewhere and so had to fit into a predominantly Anglo-Scottish environment. He concludes, however, that it did not make any difference; their experience in South Australia was, in Richards' opinion, essentially the same as elsewhere. He goes further and argues that the Irish experience differed little from that of other migrants. As such, he questions the importance of ethnicity in explaining migrant experience. In his view, "categories such as the Scots and the Welsh, even the Irish, are not the most useful analytical devices in studying migration."

However the Irish in Queensland, according to M.E.R. MacGinley, differed from those elsewhere due mainly to the timing of their arrival in that colony. As the majority of these settled in Queensland between 1860–90, they were, on the whole, more affluent than the Famine emigrants or those going to New South Wales earlier in the century. As a result many of the Irish in Queensland became leaders in their local communities and were among the first members of the Queensland Parliament. They were also more geographically dispersed than in other colonies, a result of the practice of transport ships stopping in many places along the Queensland coast and disembarking their passengers there.

Despite the variations in their experiences in different colonies, the memory of their early years in Ireland played an important part for most in determining their attitudes in Australia. In his survey of the origins of universities in New South Wales and Victoria, Barry Smith makes the point that "the closest exemplars of Sydney and Melbourne in time, and in organisation and methods of coping with denominational hostilities, were the Queen's colleges of Ireland". This was because of the large number of Irish graduates who filled foundation chairs in these universities, especially in Melbourne where three of its first four professors came from Ireland. In fact by the 1870s, twenty-six members of its Senate, the largest single group, were Trinity College Dublin graduates who "set the university in a peculiarly Irish legal, medical, clerical and political world that probably had no equal outside of Dublin". These men "lived their imaginative lives and indeed much of their physical lives remote from Australia", being in Professor Smith's opinion the academic equivalent of a military garrison on tour overseas. At the same time they were not dissimilar from that other "garrison", the squattocracy who also pined for the cherished values of their original homelands. While they provided Melbourne University with good standards, admired by overseas visitors, these were not necessarily shared by the local community. Not only these values but also their mode of expression is the subject of Jakelin Troy's article which traces the importance which the English and indeed the Irish spoken by early Irish migrants had on Australian English and also on Aboriginal pidgin. This was most pronounced amongst the poorer classes and Ms Troy challenges the view that the English spoken by London criminals transported to Australia was the dominant influence in the development of Australian English—the Irish she contends were equally important.

Whatever doubts historians may have about the contribution of ethnicity to the migrant experience, and some of these are explored by Bob Reece, there can be no doubt about the impact which their Irish origins had on H.B. Higgins and Daniel Mannix. Though differing in their Irish backgrounds, Higgins the son of a Wesleyan Minister and Mannix of an Irish Catholic large farmer, both cherished profoundly the qualities which they held inherent in the Irish cultural tradition. Higgins, one of the most distinguished of all the early Australian High Court judges, told his Australian born nephew that the Irish were "more sympathetic, have more delicacy of insight than English people". He reminded his nephew that his grandfather "used to say that he had never met people with such inate courtesy as the Connaught people". As proof of his enduring memory of his Irish antecedents, even after 60 years in Australia, Higgins bequeathed £20,000 to the Royal Irish Academy for the promotion of Celtic studies. Mannix was even more involved in Irish internal affairs. Because of his close friendship with de Valera and his conversion in Melbourne to Mr de Valera's republican values, Mannix, according to Dermot Keogh, sought to temper Vatican condemnation of the anti-Treaty side during the Civil War and later to entice de Valera to enter the Dail on the grounds of the nominal nature of the oath of allegiance to the Crown. He also strove to transplant the traditional Catholic values of his homeland to his own Australian diocese and pursued that course throughout his long life, despite the opposition of his more liberal co—religionists. Mannix was indeed the epitome of an Irish emigrant who lived in Australia but never really became part of it.

However, on balance, it would be more correct to conclude that most Irish emigrants to Australia soon identified with their new homeland. This is epitomised in Oliver MacDonagh's essay which, while not directly germane to our theme, is included for its insight into the continuing importance of the Irish-Australian connection. If this book has any contribution to make to the ongoing study of that process it must surely be that in highlighting the diversity of that experience it also confirms the enduring memory for most of their Irish origins.

All of the essays in this book originated as papers delivered to a conference on "Australia and Ireland: the Emigrant Experience" held in Dublin in April 1987. The conference was made possible by the financial generosity of the Irish and Australian governments. Valuable assistance was also received from the Australian Ambassador to Ireland, the Presidents of University Colleges Cork and Dublin, the President of St Patrick's College Drumcondra and the Provost of Trinity College Dublin. The organising committee consisted of F. X. Martin (chairman and chief instigator), David Fitzpatrick, Bob Reece and the joint editors of this volume. We would like to thank David Fitzpatrick for assistance in the initial preparation of this manuscript and Poolbeg Press for publishing it.

1.

Convicts, orphans, settlers: patterns of emigration from Ulster to Australia 1790–1860

TREVOR PARKHILL

> I often dream of going home but still dream of going back again [to Australia]. I think if I was at home I would not be content. I have plenty of money and friends and good health, and I feel thankful for it and am well content.[1]

James Johnston's message of buoyant expectation and confidence, contained in his letter home from Creswick Creek, 100 miles from Melbourne, was characteristic of the experience of the Ulster immigrant to Australia by 1860. By then, the number of voluntary settlers, whose passages were assisted by a variety of officially-sponsored schemes, out-weighed the forced migration which had dominated the flow from Ulster—and elsewhere—to Australia in the half century following the departure of the *Queen*, the first Irish convict ship which sailed from Cork in April 1791. The *Queen* sailed in the Third Fleet; there had of course been a proportion (estimated at 4 per cent)[2] of Irish convicts transported on the First and Second Fleets who had been tried in, and transported directly from, England. But of the 148 convicts who comprised the first emigrants direct to Australia from Ireland, one-sixth had been tried and convicted at assizes in the nine counties of Ulster. This seems a modest enough criminal achievement bearing in mind the turbulent politics and social disturbance of the 1790s. Both Shaw and Rude[3] have drawn careful distinctions between the different

6

categories of prisoners who occupied the holds of the prison ships—political, social and ordinary criminals. In all these categories, and in the other form of enforced migration, that of female orphans from the workhouses, there was always an appreciable Ulster representation.

This was particularly manifest in the "political" category of convicts who were sentenced for involvement in the attempted rebellions at either end of the period discussed here—1798 and 1848. The intellectual origins of the 1798 rebellion, and a good deal of the violence which erupted in the months of May and June of that year, had their roots in Ulster. Much of the leadership and articulation of the United Ireland movement was to be found in Ulster; the *Northern Star*, the newspaper of the movement, was published in Belfast on a regular basis from 1792 until destroyed by General Lake's forces in 1797.[4] Of the estimated 500–600 specifically political prisoners removed to Australia by the early years of the nineteenth century,[5] and of the further group of 4000–5000 social rebels, there are sufficient identifiable individuals from Ulster to confirm the province's tempestuous decade of upheaval and disaffection.

The case of William Orr, a watchmaker and native of the parish of Antrim, who was sentenced to transportation in 1799, demonstrates something of the social background of Ulster transportees. Although there is no doubt that Orr and his family were clearly part of the radical presbyterian tradition which featured prominently in the political disaffection in Ulster, his story suggests caution before classifying convicts as "political" or "social" prisoners. Orr's defence statement asserted that "the crimes with which I am charged are many and the evidence to support them rests entirely with one man." He further claimed that he left home following the burning of his mother's house by the army, "my brother being suspected of being concerned in the insurrection." He hoped to emigrate to America, "where he still intends to go if acquitted."[6] In the event, William Orr was charged with robbery, convicted and transported in 1799. After representations had been made on his behalf, he was allowed to return to Ireland in 1805 when the Lord Lieutenant of Ireland adjudged, as he did in the cases of many of the transported United Irishmen, that "there is reason to believe that Orr was unjustly charged with the offence for which he was transported."[7]

There was also clear and strong Ulster representation among the political prisoners transported after the failure of the 1848 Rebellion. Of the seven Young Ireland leaders who were transported to Van Diemen's Land, two—John Mitchel and his brother-in-law, John Martin—were Ulster farmers, Mitchel from Newry and Martin from Co. Antrim. Each kept diaries of their imprisonment which show them to be inheritors of the earlier eighteenth century Ulster radical tradition.[8] It is Mitchel's better known and widely read *Journal* which conveys much of the rather gentlemanly—certainly in comparison with the treatment experienced by "ordinary" felons—custodial lifestyle they were obliged to observe. In an unpublished letter to Dublin in 1852, he deplores his imprisonment: "It would be uncandid to pretend that with all the furtherances and appliances we have we are in content . . . Disguise itself as it will, Slavery is a bitter draught',[9] and complained of the reports he had heard of "the vulgar rogues of newspaper men in Ireland upholding me as the happiest man of modern times . . . .". Yet Mitchel's writings cannot help but reveal a pleasant enough existence, apart from his confinement. He records a serious consultation with John Martin

as to whether I should allow at length my wife and family to come out to Van Diemen's land. . . . To escape . . . clandestinely would indeed be very easy for all of us at any time, but it is not to be thought of. It is grievous to think of bringing up children in this island, yet by fixing my residence in this remote, thinly-peopled and pastoral district engaging in some sort of farming and cattle feeding, and mingling in the society of the good quiet colonists, we might almost forget at times the daily and hourly outrage that our enemies put upon us in keeping us here at all . . . in short, I do so pine for something resembling a home . . . and I have written this day to Newry, inviting all my household to the antipodes.[10]

This is a sentiment which is echoed by more mundane felons who were transported from Ulster but who developed an affection for their adopted country. Ticket-of-leave prisoners, or emancipated transportees, were at liberty to ask to have their families join them. A series of their communications both to their families and to the authorities in Dublin Castle survives and enables some suppositions to be made about the prisoners who settled in Australia, the capacity of a significant number to be adequate and progressive citizens in a developing environment, and the role convicts themselves had in establishing a chain of immigration to Australia from Ireland. The report of the select committee into education into Ireland,[11] which preceded the establishment of a national system of schooling in 1831–2, found that of the four provinces Ulster was the best provided for in terms of the ratio of schools to population and that, in the English language at least, Ulster men and women were the best educated in Ireland. So it is no surprise to find that some of the more discursive and informative communications were from Ulster prisoners seeking to persuade their families to join them.

Alexander Boyce, writing from Wollongong, New South Wales, 25 January 1835, to his wife in Belfast, exhorts her:

> On receipt of this letter ... address a Memorial to his Excellency the Viceroy of Ireland stating the then cause of you not coming and that you are now ready to join your husband ... granting you and your children a passage ... there has been many similarly situated and none ever had been refused ... [12]

He had written a similar letter three years previously but without reply. Although the three years of silence may betoken Mrs. Boyce's disapproval of her husband as a convict, leading her to keep quiet about the letter, generally speaking letters from abroad were circulated and known about. Had the letter been read by others in Belfast—where the regular departure of emigrant ships for the United States and Canada made the prospect of emigration a real and practicable proposition—there can be no doubt of the effect of

Boyce's assertion that

> there is no part of the world where an industrious man can do
> better. He can earn from 5s to 7s 6d per day . . . [and] he can
> take a piece of land on a clearing, lease for 7 years without
> any rent, all he grows is his own, free from tythes or taxes . . .
> there is another [scheme]—you can place yourself on a piece
> of government land which you may occupy until government
> may require it for sale and if you bid 5s per acre you can get as
> much as you want . . . [13]

O'Farrell confirms that this was an inspiration of emigration
for some if not many:

> The magnet effect did operate from Australia as emancipated
> convicts sought to persuade family and friends to join
> them—but weakly—they were too few and Australia [was]
> too far away to compete for Irish migrants with the stimulus
> of free or cheap passages. [14]

What the prisoners' testimonies, contained in the Free Settlers Papers, confirm, is the unexpected contribution male
and female emancipated convicts made to the Australian
settlement, from the point of view of becoming respectable
citizens, skilled craftsman, hard-working farmers, responsible
wives and mothers. For instance, Alexander Boyce in his
letter to his wife refers to

> a neighbour of mine here most respectably married named
> Sarah Cramshee who, at the time of her being transported,
> left a boy child . . . in the poorhouse . . . she is most anxious
> to get him out to her living as she is well off . . . she had been
> a kind friend to me. [15]

An account in the *Belfast Newsletter* of March 1825 reports
that Sarah Cramshee—"she was come of decent people"—
attacked one John McQuillan: "the prisoner Boyle held him
by the arm while Cramsie took his notes out of his pocket—
both guilty; transported 7 years." [16] O'Farrell also observes
that "In Australia . . . the emancipated convict Irish soon
developed modest but significant entrepreneurial qualities" [17]
and this is borne out in letters to Ulster from emancipated
convicts such as Robert Boyd, writing from Modbury County,

Murray, New South Wales: "I am happy to inform you that I am master of sixteen head of cattle which I have bought at different times with money earned after doing my governmental work."[18]

Between the rebellion of 1798 and the end of the Napoleonic Wars, much of the rural disturbance and "social" crime occurred not in Ulster, but elsewhere in Ireland. Clarke and Donnelly have commented on, and tried to explain "the comparative tranquillity of the north in the early nineteenth century."[19] The post-Napoleonic War slumps in Ireland, however, affected Ulster particularly severely for a number of reasons. It was the region whose agriculture was given over most intensively to tillage, so the post-war fall in prices for food-stuffs affected the Ulster tenant farmer badly, all the more so since there was no commensurate fall—the opposite on some estates—in the levels of rents, an impasse which made the spectre of arrears of rent inevitable. Ulster's economic prosperity in the later eighteenth century had been as much based on the development of linen spinning and weaving as on agricultural produce. This prosperity had seen a population increase whose "biological carryover" into the depressed years after 1815 created, in Crotty's phrase, "the cauldron of social and economic pressures which characterise Ireland during these years."[20]

It is against this background of population pressure and economic depression that the increasing number of transportations from Ulster to Australia after 1815 must be seen. According to Shaw, from 1817 to 1829 "more than a fifth of the 9,500 male Irish convicts transported came from Dublin, and nearly one quarter (some 2,300) from Ulster."[21] A study of the assize books of courts in Co. Antrim suggests that the "comparative tranquillity" of Ulster which Donnelly and Clark saw in their study of agrarian violence was counterbalanced by the number of larceny offences for which transportation was adjudged an appropriate punishment.[22] For example, of the 130 convictions at the Co. Antrim assizes in Carrickfergus in 1827, 80 were for grand larceny—that is, theft of goods to the value of more than 12 pence. Of these,

40 were sentenced to transportation. No other crime had more than seven convictions and those associated with Shaw's classification of "social" or "political" crime—arson, riotous assembly, houghing of livestock, murder etc. were insignificant in number. A scrutiny of newspapers in Ulster for the period 1830–45 has produced a total of 1,190 cases of sentence of transportation, which must be an underestimate by at least 50 per cent of the total.[23] However incomplete, this survey has a usefulness in showing the geographical spread of transportation—25 per cent from Belfast, 13 per cent from Co. Antrim, 12 per cent each from Co. London-derry and Co. Tyrone, 7 per cent each from Co. Donegal and Co. Armagh, and 2 per cent each from Co. Down and Co. Fermanagh. Of the 1,190 transportees from Ulster, 25 per cent were women, and this echoes Shaw's estimate that "a quarter of all the Irish transported were women, or twice the proportion of the British convicts."[24] Consequently, says Shaw, three-eighths of female prisoners in Australia were Irish, compared with only one quarter of all male convicts.

The predominant image of Australia in pre-famine Ulster must have been exclusively related to its penal role, but the Free Convicts Papers suggest that the stigma of transportation was not sufficient to deter families joining husbands and fathers (although one wife in her reply refers to the disgrace her husband has brought on her). It would be easy to make too much of the typicality of the convicts' communications and their readiness and ability to prosper from a seemingly hopeless position. But they must have done a good deal to correct the notion of the permanence of transportation and they began the process, which would be later echoed in shipping advertisements, published letters giving details of loan and free passage schemes, and in letters from emigrants themselves, of conveying the message that Australia *did* provide opportunities for enterprising individuals. All that, however, was for the 1830s and later. Until then, it tended to be men of some substance who were favoured by free land grants that served to make them leave the fruits of the success they had already achieved in Ulster. Henry Osborne left his father's substantial Co. Tyrone farm in 1828 and invested the £1,000 his father gave him as a farewell gift in Irish linen which, on his arrival in Sydney, he is reputed to have sold at a fine profit.[25] Osborne received two land grants, each of 2,560 acres at Marshall Mount, some twelve miles south of Wollongong in the finest dairy country to be found in the Illawara district. Osborne's experience on the land in Ireland—the quality of land on the family farm in Dernaseer, parish of Dromore, suggests he would have been well acquainted with mixed pastoral and arable farming—plus the right to about 30 convict labourers with his first grant, helped put his farming venture in Australia on a sound footing. He later acquired vast tracts of land between the Murrumbidgee and Murray rivers, and continued to acquire land as one of the stockowners who forced the New South Wales government to extend the "limits of location" of pasture land to the extent that, by 1850, 73 million acres of Crown land were leased to less than 2,000 farmers—an average leasehold of 30,000 acres. By 1854, Osborne himself held 261,000 acres at less than one-fifth of a penny per acre per year, including land which contained valuable coalfields at Newcastle. By 1856, three years before his death, he was referred to in a Sydney newspaper as "among the wealthiest of our country gentlemen."

Tasmania, clearly associated in the public mind with penal settlement, also attracted enterprising Ulster settlers endowed with capital. Samuel Dawson wrote the following to his father-in-law in Belfast, Dr. Robert Tennent—who may well have been the source of Dawson's means—from Claremont, Tasmania, in 1835:

> Although my property here is of considerable value, and yearly increasing therein . . . as yet all has been outlay with me but thank God I have now conquered most of the difficulties attending a settler, so that I may reasonably work for some return for all my great labour and expenditure of capital upon my farm . . . at Tempo [one of his two estates, named after the Tennent estate in Co. Fermanagh] I have about 300 head of cattle and several valuable horses, the increase from which must, by and by, be considerable.[26]

Case histories such as Osborne, the Wilson family from Broughshane, Co. Antrim and in the 1870s, Sir Samuel McCaughey from Ballymena—all of whom came from Ulster and built land business empires in Australia—are exceptional in every sense but not so rare or unique as to be discounted. Just as exceptional, at least in terms of the adaptability they brought to the developing settlements, were the immigrants from throughout Ireland whose passages to and establishment in Australia were directly aided by the colonial authorities. Fitzpatrick has commented on the eagerness with which the Australian Irish exploited government nominated schemes.[27] Ulstermen took advantage of the various assisted passage schemes which operated from the early 1830s to New South Wales and, later, to South and Western Australia, including a loan system for skilled tradesmen and their families in 1832–36, a Bounty System, 1836–45, and the remittance or nomination system, 1848–86.[28] The proportion of Ulster people who benefited from assisted passages is uncertain. O'Farrell says that "a further distinctive strand of Irish migration to Australia was that of Protestants from Ulster, an element fluctuating between 10 and 20 per cent of the Irish total."[29] However, for the pre-famine period, certainly, the percentage of Ulster people in the gradually accelerating stream of free emigrants to Australia must have been much greater than 20 per cent. W.F. Adams, in his seminal work on Irish emigration to North America between 1815 and 1845, estimated, as precisely as the sparse pre–1851 statistics allowed, that one million people emigrated from Ireland.[30] More recently, Clark and Donnelly have put the Ulster contribution to this figure as high as 40 per cent, so there is no reason to assume that the Ulster proportion of Irish emigration to Australia before 1845 numbered less than that amount, given the extent of the traffic suggested by sources here and in Australia.

Among the sources which assist a study of pre-famine Ulster emigration are the Ordnance Survey Memoirs, compiled in the 1830s.[31] The Memoirs contain information garnered from each locality, but it is only for the Ulster counties of Londonderry and Antrim that the information and details on the subject of emigration are at all helpful to research. Three parishes in Co. Londonderry—Coleraine, Kilcronaghan and Maghera—are noted as having members who left for the new colonies. In the case of all ten emigrants, comprising one family group and the rest young single males, average age 22, the destination was Van Diemen's Land. From the Co. Antrim parishes of Ahoghill, Killead and Templepatrick, a further ten individuals are noted, eight of whom went to Van Diemen's Land and two (apparently a father aged 50 and a son aged 22) to Sydney. One of the individuals in the parish of Templepatrick is described as a "farmer with £100 capital"; a sum in all probability raised from the sale of his tenant right.

There are other instances scattered throughout estate papers of the raising of capital by the sale of a tenant's "right" to receive compensation for improvements he may have made to his property during his tenancy. On the Stuart estate in Co. Tyrone a rental contains observations in the agent's hand such as, "James Alcorn held about 33 acres . . . by lease at £24.12s.6d; they went to Australia and sold with my consent to John Perry for £315."[32] There are other references to the landlord's consent to the "sale" of land: the land, since it was his, was not being sold; it was the tenant's interest in it for which the incoming tenant was paying about £10 per acre. The Devon Commission, a parliamentary enquiry on landholding in Ireland which took evidence in centres throughout the island in the early 1840s, found that in many areas of better quality land, tenant right could sometimes raise a tenant £30 per acre. There are a significant number of references in the inquiry's evidence to the value of the tenant right in assisting emigration and, although only North America is mentioned specifically in this respect, the sale of tenant right on a substantial farm was clearly sufficient in some cases to be applied to a farming family's passage to Australia. However, Lord Dungannon's agent felt that there was a detrimental side to this Ulster custom:

It is carried to too great an extent . . . the tenant, in some instances, sells at an enormously high price and he puts the money in his pocket and emigrates to America or some other part of the world and takes it with him.[33]

In the case of emigration to Australia, even where an intending emigrant and his family were having the bulk of their passage paid for by the colonial government, it remained the case that no emigration, by whatever scheme of assistance, could be contemplated without sufficient ready money to meet the expenses of the various stages of a family in the journey—from Ireland to London and thence to Plymouth followed by the lengthy 14–16 week voyage to Australia. The burden of the costs incurred in emigrating to Australia was sufficient to provoke Vere Foster in 1854 to subtitle one of his pamphlets on emigration to America, in which series he gave detailed practical advice for intending immigrants on the best means of travel, *The Advantages of Emigration to America rather than to Australia*.[34] He listed a variety of "advantages" in favour of the traditional emigrant's route, including the better prospects of work in the cities: "In America, a very large number of emigrants are much more sure of finding employment owing to there being a much larger resident population to give employment." Foster was principally concerned, however, to alert migrants to the equation that "the same money which is required for the passage of one person to Australia being nearly sufficient to carry five to America." The advertisements for sailings to Australia which appeared in the Irish press were always at pains to assure readers that the waiting time for the departure of sailing ships, a perplexing aspect of emigration which travellers to North America had found expensive since they were obliged to stay in lodging houses in the ports, was minimal. The advertisements which began to appear in Ulster newspapers in the 1830s took care to assure that

persons from all of the Three Kingdoms can join these vessels [bound for Australia] at a small cost at London or Plymouth where they can embark with certainty on the days stated, and avoid all further expense . . . limited number of married mechanics, agriculturists and shepherds will, on certain conditions, be allowed a free passage by these ships.[35]

The increasing availability of assisted or sponsored passages from the 1830s went some way towards overcoming the difficulties of the cost of transport. At a local level in north-west Ulster, there were more specific "packages", designed to attract people with farming and artisan experience and their families, advertised in the *Londonderry Sentinel* throughout the 1830s. Those named in the lists of emigrants for Van Diemen's Land and New South Wales in the Ordnance Survey Memoirs may have been early beneficiaries of a scheme thus advertised. The *Ellen*, 600 tons burthen, was advertised from July to September 1836 with the attraction that

> Her Majesty's government in order to encourage the emigra-
> tion of industrious young married couples to the Australian
> colonies will now grant towards the expenses of their passage
> a bounty or free gift of £20 for each married couple without
> regard to their trade or occupation . . . thus a man and wife
> who are possessed of £18 may be conveyed free to Van Die-
> men's Land or Sydney with all provisions for the voyage . . . [36]

In the later 1820s and 1830s, the north-west of Ulster, including the countries of Londonderry, Donegal and Tyrone, had been badly affected by the accumulating difficulties facing agriculture throughout Ireland and, more crucially, the downturn in the economic viability of the domestic linen industry, which had become more and more a declining source of income. The industrialisation processes which particularly affected the spinning of yarn from the 1820s onwards, had forced a large number of smallholders to entertain emigration as an alternative to the quandary of reduced income, increased rents and sizeable families to feed. The same newspapers which advertised Australia's advantages also carried notices from 1828 on, inserted by the Canada Land Company—whose London agent was A. C. Buchanan, himself a native of Co. Tyrone—looking for farmers and labourers with families, on the premise that family units would be a more stablising and reliable form of immigration than young mobile single people. It was with this class of tenant in mind that the notice in the *Londonderry Sentinel* for the *Ellen* also had a specific message for the overseers of parishes and others [who] now have an opportunity [of ameliorating] a condition of the poor classes by transferring the surplus to New Holland which contains an immense tract of rich land and the climate which is so healthful as 'tis lovely, where the expense of living is scarcely equal to one-third of what it is in Ireland and where there is full employment for all at higher wages.[37]

It was this sort of rhetoric—which also aimed to combat the image of the penal colony—that David Fairley, a young carpenter in the city of Derry, and his wife responded to in the mid–1830s. They emigrated armed with recommendations for his clergyman and employer sufficient to meet the requirements of the Bounty scheme for free passage to New South Wales, which praised Fairley

as a young man understanding his trade, under the age of twenty-six and most desirable as a person calculated to meet the views and plans of Government in providing and inducing young tradesmen to emigrate to New South Wales and settle in that infant colony.[38]

Generally, it is letters from immigrants detailing their observations on their new life which have proved to be most useful source materials. David Fairley did write home as soon as he landed in Sydney, and his letter was, unusually, published immediately in the Sentinel.[39] When his brother James replied to it, he remarked:

Mr. Stark was very glad to hear of your welfare and came for the letter and he kept it for 2 weeks. The most of all the gentlemen in Derry had it and thought [it] the greatest wonder ever witnessed.

Rodney Green, in his essay on emigrant letters published in 1966,[40] stresses the value immigrants' letters had in maintaining the impetus of emigration. Their example continued to be a source of curiosity and inspiration to those who remained at home. There can be no doubt that the publicity of an emigrant's letter, both within a local circle of friends and to a broader readership, demonstrated to many the practicability of a root and branch family emigration.

Fairley's published letter pulled no punches; he refers to a "very favourable passage but a great many deaths—twenty-five children and five adults, four women and one man." but the letter must have influenced the inclination to emigrate of a considerable number of families in north west Ulster.[41] It would, he wrote, give him "great pleasure to see all my brothers and friends here, where there is some reward for labour and industry." He then gave practical details on wages and living standards:

> I joined the government work with the rest of my shipmates, as a bricklayer, at two guineas per week, which is regularly paid every Saturday. A great many of the carpenters went to country gentlemen at the same wages but [also] found in house and fuel . . . where we are employed in the Governor's botanic gardens . . . we could reach almost off our scaffolds to the lemons and oranges, fig trees, pomegranates, peaches etc. and the parrots sitting on the trees beside us in flocks . . . all differing from the northern part of the globe.

Just as helpful, from the point of view of determining a clearer picture of the conditions in Ireland which emigrants were leaving and the perennial question—were they pushed by those conditions or, rather, were they pulled by the prospects of their new country?—are what Rodney Green has termed "reverse" emigrant letters. James's letter to his brother is just such an example:

> There's a great number going out by the Parland ship this year. James Bradely, a carpenter, is going out . . . there is three carpenters going from this town to Sydney . . . and William McCullough the shoemaker with whom we send this letter. You may tell Mr. Presday's friend that he is well and is a high up man in Derry.[42]

For several years in the decade prior to the Famine, a number of ships bound for Australia, among them the *Parland* which James Fairley refers to, carried tradesmen and farmers, with their families who were going to join, at least in the first crucial days on arrival, brothers, relatives, friends or work colleagues. This form of chain migration had already been established from Ulster to North America and it was its own guarantee of keeping the emigration movement to New South Wales going.

Although O'Farrell says that "very few Famine refugees came to Australia from Ireland,"[43] the constant trickle from the west of Ulster which has already been identified in the pre-Famine period continued throughout the 1840s and 1850s. But the Ulster emigrants to Australia were more displaced persons than refugees. Displaced by economic and social factors—pressure of population and rents, removal of the crutch of domestic industry—the experience gained through more than a century of reactive emigration became apparent in the carefully-staged migration to Australia of family and close friends.

Fitzpatrick's view is that chain migration not only assisted family but also community emigration[44] and certainly the Australian immigration sources, which are generally more helpful than their American counterparts in recording an immigrant's precise place of origin, reveal, in the period from 1848 and continuing into the 1860s, a regular stream of immigrants from a broad arc in south and west Ulster, taking in Lisnaskea, Enniskillen, Lowtherstown, Kesh, Strabane, Derry City and Donegal. The extent to which farming communities, both Roman Catholic and Protestant, particularly in Counties Tyrone and Fermanagh, transferred themselves to a relatively compact area of New South Wales, suggests a very strong communal tide. The recreation of a "home from home" in a new country of settlement was a feature of Irish settlement in urban America, illustrated in the lists of names contained in emigrants' letters home of people the writer has seen and who would be known at home. There is a sense of this already happening in Australia in David Fairley's letter of the late 1830s, but there is not the same continuation in later letters of this "urban village" idea. O'Farrell prefers the Canadian model for comparative purposes, where "the Irish chose not to live in villages of the close kind but to live apart from each other."[45] Emigrants of Ulster origin generally did not remain in groups, even when they emigrated with friends and relatives, or with people from the same region.

The Ulster migration to Australia, at its most dense from the west and south of the province, continued throughout the 1850s, a period for which there are more sources to make generalisations about the character of the emigrants themselves. O'Farrell makes the point that, not only did the "mass Irish population [come] from the 1850s ... in search of gold, land, fortune, and adventure," they were a "much more accomplished, venturesome and happy lot than those the Famine had dumped on America."[46] Letters back to post-Famine Ulster tend to have a ring of confidence, not only in their description of success, but also in their readiness to disclose doubts, uncertainties and misfortune and to overcome them. James Johnston, who earlier confessed himself as being very content with his new life in Australia, had emigrated in 1859 or 1860 from the family holding of some 30 acres in Crevenish, near Kesh. He is representative of the migration from western Ulster in most respects except that he travelled singly and with no intention apparent in his letters to assist other members of his family to join him. As it did for many, the lure of gold proved irresistible: "I have a good mind to try my fortune at the digging for a while. I never saw anyone from home that I knew yet."[47] (It was the Munster-Irish who dominated immigration into Victoria— from where Johnston was writing—in the 1850s and 1860s, while the Ulster immigrants tended to gravitate towards New South Wales). Having served notice of his fortune-hunting, James Johnston's next surviving letter, some four years later from Hardie's Hill, Victoria, reports:

> We have been pretty lucky in speculating since we started it. We are in weighty [?] now in four different mining companies; if they turn out well, which they are seeming to do well, we will be able to go home ... they cost us a deal of money but any speculation we make we can pretty near double our money, but the right time is not come yet. If a man has money here he can make money but without it he can do nothing.[48]

This success story had a poignant ending, however. Having assured his parents that "we will both go home together again

if things go well again this year . . . I send my respects to
Father, Mother Belle, Mary and William and hope soon to
meet again if not here I hope in a better world where toils
and trails is no more," the next chronological item in the
collection is a short note, an obituary of sorts, to the effect
that James Johnston had died of gangrene poisoning after a
perfectly innocent knife-wound he received while opening a
sack of grain.[49]

There were examples of other Ulster gold diggers who also
made good, if not by turning up the yellow nuggets, at least
by eventually establishing for themselves a way of life and
means of earning a living that was to a large degree dependent on the trades and skills they took with them to Australia.
Among these are Hugh Maguire, of Strabane, Co. Tyrone
and James Getty of Ballymoney, Co. Antrim, who both found
themselves in Melbourne in 1852–3 and whose correspondence relates their separate workings in the gold-fields and
their frequent return trips to the base of Melbourne. Maguire
is soon confessing his lack of progress:

> As far as my own success upon the diggings I must candidly
> say that up to the present time it has fell far short of what I
> expected. I was fourteen months in the diggings . . . yet I
> have been only able to come to Melbourne with about sixty-
> five pounds sterling.[50]

And although he affirms that he did not "mean to give the
diggings up, however, as I hope by perseverance to outhector
fortune and yet return a lucky Gold Digger," by 1860 his
letters home suggest his employment, which he has clearly
been in for some time, is as a traveller for a clothing firm (he
had been apprenticed to the drapery business in Strabane).

James Getty trained as a millwright in Ballymoney, Co.
Antrim and the letters he received while in Melbourne
between 1853 and 1859 from his family give useful detail on
his progress in the coalfield and then at his trade in
Melbourne.[51] These collections make it clear that the possibility of removal to Australia is merely an additional string
to the bow which played the refrain at the emigrant's wake:
both the Maguire and Getty collections refer to migration to

the United States (where some family members have clearly been long established) as well as to Australia, and there is even reference made to a family which, having left for America, then found its way to Australia. Although there is no direct evidence in either of these collections of named individuals being nominated for assisted passages, there is a raised sense of expectation in the families of joining Maguire and Getty, and this is strongly evident in the "reverse" emigrant letters of the Getty family:

> . . . would I not make as good a partner as any you have got yet. If you think so, I will go [to Australia] for it is losing time stopping in Ireland for you can make more money in one month than we can all make in one year.[52]

The social and economic difficulties of the 1840s saddled landlords and tenants alike for years after with the bequest of arrears of rent. So it was not merely philanthropy which was behind the assistance offered to tenants on the Shirley estate in Co. Monaghan in 1849 when their passages to South Australia were arranged. Major Shirley had, in fact, been assisting passages for tenants to Canada from the mid–1840s, even (apparently) before the full onset of the Famine. In fact, the ticket stubs containing the names, ages and addresses of the beneficiaries whose emigration to South Australia was being aided were originally to be used on the Canada passage, and only manuscript lists of families confirm that, in the end, a tightly-knit rural community was transplanted to Australia, helped as much by the colonial authorities' schemes as by the munificence of landlords such as Shirley in Co. Monaghan, Caledon in Co. Tyrone and others.[53] In all probability the Shirley tenants' passages were assisted by the South Australian government, although the landlord may have assisted with their outfitting or journey to the point of embarkation.

There were other schemes, not government-sponsored, to help with emigrants' passages to Australia. One of the most prominent of these in the later 1850s and 1860s was the Donegal Relief Fund. It raised money from the growing numbers of Australian-Irish with the specific purpose of helping to alleviate the distress which continued to be experienced on the west coast of Ulster and, in 1859 alone, is reported to have been responsible for the passages of one third of the 2,544 Irish who landed in New South Wales under the government's assistance scheme.[54] In all, five shiploads of Donegal migrants arrived in New South Wales and Victoria, the most renowned carrying refugees of what were to become known as the Derryveagh evictions. In 1861, 47 families on the estate of John George Adair in Co. Donegal were evicted on his orders, in the belief that a number of them had somehow been involved in the murder of his steward.[55] The consequent bitter scenes attracted much interest and it was the response of the Donegal Relief Committee to pay for the passages of 143 young men and women—mainly single people, there were only four families among them—who had not been reinstated on the Adair estate.[56] They landed, on the *Abyssinian*, in May 1862, the majority of them to take up jobs as servants and farm labourers, although the first task for many of these native Irish speakers would have been to improve their command of the English language.

Of the various assisted passage schemes in Ireland and in Australia, the female orphan scheme, which is considered elsewhere in this volume, was the shortest-lived and the most controversial. The emigration of female orphans from some Ulster workhouses to Canada had in fact been taking place from the mid 1840s. The administrators of workhouse policy were guardians of the public purse as well as of the inmates, and their task was to make economic use of the poor law rates levied to fund the workhouse. In their view, and in that of the Poor Law Inspectors, orphans had to be considered residents and, therefore, long-term drains on public money. The Poor Law Commissioners had recommended, before the female orphans to Australia movement was instituted in 1848, that local guardians should

> send as emigrants to Canada, at the cost of the Electoral Division, anyone of the able-bodied inmates of the workhouse, especially females . . . In this mode [continued

Mr. Edward Senior's memorandum] some of the permanent deadweight in the workhouse may be got rid of at a cost to the Electoral Division of about £5 or about one year's cost of maintenance.[57]

The emigration of female orphan paupers had, therefore, been in operation from a number of workhouses in the north-west of Ulster, Londonderry, Coleraine, Limavady, Strabane and Ballymoney among them. This had, of course, been the area trawled in the 1830s and early 1840s by the Canada Land Company, so it is no surprise to see A. C. Buchanan's name mentioned in the discussions in the workhouse minute books. Of the 4,000–odd orphans which Trevor McClaughlin of Macquarie University has calculated were sent, nearly 900 (just under 25 per cent) came from Ulster, so in numerical terms at least Ulster was, if anything, under-represented.[58] But it was the Belfast contingent on board the *Earl Grey* who attracted most attention, not least in the New South Wales Commission of Inquiry and Report, and in the editorials of the *Sydney Morning Herald*, for their allegedly raucous and licentious behaviour. The inquiry into the *Earl Grey* affair chose to offer a redemptive explanation for the Belfast orphans' behaviour, attributing it to "the peculiar circumstances of that town, wherein there is a great and constant demand for the labour of young girls in factories, the effect of which is to expose them at an early age to the contamination of evil example, and to familiarise them with the use of improper language."[59]

The real concentration of Ulster immigration into Australia was to come in the 1880s and 1890s. This article has sought to show the various types of emigrants and the schemes which assisted emigration, from the early days of settlement until the more traditional pattern of emigration was established in the 1860s. Before that, political prisoners, ordinary felons, tradesmen, already-established business and farming figures, orphans and what O'Farrell has described as "the rank and file of the migrant army" from Ulster have left behind evidence in a variety of forms which is useful in a number of ways. It throws light on the social and economic conditions in Ulster which prompted widespread migration. It also helps an understanding of the process of emigration and the central role of assistance, both from the state and from friends. It may be said that the evidence is, in the main, that of achievers, but enough examples have been instanced to demonstrate the constructive part immigrants from all categories—political prisoners, convicted felons, orphans, assisted migrants and settlers of independent means—had to play in establishing the Australian colonies.

References
1. PRONI, T3602/1.
2. A.G.L. Shaw, *Convicts and the Colonies* (London, 1966), p. 166.
3. G. Rude, *Protest and Punishment: the story of the political and social protesters transported to Australia, 1788–1868* (Oxford, 1978).
4. PRONI, N11.
5. Shaw, op. cit, p. 182. See also Edith Mary Johnston, "Violence Transported: Aspects of Irish Peasant society" in Oliver McDonagh and W.F. Mandle, (eds.) *Ireland and Irish-Australia* (London, 1986).
6. PRONI, T1956.
7. ibid.
8. John Mitchel, *Jail Journal*; and PRONI, D560, Diary of John Martin.
9. PRONI, T413/2, 4 October 1852 to "Miss Thomson," Dublin.
10. Mitchel, *Jail Journal*, p. 245.
11. H. C. 1826–7, XII.
12. PRONI, T3650, quoted in B. Trainor "Sources for Irish-Australia Genealogy in PRONI" in *The Irish Australians*, Ulster (Belfast, 1984).
13. PRONI, T3650, 25 January 1835.
14. P. O'Farrell, *The Irish in Australia* (Sydney, 1986), p. 62.
15. PRONI, T3650, 25 January 1835.
16. *Belfast Newsletter*, 29 March 1825.
17. O'Farrell, *The Irish in Australia*, p. 63.
18. PRONI, T3650/7.
19. Samuel Clark and James S. Donnelly Jr, *Irish Peasants: Violence and Political Unrest 1780–1914*, (Manchester, 1983), p. 149.
20. R. Crotty, *Irish Agricultural Production: Its Volume and Structure* (Cork, 1966), p. 89.
21. Shaw, *Convicts*, p. 179.

22. PRONI, ANT2/2A/1.
23. Compiled by Nigel McCarley, ACE researcher for the Ulster Historical Foundation 1985–6. I am indebted to him and to Dr B. Trainor for permission to consult this work.
24. Shaw, *Convicts*, p. 183.
25. O'Farrell, *Irish in Australia*, pp. 24–26. See also Pat MacDonnell "The Land that Osborne Left," *Familia: Ulster Genealogical Review*, Vol. 2, No. 3 (1987), Ulster Genealogical and Historical Guild.
26. PRONI, D1748/B/1/51/1–5.
27. D. Fitzpatrick, *Irish Emigration 1801–1921*. (Dublin, 1984).
28. For a summary of the various schemes see Richard Reid, "From Ballyduff to Boorowa—Irish Assisted Emigration to NSW 1830–1896" *The Irish Australians*, (UHF and Society of Australian Genealogists, 1984).
29. O'Farrell, *Irish in Australia*, pp. 100–102.
30. W.F. Adams, *Ireland and Irish Emigration to the New World, 1815–45*, (Baltimore, 1980).
31. PRONI, MIC 6. Originals in Royal Irish Academy, Dublin.
32. PRONI, D847/57/7.
33. Devon Commission pt 1, p.604, 1 April 1844, Q37.
34. PRONI, D3618/D/9/14.
35. *Belfast Newsletter*, 17 April 1838.
36. PRONI, N12/1/1, 23 July 1835.
37. PRONI, N12/1/1.
38. PRONI, T3635/1/1.
39. *Londonderry Sentinel*, 24 February 1838.
40. E.R.R. Green, "Ulster Emigrants' Letters" in *Essays in Scotch-Irish History*, (London, 1969).
41. Letter from David Fairley, *Londonderry Sentinel*, 24 Feb. 1838.
42. PRONI, T3635/2/1.
43. O'Farrell, *Irish in Australia*, p. 63.
44. Fitzpatrick, *Irish Emigration*, pp. 21–22.
45. O'Farrell, *Irish in Australia*, p. 62.
46. ibid., p. 63.
47. PRONI, T3602/1.
48. ibid.
49. ibid.
50. PRONI, D1420/2.
51. PRONI, T2052/1–4.
52. PRONI, T2052/1.
53. PRONI, D3531/P/1–5; also described in Nigel McCarley, "Where did they go?" *Familia: Ulster Genealogical Review*, Vol. 2,

No. 2 (1986).
54. O'Farrell, *Irish in Australia*, pp. 69–70.
55. W.E. Vaughan, *Sin, Sheep and Scotsmen: John George Adair and the Derryveagh Evictions, 1861*, (Belfast, 1983); see also W.E. Vaughan, *Landlord and Tenants in Ireland, 1848–1904*, (Dublin, 1984), pp. 10–12.
56. O'Farrell, *Irish in Australia*, pp. 69–70.
57. PRONI, BG5/A/2.
58. I am grateful to Trevor McClaughlin, Senior Lecturer, Department of History, Macquarie University for a preview of the results of his research on the female orphans.
59. NSW Legislature Report and Proceedings, June 1850.

2.
The emigration of Irish workhouse children to Australia in the 19th century

JOSEPH ROBINS

The aim of this article is to describe a scheme, and the social circumstances that gave rise to it, for the emigration to Australia of young female orphans from the Irish workhouse during the period 1848–1850. Apart from its unusual and dramatic nature, the scheme is of interest as an example of government attempts to solve two social problems simultaneously:—the Poor Law problem of the burden of a huge number of children in Irish workhouses and the colonisation problem of easing the dire shortage of wives for the male population of Australia. Judy Collingwood, in the article which follows mine, will view the scheme and its outcome from the Australian end. I shall confine myself as far as possible to the Irish side of the story.

There are two aspects to this account. Firstly, I will deal with the circumstances in which a great many children were thrown on public charity during the period under consideration. The main influence was, of course, the impact of the Great Famine but there were other influences existing prior to the Famine and within the Famine years themselves which led to the accumulation of a great number of workhouse children. I will give you some impression of the Irish workhouse system to illustrate why the prospect of a new life elsewhere must have been attractive to the children who were trapped in the system. Secondly, I will deal with the manner in which the orphan emigration scheme to Australia was organised and operated.

It is relevant first of all to look at the demographic pattern prior to the 1840s. Large numbers of children had become a feature of the typical Irish family. Despite frequent fever epidemics and a level of subsistence never far from starvation, the population of Ireland increased rapidly during the early decades of the nineteenth century. The poor married early to reproduce abundantly. John Carr, an English visitor, noted in 1860 that "the want of an establishment never affects the brain of an enamoured rustic."[1] A mud cabin was quickly constructed and in this spartan abode the newly-married couple set about procreating a large family. By 1841 the population had risen to 8.2 million compared with about 3 million a century earlier.[2]

Obviously in the prevailing social conditions—a level of subsistence hardly above starvation level, intermittent famine and epidemics—it was to be expected that there would be large numbers of children whose care would fall upon public charity. While, however, there were some minor institutional provisions for children, the position generally during the 1830s was that there were few havens for them.[3]

There was, as yet, no poor law system. Prior to the 1830s the main government-supported institutions for the care of pauper children had been the charter schools, the Foundling Hospital in Dublin and, to a lesser extent, the Cork Foundling Hospital. The schools and the hospitals had operated throughout the eighteenth century primarily as centres to proselytise Catholic children, that was to secure their conversion to the Protestant faith. They were considerably resented by the majority population and gave rise to a deep distrust of government-supported institutions in general. Eventually, however, with the gradual emancipation of the Catholics the charter schools and foundling hospitals became an embarrassment to the government which was now anxious to show its impartiality in religious matters. The foundling hospitals were closed and the charter schools, which were operated by a Society consisting of members of the Protestant ascendancy, had the government's financial support withdrawn from them.

As already noted there were few havens for the homeless child in the 1830s. Francis White, secretary to an *ad hoc* board of guardians established to deal with a cholera epidemic, reported in 1833 that about 1,000 children from poor families who had been orphaned in Dublin by the epidemic had become wandering beggars "during a life of the most awful and precarious existence."[4] In rural areas the picture was similar. For instance, in Aughvale parish in Co. Mayo a large proportion of 300 children who had lost their parents in an epidemic had become beggars. And a similar picture emerges about other areas from government reports of the period on Irish poverty.[5]

Despite earlier government reluctance to provide a Poor Law for Ireland it had become inevitable by the end of the 1830s in a situation where the population was continuing to increase and social conditions were rapidly deteriorating. The Irish poor law system was established by the Poor Relief Act of 1838. It consisted of 130 unions—groups of parishes— in each of which a large workhouse was to provide for the relief of paupers from the area. As a system of public charity it was extremely harsh both in concept and operation. It was based largely on the misbegotten belief that it was required to deal with a work-shy population, who would abuse it, if there was any opportunity to do so, to the great cost of the property-owning, tax-paying classes.

The workhouses were spartan centres with a regimen that was deliberately "irksome" that is, organised in such a way as to goad the pauper into making his departure as soon as possible. The buildings were cold and unfriendly with mud floors; they were surrounded by high prison-like walls; all inmates had to wear the rough workhouse garb which carried the name of the union imprinted on it in large letters. There were two poor meals a day. The strict rules, if broken, could be punished by imprisonment in the local gaol.

Under the workhouse rules at this period, the whole family had to enter together; as they entered, they were broken up and segregated in different parts of the institution. There was no question of a father putting in his family while he sought a livelihood outside to enable him to take them out again. They did not have the choice of receiving relief outside the workhouse. For them the "workhouse test" operated: the choice of suffering the indignities of the workhouse or starving by the roadside. Later a restricted form of outdoor relief was introduced, but the main thrust of Poor Law policy remained firmly based on admission to the workhouse.[6]

Another deterrent provision, initiated as the numbers entering the workhouses started to alarm the authorities, was the obligation on a family to give up any land it might possess in excess of a quarter acre. Of all the punitive provisions of the Poor Law this was probably the most resented by the Irish peasant. Whole families died at the height of the Great Famine rather than give up their patch of land for the modicum of food they would receive in the workhouse.

The "poorhouse," as it came to be called, became an object of shame resented by every self-respecting individual and shunned even by many of the hungry during the conditions of deprivation which prevailed in Ireland not only during the famine years 1845–1849, but for several decades subsequently. However, the workhouses, when they opened in the early 1840s, did meet an immediate need. While they were shunned by the self-respecting, there were many who could not be choosers. Unmarried mothers and their infants sought their protection from a disapproving society. But the largest group of all were orphaned and deserted children. There was very little public provision for them immediately prior to the introduction of the Poor Law. With the opening of the first workhouse, the Catholic clergy and others concerned with their welfare directed children in need of care towards the workhouse. The fear that these new institutions of the State would become proselytising centres, as had been the experience of the past, rapidly disappeared as it became obvious that the central Poor Law Commissioners were determined that no matter what other indignities they might impose on the individual, his religion should not be placed under any threat.

Furthermore, the Catholic authorities were particularly worried about the activities outside the workhouse of the Protestant bible societies, evangelical organisations whose primary aim was to attract Catholics. The increasing wretchedness of the rapidly expanding and impoverished population, culminating in the terrible climax of the Great Famine, offered the societies an obvious means of weakening resistance to their message without undue violence to their conscience. The feeding of the hungry and the clothing of the naked had always been recommended Christian works of mercy. The bible societies turned to this work with great enthusiasm. If there were those outside these organisations who saw in this development a cruel device for winning the hungry Catholic from his religion, there were others within the societies who regarded as divinely inspired the opportunities offered by conditions of mass starvation. Revd Alexander Dallas, the driving force behind the Society for the Irish Missions to Roman Catholics, noted the terrible metamorphosis which famine had brought about in the character of the individual, particularly the manner in which his whole mind and feelings were submerged in a fierce craving for food. He wrote:

> In this way the preparation already made by God for the reception of His divine teaching was facilitated by the fearful judgment spread over the land.[7]

The "Souper," the Catholic who had changed his religion so as to be assured of a meal, now became an unhappy figure of the period; an outcast among his former co-religionists, an unreliable and incongruous convert among those he had joined.

Much of the efforts of the societies during the 1830s and 1840s were directed at Catholic children. In general they offered at day schools an education, a meal and clothing in return for conversion to the Protestant faith. In some areas, along the famine-striken west coast in particular, large colonies of children were established by the societies where there was residential accommodation as well as day schools. In a colony in Achill Island the Protestant clergyman in

charge claimed in 1849 that "almost the whole rising generation" of the surrounding area had been under his instruction
for the previous three years.[8] This situation was a major influence in driving children into the workhouses.

During the period 1840 to 1842, it was found that a large
proportion of all those seeking admission were children. By
early 1846, with the Famine under way but not yet making a
major impact, more than half the workhouse population
consisted of children. In February 1847 there were 63,000
young children among the workhouse population of 116,000.
By the middle of 1849 the number of children had increased
to over 90,000. While many of them would have been
accompanied by a parent or parents, most of them were
orphaned or deserted children. Some unions were almost
overwhelmed by the number of children in their care. In
Midleton workhouse and its auxiliaries in July 1848 there
were 1,397 children. In Cork workhouse and its auxiliaries
there were, early in 1849, 1,580 girls and 1,620 boys. About
the same time there were 1,157 children being maintained in
Tullamore workhouse.[9]

Edward Senior, one of the Irish Poor Law Commissioners,
reporting to a parliamentary committee at this time, said that
the burden of children was constantly increasing in every
workhouse in Ireland; that whole families were being swept
away by the famine fever but many of the children were
surviving.[10] This is confirmed by Sir William MacArthur's
medical account of the famine. He states that because of the
strain imposed on the heart by typhus, the resulting mortality
was heavier among the middle-aged and the elderly than
among the young.[11]

Not all the unaccompanied children entering the workhouses had been orphaned. Large numbers had been deserted
by their parents. This was one of the saddest consequences of
the disruption of family life by the Famine. Desertion was not
always callous or complete. Often the parents left their
children "on the union" because the workhouse provided a
subsistence which was not available outside, and in the hope
that when the better times came the families would be

reunited. Some parents actually entered the workhouses with their children and then, slipping over the workhouse walls at night, they left the children behind them and, heading for Dublin or Cork, set out as emigrants to America. Their intention was to send for their children when they obtained a livelihood for themselves. Many succeeded and the workhouse records of the period give details of children being sent to join their parents in America. But some parents died on the emigrant ships and others in the pestilential immigrant camps of Grosse Isle and Staten Island. Others simply disappeared and many of the abandoned children of the Famine were faced with a childhood in the workhouse.

By the beginning of 1848 the government was painfully aware that the many orphan and deserted children being admitted to the workhouses were creating a major social problem for it. The absence of any large-scale system of voluntary charity to which the children might be transferred, the deep official distrust of outdoor relief, the extremely limited opportunities for securing employment for young people outside the workhouse, the behavioural and moral deterioration of the children as their workhouse stay lengthened, all made it obvious that the problem would be a long-term one unless some special measures could be devised. It was in these circumstances that the government introduced a scheme in 1848 to encourage young female orphans to emigrate to Australia. The scheme was epic in nature, involving the carriage across the world of shiploads of young teenage girls. It was also an illustration of government ingenuity in attempting to solve simultaneously some of its colonisation and Poor Law problems.[12]

The circumstances in Australia which gave rise to the need for such a scheme can be stated briefly. By 1841 the population of New South Wales, the main area of population, had increased to about 117,000. Despite various schemes during the previous decade aimed at encouraging more female immigrants, there still remained a great dearth of females. In some areas in the interior over 80 per cent of the population was male; in others women were "as scarce as black swans in Europe." In these abnormal conditions homosexuality was widespread except in the areas where there were aboriginal inhabitants. Here, white men and "gin" women cohabited freely. Venereal disease spread rapidly among the natives. Great numbers of unwanted illegitimate half-caste babies were murdered and local religious and lay leaders were convinced that nothing could improve the abysmally low morality prevalent in the bush but a plentiful supply of white women.[13]

Fitzroy, the New South Wales governor, pressurised the Colonial Secretary, Earl Grey, who, anxious to meet Australian demands, asked the Emigration Commissioners to investigate the suitability for emigration of Irish workhouse orphans. By March 1848, the Emigration Commissioners had worked out a scheme with the Irish Poor Law Commissioners. It involved the selection of young orphan females between 14–18 years of age who would be sent as emigrants to the Australian colonies where, it was hoped, they would in time become the wives of settlers.[14]

The Poor Law guardians for each workhouse were asked to put forward the names of suitable girls. The response of the boards of guardians was, generally speaking, enthusiastic; the scheme was welcomed as a contribution not only to improving the future prospects of the young girls concerned, but also to the reduction of workhouse populations and the huge burden that they had imposed on the rates.

There was here and there a dissident voice. *The Nation*, organ of the Young Irelanders and vehemently and defiantly critical of government policy in regard to Ireland, described the scheme as "one of the most diabolical proposals ever made or conceived since Cromwell's time" and urged that it be resisted by every board of guardians in Ireland.[15] A provincial newspaper, the *Tipperary Vindicator*, claimed that the scheme was establishing a form of white slave traffic and that the girls were being exported to Sydney like Circassian beauties to Turkish towns to pander to the vices of the richer settlers. The same newspaper reported the resignation of a member of the Roscrea board of guardians, because he objected to the Poor Law Commissioners sending girls to Australia to become the wives and mistresses of "bushmen or savages."[16] But these objections were isolated and made no impact. Conditions in Ireland were too terrible for any substantial body of opinion to develop on this matter. Many persons had their personal tragedies to contend with and for the great bulk of the population parting with those close to them either by death or emigration had become a routine feature of their lives. The orphan scheme went largely unnoticed.

By May 1848 sixty-eight unions had provided the Poor Law Commissioners with lists of children suitable for emigration. A total of 2,052 female orphans had been nominated. The Emigration Commissioners instructed their agent in Dublin, Lieutenant Henry, RN, to call on the workhouses to inspect the orphans who had been proposed. The method of selection adopted by him was a simple one. As the girls sat in the workhouse he walked amongst them making his choice. It was decided that 2,500 girls should initially be selected and sent to Australia in twelve ships.[17]

The Poor Law Commissioners planned the scheme very meticulously. For instance, the unions were instructed to give each girl an outfit consisting of six shifts, two flannel petticoats, six pairs of stockings, two gowns and two pairs of shoes. Episcopalian girls were to be given a bible and a prayer book; non-conformists a bible and a psalm book; and Catholics a Douay bible and a prayer book. The guardians were also to provide wooden boxes of good material with strong locks into which the girls were to pack their belongings. Children from the eastern and western counties were to be taken to the North Wall, Dublin, from which a steamer made the trip to Plymouth twice a week, the cost of the fare being 13s. 6d., including the price of food. Girls from unions in the southern counties were to be taken to Cork for embarkation from Penrose Quay. Generally it cost unions about £5 to outfit each girl and send her to Plymouth.[18]

Some unions attempted to skimp on the clothes with which the orphans were to be provided and the Emigration Commissioners had to buy additional items for them. But other unions took a greater interest in preparing the girls for the journey. A party from Carlow was described as "comfortably if not respectably clad," whilst nineteen girls from Omagh were of "exceedingly clean and respectable appearance being comfortable, neatly and rather picturesquely dressed in tartan cloaks and straw bonnets."[19] A group of twenty-five girls from Mohill workhouse were described by the local poor law inspector as fine healthy young women. "I cannot say much for their education," he added, "several of them I think had very little, others had a tolerable amount."[20] The Dublin correspondent of the *Wexford Guardian* watched girls from various unions embarking on the Dublin quays and noted that they were for the most part good-looking, well-dressed young girls.[21]

But not everyone was impressed by their looks. An Anglican clergyman who saw them at Plymouth said they were very strong, short, with a thick-set frame of body and stout-limbed. "They certainly, poor things, could not boast of much beauty or personal attractions. . . . On the whole I would say they were better calculated for milking cows and undergoing the drudgery of a farm servant's life than to perform the office of lady's maid." An emigration agent at Plymouth claimed that because of the poverty they had endured they were inferior to English workhouse girls in physical development and personal appearance, and the Emigration Commissioners, in a report to Earl Grey about the girls dispatched on the first two ships, described them as "wanting in the orderly and tidy appearance" which characterised English female emigrants and as "generally short and not at all well-looking." In view of the reports about them it was decided that the Irish workhouse girls should be allocated to separate ships, as the Emigration Commissioners were of the opinion that "their habits and manners make them very unacceptable companions to English emigrants."[22]

The authorities gave a great deal of attention to the preparation of the girls at Plymouth and to safeguards for their welfare on the long voyage to Australia. Their health was examined and they were inspected for personal cleanliness. For the purpose of maintaining general discipline on board, a surgeon-superintendent, a matron, a number of sub-matrons and, where possible, a religious instructor were appointed for each ship. The surgeon-superintendent, who was assigned the main responsibility for the welfare of the girls, was to receive a payment of 10s., later increased to 12s.6d., for each emigrant landed alive. The remuneration offered to the instructors was a free passage to Australia plus a fee of £10, but there was great difficulty in obtaining teachers on these terms. The diet drawn up for the voyage was better than that devised for ordinary emigrants and included a daily ration of a half pound of beef, pork or preserved meat, as well as bread, sugar, tea, coffee and other items.[23]

On 4 June 1848 the first ship, the *Earl Grey*, sailed from Plymouth to Sydney with 185 girls from ten unions on board. It was followed during the next few months by the *Roman Emperor* destined for Adelaide with 224 girls; the *Lady Kennaway* with 191 girls for Port Philip; and two further ships to Sydney, the *Inchinnan* with 164 girls and the *Digby* with 223 girls.[24] Only one of these vessels went to South Australia: there were influential circles in England anxious to protect the new settlement at Adelaide from pauper and convict immigration and to set it aside for a socially superior type of colonist. Irish settlers in particular were discouraged. Strong protests had been made by British sources to the Colonial Office against sending workhouse inmates to this colony and the Emigration Commissioners had prudently decided to delay sending further orphans until they had judged the reaction to the first consignment.[25]

The first Irish orphan ship to reach Australia, the *Earl Grey*, anchored in Sydney on 7 October 1848. Two of the girls had died on the journey, one a thirteen and a half year old girl from Armagh who had given her age as fifteen in order to be selected. To the consternation of the colonial government authorities, Dr Douglass, the surgeon-superintendent in charge of the girls, reported immediately on arrival that those on the boat were not orphan girls as they were supposed to be but were prostitutes and beggars. He claimed that the Emigration Commissioners had been grossly deceived, either by the local boards of guardians in Ireland or by the government official who had selected the emigrants. The astonished governor asked the local emigrant committee to investigate the allegations and some weeks later it reported that it had established beyond doubt "that great injustice has been done to the colony." The committee found that fifty-six of the girls, all from Ulster, were of undesirable character and that

> their violent and disorderly conduct on the voyage, their habits of pilfering, and their grossly profane and obscene language were such as to admit of no other conclusion than that they had mixed with the lowest grade of society and that many of them had been common prostitutes.

According to the committee some of the "girls" had long passed girlhood, a number of them had emigrated under assumed names and two were married women who had run away from their husbands. Forty-nine of the troublemakers were quickly dispatched under police escort into the interior, twelve to Maitland and thirty-seven to the Moreton Bay area, a district still being used as a convict settlement. The characters of the girls proved no obstacle to them; all but one were quickly hired for high wages. The remaining girls on the ship, who had behaved in a satisfactory manner during the voyage, were retained at the orphan depot for one week so that their personal traits might be observed. As soon as they were open to engagement, all were rapidly hired, mainly by persons from Sydney and its immediate environs, and many of them were later reported to be giving great satisfaction to their employers.[26]

When Earl Grey, the colonial secretary, received news of the disastrous start to his scheme he immediately wrote to the Irish Lord Lieutenant, Clarendon, accusing the Irish Poor Law Commissioners of culpable negligence and urging an investigation into the manner in which the girls had been selected. The subsequent enquiry, culminating in a lengthy report, produced little but disclaimers by all concerned about negligence in the affair. Lieutenant Henry, who had selected the girls, said in explanation: "meditating on the mournful matter what, I ask myself, can I say beyond giving utterance to profound and painful feelings." He claimed, however, that his conscience was clear and that he had chosen them according to their personal appearance, which gave no indication that they were anything but girls of upright character. The Poor Law Commissioners conceded that some minor abuses had taken place but suggested that Dr Douglass, who was mainly responsible for the allegations, had unjustly accused the girls of immoral conduct simply because of their bad language, a normal trait in Belfast factory girls. Earl Grey, anxious to continue and defend the scheme, accepted the Commissioners' views and in a dispatch to Fitzroy conceded that some irregularities had occurred but claimed that Dr Douglass's charges generally were too sweeping.[27]

At the end of 1843, 992 orphans from forty-four unions, as well as five girls from the Dublin Mendicity Institution, had been dispatched from Ireland. There was great pressure from the boards of guardians and other sources to extend the lists beyond the number of 2,500 originally fixed. Excitement about the scheme ran high in many Irish workhouses. In Mallow the guardians found that orphan girls in service in the district were leaving their posts and endeavouring to be accepted in the workhouse so that they might be selected for emigration. In Cork workhouse a young girl, enraged at being rejected for emigration, wilfully destroyed a new gown intended for one of her more fortunate comrades. The guardians decided to prosecute her.[28]

Because of the many protests from local guardians about the slow rate at which the emigration was being conducted it was decided to depart from the original intention of sending all the orphans on special ships, and to send smaller groups with other emigrants. The government also decided to extend the scheme to include a further 2,000 orphans. Dublin Corporation, anxious that every device should now be availed of to transport as many children as possible, proposed that the emigrant ships should sail direct from Irish ports to Australia instead of from Plymouth. The Emigration Commissioners pointed out, however, that since the scheme was being paid for out of colonial funds, they would not feel justified in making any change in the arrangements which would add to the costs.[29]

The Irish Poor Law Commissioners were anxious that the extension and acceleration of the scheme should not give rise to the careless selection of orphans. The Commissioners continuously urged on local guardians the importance of selecting only orphans of unblemished moral character and sound health. This policy appears to have been conscientiously applied by the guardians and complaints regarding the girls who continued to arrive in Australia during 1849 and early 1850 were relatively few.

But the good character of most of the girls was not enough to remove resistance to the scheme. Despite the fact that the first parties of girls were quickly accepted and absorbed by the New South Wales and South Australian settlers, the antipathy towards them which had always existed soon became more overt. By the beginning of 1850 the Australian authorities, bending to local pressures, had decided that they had enough Irish orphans and the British Government accepted that the scheme should be terminated. The final group of Irish workhouse orphans was dispatched in April 1850.[30]

Altogether 4,175 orphan girls had been sent from Irish workhouses during the two years that the scheme had been in operation. Sydney had received 2,253 of them, 1,255 had gone to Port Philip, 606 to Adelaide and the remaining 61 had been taken to another country, to the Cape of Good Hope. Some undoubtedly fell by the wayside. At the end of 1850 the local Apprenticeship Board in Adelaide, which supervised the placing of the girls in that area, issued a report about the 600 orphans who had arrived there. Thirty-two of them had been brought before magistrates for various crimes. Six others were mothers of illegitimate children. A further six were living in the bush "in a state of adultery." Forty-three were prostitutes in or about Adelaide.[31]

It is clear, however, from this and other reports that the majority behaved well, gave satisfaction as servants, married, as it was hoped they would, and brought up their families in better and happier circumstances than mid-nineteenth century Ireland could offer them. Most of them had spent several years under workhouse discipline. Young and ignorant, thrown into the harsh environment of a developing country where there still existed what a contemporary account referred to as the "contaminating residuum" of its penal colony days, it was to be expected that not all of them would have the fibre to withstand its inherent dangers. Religious and racial antagonists seized on their inadequacies and were sufficiently influential to incite indignation whenever an opportunity arose.

But probably the main influence operating against the scheme was not so much that it related to immigrants who were both Irish and Catholic, but that the the colonists had now developed an *amour propre* which rejected the idea that their developing state should continue to be built up on the unwanted produce of the workhouses and gaols of Britain and Ireland.

And what had the orphan emigration scheme contributed to the problem of the Irish workhouses? Very little. When the last orphan ship sailed in April 1850 it left behind in these workhouses over 104,000 children, a great many of them orphaned or abandoned.[32] A great number of these children would spend the rest of their childhood within the workhouse walls. And later they would become statistics in the annual reports of the Inspector of Prisons as, passing out of the workhouses, they passed into the prison system the only life for which many of them had been fitted by their workhouse experience. In the light of what happened these lost children of the famine years, one is compelled to say that those who found a new and happy life in Australia were lucky ones.

References
  1. John Carr, *The Stranger in Ireland* (London, 1806), p. 152.
  2. L.M. Cullen, *An Economic History of Ireland Since 1660* (London, 1972), p. 118.

3. Joseph Robins, *The Lost Children* (Dublin, 1980), pp. 10–100.

4. Francis White, *Report and Observations on the State of the Poor of Dublin 1833* (Dublin, 1833).

5. *First Report of Commissioners for enquiring into the Conditions of the Poorer Classes in Ireland*, pt. 1, app.A, pp. 1–186. H.C. 1835 (369) xxxii.

6. Robins, *Lost Children*, pp. 176–182.

7. E.J. Quiqley, "Grace Abounding," in *Irish Ecclesiastical Record*, fifth series xx, ii(21) pp. 506–7.

8. *Achill Missionary Herald*, 30 July 1849, p. 97.

9. Robins, *Lost Children*, pp. 178–182.

10. *Third Report, Select Committee, House of Commons, Poor Law (Ireland)*, March 1849, q.2336, H.C.1849(137), xv, pt.1.

11. William MacArthur, "Medical History of the Famine," in R.D. Edwards and T.D. Williams (eds.), *The Great Famine* (Dublin, 1956), pp. 275–280.

12. Robins, *Lost Children*, pp. 176–270.

13. Russel Ward, *The Australian Legend* (Melbourne, 1958), pp. 88–104.

14. Robins, *Lost Children*, pp. 200–203.

15. *The Nation*, 26 Feb. 1949, p. 137.

16. *The Nation*, 2 Jan. 1849, p. 2; 24 Jan 1849, p. 2.

17. Chief Secretary's Office, Registered Papers 05208/1848; 0825/1849. Oliver MacDonagh, "Irish Emigration . . . during the Famine" in *The Great Famine*, p. 355.

18. Robins, *Lost Children*, p. 204.

19. *Longford Journal*, 17 Mar. 1849 p.4; 13 Oct. 1848, p.4.

20. *Minutes of Evidence, Select Committee, House of Commons, on the Poor Laws (Ireland)*, 1849, q.13489, H.C. 1849 (572), xv pt.2.

21. *Wexford Guardian*, 2 Sept. 1848, p. 3.

22. Rev. T. Childs and Lt. Carew to Emigration Commissioners, 5 Aug. 1848; Earl Grey to Governor Young, 29 Aug. 1848; *Emigration (North American and Australian Colonies) Despatches*, pp. 229–230, H.C. 1849 (593), xxxviii.

23. Robins, *Lost Children*, p.206.

24. Registered Papers 0825/1849; 01302/1849.

25. James F. Hogan, *The Irish in Australia* (London, 1888), pp. 195–203.

26. Governor Fitzroy to Earl Grey, 19 Dec. 1848, *Papers Relative to Emigration to the Australian Colonies*, H.C. 1848 (593), xxxviii.

27. Registered Papers 09048/1849; 06888/1849; 07446/1849; 0999573/1849.

28. Robins, *Lost Children*, pp 212–3.

29. Registered Papers 0825/1849; 04674/1949. *Second Annual Report, Irish Poor Law Commissioners*, par.18.
30. Robins, *Lost Children*, pp.214–21.
31. *Third Report, IPLC*, Table xvii; Young to Grey, 2 Nov. 1850. *Emigration (Australian Colonies) Despatches*, H.C. 1851 (347, pt.2, xi.
32. Third Report, IPLC, p.2.

3.
Irish workhouse children in Australia

JUDY COLLINGWOOD

The Times remarked in June 1848 that "emigration is the question of the day" and went on to lament that while "the colonies are crying out for more labour, and the parishes for the lower rates, it is much to be feared that both parties will be content with a shipment of pauper outcasts, the dregs of the streets, the leavings of the Unions, and the sweepings of the gaols. . . . "[1] Indeed, with a seemingly insatiable demand for domestic servants in the Australian colonies, and the Irish workhouses filled to capacity, as Dr Robins has shown, it would seem that in the case of Ireland at least, emigration presented a perfect opportunity to ameliorate the want of labour on the one hand and the hardship and distress endured by the inmates of the unions on the other. Sir William Meredyth Somerville, Chief Secretary of Ireland, believed "its effect will be good—and its benefits universal—to the poor destitute creatures themselves—to society here, to society in the colonies—and last not least to the State itself. . . . "[2] He went so far as to suggest that if carried out in "a benign, confiding, parental spirit," the plan "will give a different tone to public feeling in this country towards England."[3] He believed the state should come forward and act on behalf of these children—"more fortunate than thousands who have been swept away by the ravages of pestilence and famine, they remain, friendless and deserted, to be adopted I hope by the State, whose children they are, and to whom alone they can look for aid and assistance. . . . " The government must,

46

however, "appear to be guided rather by considerations of Imperial Philanthropy than of Poor Law Administration. . . . "[4]

In formulating the scheme for the emigration from Irish workhouses to Australia of young orphans, Charles Trevelyan, Assistant Secretary at the Treasury and a leading figure in the administration of relief for Ireland during the Famine crisis, anticipated some of the prejudices which would face this proposal. The emigrants must be "tolerably well taught and well trained; for it is the money of the Colonies which we are spending and they criticise very severely the Class of persons whom we send out." Recognising that paupers already had a bad name in Australia, it was necessary for all concerned "to endeavour to obviate this, and to give the poor Children that religious and intellectual instruction which is the only Stock in trade with which they will be started in life."[5]

As well as charges of disposing of paupers, Trevelyan anticipated complaints of a sectarian nature. His correspondence with Somerville is revealing of his attitudes to the Irish and to the Australians:

> The Australians although not quite so fond of a grievance as the excitable & imaginative Irish, will, nevertheless, see that the idea of the Irish Workhouses being cleared at their expense is too good not to be made the most of for their own benefit, . . . [6]

The first "shipments" should therefore be made "as acceptable as possible."

> The perfect thing would be to send two ship-loads of *Protestant* Female Orphans—(you must keep this a great secret from Bishop Murray, and everybody except Redington)— and after that they could not complain at our having our own way.[7]

Protestant and Roman Catholic orphans, he thought, should be sent in separate ships if there were enough of the former to fill one, but the point was that "the Protestant Orphans should be sent among the first."[8] Clarendon, the Irish Lord Lieutenant, was very much alarmed by this idea of giving the scheme "a Protestant character," which he felt would be "not only fatal to the plan as regards Ireland but would create a Sectarian uproar and pabulum for MacHale & Co [the Catholic Archbishop of Tuam] that would be very ill compensated by any benefit to the children or relief to the Unions. . . . " He declined to have anything to do with it if such was the plan, envisaging mis-representation by "these people who love always to quarrel with their bread and butter rather than to eat it," and MacHale firing off "another anathema to Rome against the anti-Catholic system of the English Government." It would not be difficult, he thought, to show the colonists that "a Catholic girl or boy of 14 is just as convenient for purposes of Colonization as a Protestant."[9] Trevelyan hastened to defend himself on the charge of "Ultra Protestantism"; he had meant to suggest that since the colonies were paying, "we should endeavour to make it as acceptable to them as possible, and especially to give them a favourable impression of it at first."[10]

Another correspondent thought the original understanding was that the English Treasury would pay a bonus of £5 per head and apprentice orphans under 15, and was dismayed that this had been dropped. "It needs fully this gilding," he said, "to make the Colony swallow a Roman Catholic Pill." Without it the colonists would think they were shouldering the entire bill, which would produce "Immense indignation."[11] Many colonists were indeed under the impression that the British government intended to foot the bill for the scheme, and the Orphan Committees which were set up formally proposed that the Poor Law authorities contribute more to the cost of passage than only the expense of outfitting and sending the girls to Plymouth, but without success.[12]

In July Edward Senior wrote to Trevelyan congratulating him on the scheme, which had enjoyed "the rarest of all success, it has been as useful as popular, and I do not remember any Government measure so universally praised." In conclusion, however, he sounded an unconsciously ominous note in view of subsequent condemnation of this orphan migration: "Ten years experience in my present office . . . ," he wrote, "has convinced me that pauper children do not graft into society—

that the want of domestic, or parental education, can never be filled up—and that your only alternative consists in vice at home, or employment in the colonies, and that *a child brought up in a work house who remains there till the age of 18 is generally morally ruined.*" [13]

Such a view fits ill with the mission entrusted them by "KEF," who wrote three tracts directed at the orphans and matrons proceeding to Australia under the scheme: "The absence of female society in Australia," he informed them, "has made the settlers wild, reckless men; it should be the province of the young women who now emigrate to win them back to home ties and duties, and to revive in their hearts many pure and hallowed feelings, which have long lain dormant." [14] More sensible was his advice not to consort with the crew, not to linger about the forecastle deck at night and to dress with modesty, for "a very trifling act, the very appearance of evil, will cause a young maiden's virtue to be doubted." [15] This was particularly pertinent advice in view of the scandal surrounding the conduct of girls on the *Subraon* which preceded them to Australia in 1848.

Inmates of English workhouses were also sent to Australia, but the numbers were small and they generally went in separate parties. In 1848 only 19 were sent, in the *Ramillies* to South Australia, and in 1849 a further 23 went to South Australia in the *Eliza*, with 29 going to Sydney in the *Diana* and 21 accompanying a group of Parkhurst boys to Western Australia in the *Mary*.

In spite of the careful precautions taken in ensuring personal selection of the orphans by Lieutenant Henry, the Commissioners' agent at Dublin, the Colonial Land and Emigration Commissioners were greatly embarrassed to receive a report of extensive misconduct aboard the *Earl Grey*. Such disorderly behaviour was not restricted to Irish immigrants. Several girls from the St. Marylebone workhouse sailing to Adelaide on the *Eliza* were charged with "the use of low and vile language in their intercourse with each other and within hearing of respectable married women—with making a continual noise on the lower deck even during the hour of labour of one of their own sex and with a general bearing altogether inconsistent with propriety . . . " and "the utmost difficulty is required to limit them within anything like reasonable bounds from their decided preference for the society of the Sailors before the mast."[16] One, Eliza Lee, was taken off the ship at Plymouth as an example to the others. It was alleged she had shown "gross insolence to the Surgeon Superintendent and the Captain of the Vessel and had excited the others to insubordination."[17] Similarly, girls from the Holborn Union sent to Fremantle in the *Sophia* in August 1850 had caused "some trouble" and had been "punished by privations." The Surgeon was later reprimanded for cutting off the hair of Keziah Bennett while inebriated.[18]

As well as condemnation of conduct on the voyage, complaints of ill-health were also received. Margaret Gorman, from the Donegal Union, arrived at Melbourne on the *Lady Kennaway* and was alleged to be an "imbecile on arrival and quite unfit for service." Though an inquiry was carried out, the Commission agreed that the workhouse was probably "covering up," but stated lamely that "she must have become imbecile through fits during the voyage."[19] Her medical state does not appear to have impaired her chances of future happiness, for she was subsequently reported to have married a "labouring man."[20] Another case of imbecility appeared in the *Derwent*, in Eliza or Elizabeth Armstrong, who came from the Lisnaskea Union. The commissioners explained that the embarkation of the girl "was an accident arising from a want of recollection on the part of the Medical Officer of the Workhouse," who had apparently forgotten that 12 months prior to her admission to the workhouse he had signed a medical certificate admitting her to Enniskillen Gaol suffering from "mental aberration of a violent nature, which made it unsafe to leave her at large."[21]

On arrival in the Australian colonies, the girls became the responsibility of orphan committees which established receiving depots for them and arranged for their apprenticeship and hiring and generally acted as guardians. These were to include representatives of religious denominations, but a longstanding hostility between the primates in New South Wales resulted in the Anglican Archbishop Broughton refusing to serve on the same committee as the Catholic Archbishop Polding.[22] In South Australia one lay colonist approached to serve on the committee declined on the grounds that he entertained "some doubts as to the propriety of sending such Emigrants to the Colony , at least in any considerable number." In his opinion the married mechanics and labourers were the best class of emigrants.[23] The committees found little difficulty in placing the orphans, the Melbourne committee reporting "that in most instances they have conducted themselves so as to meet their employers' approbation; the main objection which appears to be entertained against them is, that they are comparatively uninstructed in the duties of domestic service."[24]

Feelings of dissatisfaction soon appeared, however, and the colonists began to ask for the suspension of the scheme. Complaints centred on the expense of the orphan immigration and the ignorance of the orphans of domestic service. In November 1849 the Melbourne committee advocated suspension, adding that with each succeeding ship the prospective employers coming forward were of a "lower rank and less desirable class than those preceding," and that demand had substantially fallen off.[25] The Sydney committee indicated that there was sufficient demand for a further party of 800 from England and Ireland, in spite of their "inferior usefulness."[26] When this quota was exceeded in spring 1850 the Sydney committee called for suspension. In South Australia also, the orphan board called early for suspension, "until the relative proportion from Great Britain shall have been sent out."[27]

The difficulties facing the orphan committees were formidable. Moorhouse, the Protector of Aborigines in whose charge the female orphans had been placed, reported that in the case of the *Inconstant*, which arrived in Adelaide on 7 June 1849, the vessel was "clean and under good discipline," and apart from one insane and one who died of typhus, the 195 orphans were healthy. Their unsuitability for country occupations, for which they were chiefly required, delayed their placement. Of the girls in the *Roman Emperor*, 150 had been "accustomed to farm work & could milk and wash, but out of these by the *Inconstant* only about 35 can milk cows and the remainder shew no disposition to learn; many of these also know nothing of washing clothes & this causes the colonists to shew indifference about hiring them."[28] As guardians of the orphans the committee was naturally expected to keep them under close supervision. Dispersal to the country districts made this extremely difficult. In March 1849 it was reported that "from 40 to 50 Orphans had left their places since last meeting, some of whom had been bound by Indenture but most of them had not." The system of indenture appeared to the board to be "imperfect in its operation" and they decided that it should be continued only where employer and orphan agreed to it, or in the case of an orphan under the age of 14. Their reasons for taking this decision were that only about a third of employers executed the indenture—"The Orphans themselves have a decided objection to be apprenticed and instances have occurred of some good and useful girls becoming perverse and unruly when their employers had bound them." Where indentures had been signed and the orphans ran away from their situations, masters were reluctant to go to the trouble of beginning legal proceedings—one girl who did so received one week's imprisonment for breaking her indenture. Many girls had left their situations and not returned to the depot, and it was felt that apprenticing the older girls was "not in the present state of the Colony practicable or necessary in consequence of the facility of procuring respectable situations."[29]

Replies to enquiries of magistrates regarding any complaints brought to them and of "the opinion of the neighbourhood upon the conduct and respectability of the orphans," as in the case of those on board the *Roman Emperor*, illustrate the difficulties of keeping track of their charges. The board regretted that their enquiries had "not been so punctually replied to, as could have been desired, 65 circulars were forwarded and only 21 answers have been received. 219 Orphans were the subject of inquiry and only 56 are mentioned in the returns being about one fourth of the number." Of these, 28 were given a good character, 20 indifferent and 8 bad. In addition, the board had heard through an "authentic channel that there are 21 of the Irish Orphans upon the Streets of Adelaide; indeed there appears to be a greater number of orphans than any other class of females and it is supposed that this may be traced in a great degree to the want of immediate parental control." This led the board to express their belief that the best means of introducing "a moral industrious community to our shores" was through the emigration of families selected from the rural population of Britain and Ireland. Orphans arriving on the *Elgin* on 10 September were reported to be having greater difficulty in finding employment, and although apparently more carefully selected than their predecessors in the colony, 109 were still unhired nearly one month later. This was attributable to the "supply of Irish female servants being slightly in advance of the demand."[30]

Charges were reported in the *South Australian Register* that the depot was a brothel and that the girls' rations had been stopped and punishments inflicted for trivial offences. The board were satisfied that these accusations had been laid by girls who had been turned out of the depot for refusing offers of "respectable service. Their Statements when placed in juxtaposition with their employers' are worth but little, and the Board is compelled to admit that these orphans have shewn little or no regard for truth." A charge that the matrons and Mr Moorhouse, the Protector of Aborigines, had called the orphans "Irish Brutes" was denied, but they admitted to addressing them "under certain provocation," as "dirty brutes." The board thought that "tho' this expression of opinion is to be regretted, yet it was naturally provoked by the extreme filthyness and unimaginable indelicacy of some of these workhouses girls."[31]

In New South Wales girls of 17 entered an ordinary agreement for one year at a wage of £10 to £15. Trained servants could command £27 to £31. The occupation of the majority was stated on the passenger lists as house servant, housemaid or nursemaid, though this may reflect the view of the Poor Law authorities of the work for which they would be suited, rather than any prior experience. In any event, in spite of low wages and the obligation imposed on the employer to provide training, complaints of the uselessness of the orphans for household duties were general. The chief magistrate thought such criticism unjustified: "They got servants at a very low rate of wages, and presumed they were able to perform all the duties of proper servants, and when they found out that this was not the case they were disappointed and wished to get rid of them."[32]

In general employers returned their servants on grounds of ill-health, misconduct or want of means. No employer was permitted to turn an apprentice out. In Sydney, if a master or mistress wished to transfer an apprentice, they must themselves find her a new place. In country districts, if there were good cause for cancelling the indenture, the girl would be escorted back to the depot. It seems that many deliberately behaved badly in order to be sent back to town. Some offers of marriage were received for girls in the depot at Wollongong. The committee felt it was better that they should go into service first when they would have opportunities of "forming matrimonial connections based upon previous acquaintance with their husbands."[33] Many of the girls did marry very soon after arriving on the colony, some to Ticket-of-Leave men. While still under the care of the committee they needed permission to marry, and this was generally, but not always, granted. Others not so lucky were seduced by their employers or fellow servants, and in one case a long legal wrangle was entered into for maintenance of a child born as a result of such a relationship. It appears likely that the mother never received the small sum paid by the father after the child's birth, as it was still on the books in 1867, along with monies owed to a further 170 orphans. Wages were not paid directly to the apprentices and could be withheld by the committee as an inducement to good conduct, evidently not always a successful ploy. Others may have absconded or left the colony.

For their part, the girls complained of ill-treatment or non-payment of wages, as in the case of Betty Just. Out of the £3.15s.0d. wages owed by her employer Parry Long, Betty received £2.2s.9d. after payment of legal expenses incurred to recover the money. A common practice among employers was to debit the girls with "so many complicated and petty sums" that the Water Police Magistrate felt obliged to rule that wages must in future be paid in full and employers must not purchase clothes for their apprentices.[34]

Underlying opposition which had been voiced by some colonists from the inception of the scheme gradually became widely expressed. This centred not only on the idea that the orphan immigration was more costly to the colonists than ordinary emigration, but on racial and religious prejudices, the chief exponent of which was Dr Lang. Lang began his opposition while in England, even before the first orphans had reached Australia, and included the plan in his general condemnation of Caroline Chisholm's scheme for female Catholic emigration. In a series of letters to the *British Banner* he trumpeted: "These young women, who are almost exclusively Roman Catholics . . . have been selected as free emigrants for Australia, expressly with a view to their becoming the wives of the English and Scottish Protestant shepherds and stockmen of New South Wales, and thereby silently subverting the Protestantism and extending the Romanism of the colony through the vile, Jesuistical, diabolical, system of 'mixed marriages'. . . . "[35] Lang demanded to know "what right" Grey had to use revenue for Irish orphans which had been provided "almost exclusively" by English and Scottish Protestants, and he believed that Protestant women were being deliberately restricted in preference to Irish Catholics. That Lang's opposition was based largely on racial and religious grounds is clear from his proposal to the vestry of the parish of Marylebone, whose request to the government for the emigration of juvenile paupers had been turned down before the Irish scheme was established, and in which he envisaged the wholesale emigration of Marylebone paupers to New South Wales. He was not proposing that the parish pay more than £5, as the Irish unions were doing, the emigration to be financed through the purchase of land which would be let to emigrants from Scotland and the north of Ireland.[36] The advantages to Great Britain were set out: "The proper remedy for Chartism, as well as for juvenile vagrancy and delinquency, is Emigration; and in the Australian Colonies alone there is room enough and to spare for all of these really dangerous classes that Great Britain could desire to be rid of for a century to come." In addition the boys would become consumers of British produce, producers of raw material for national manufactures while the girls would very soon become "colonial wives and mothers, with plentiful, peaceful, and happy homes."[37] The Commission expressed the view that "until Dr Lang's letter appeared, the idea of their producing any effect on the religious persuasion of the Australian colonies probably never occurred to anyone,"[38] but it is clear that Trevelyan at least had been more attuned to the likely reaction.

Fears of Catholic inundation resulted in a public campaign which revealed the nature of colonial prejudice against Irish Catholic immigrants, and which was all the more vehement because the subjects of it were pauper women. The *Sydney Morning Herald* expressed it thus: "for Irish emigrants we read Irish paupers, misnamed female orphans."[39] The really vehement attacks came from the *Melbourne Argus*, with charges such as this: " . . . it is downright robbery to withhold our funds and lavish it upon a set of ignorant creatures, whose whole knowledge of household duty barely reaches to distinguish the inside from the outside of a potato, and whose chief employment hitherto, has consisted of some such intellectual occupation as occasionally trotting across a bog to fetch back a runaway pig."[40] When the Irish rallied to defend their own the *Argus* scoffed: "but Paddy, dear funny Pat . . . boldly takes his stand by his thick-waisted orphan, and rashly risks the character of the whole body of the bright-eyed daughters of Erin, upon his success in proving the dumpy darling a Venus de Medici in personal beauty, a

Lucretia in purity and propriety of conduct, and a Mrs Rundell in housekeeping and culinary skill."[41]

To charges that the orphans' main aim was to marry and convert "irreligious" bushmen with the result that "the mother will dictate religion to the family and every one of those girls will some day be the centre of a Roman Catholic circle,"[42] a "Bushman" wrote to the *Sydney Morning Herald* that his understanding of the scheme was that it was expressly designed to provide wives for isolated men of the interior, and he could not understand why the press should throw an obstacle in the way of "so laudable an end as that of equalisation of the sexes."[43] Another writer condemned the author of a *Herald* article as an "intolerant and bigoted persecutor", while the *People's Advocate* expressed the view that in the absence of applicants from Scotland and England: "We must then look to Ireland; and instead of opposing female immigration from that country, chiefly on the ground that it is Irish, as the *Herald* does, we ought to be thankful that we have such a country to fall back upon."[44]

However, in the face of this mounting condemnation of the emigration of Irish female orphans, the scheme was dropped, in spite of objections by the Irish community. The Celtic Association was successful a few years later in obtaining a review of the scheme, by conducting a thorough investigation, interviewing immigration agents and registry office keepers, employers and prominent spokesmen of the Irish Catholic community. The report of the Select Committee on Irish Female Immigration was a compromise on a sensitive issue, but succeeded in vindicating the Irish orphans, stressing that they were accepted as "apprentices to the vocation of domestic service," and recommending for the future a more comprehensive dispersal into country districts and a separate classification for town and country servants.[45]

Officially the scheme was suspended on account of the orphans' ignorance of domestic service, yet the fact that the orphans were initially well received suggests that lack of training served as a justification rather than a cause of dissatisfaction. Moreover, a stated preference for women who

came as Bounty Immigrants at the same time holds little
weight, for the colonists also complained of their uselessness.
As Paula Hamilton suggests:

> It may be thought peculiarly unreasonable to complain of
> lack of training in girls destined to be apprenticed, and
> therefore by definition untrained; it might seem to reflect
> incapacity to give training on the part of the colonists as
> much as incapacity to receive it on the part of the Irish. But
> this would not be wholly fair. Colonists had not foreseen the
> wide cultural gap dividing them from Irish girls drawn from
> the poorest peasant backgrounds, and were often at a loss to
> know how to begin bridging it. Certainly there is ample
> testimony to show that, treated with patience and sympathy,
> these women would become good servants. In reality, most
> colonists were unwilling to employ them because their initial
> preconceptions were reinforced by the campaign against the
> orphans.[46]

The orphans were acceptable only because their labour was
cheap and there was no satisfactory alternative at the time,
but the strength of the campaign shows, I think, how
national and religious prejudices finally outweighed economic
considerations. The campaign was used to fight for colonial
control over emigration but the scheme was finally defeated
by factors which were already foreseen at the time of its
inception: religious prejudice, cost to the colony, and the
supposed inferior moral standards and usefulness of the Irish
female orphans. More sensitive handling, and a leavening of
other categories of migrant could have gone some way
towards mitigating these factors. Instead they were exacer-
bated by the tendency of British officials, once having identified a potential market for migration, to swamp it. The
orphans were highly visible on account of their large numbers
and the actions of the few condemned the many. Individually
most probably settled into the Irish Catholic community,
making useful Australians and a valuable economic and
social contribution to the development of the colonies.

References

1. *The Times*, 16 June 1848.
2. Sir William Meredyth Somerville to C.E. Trevelyan, Private, 28 December 1847, PRO T64/368A.
3. ibid.
4. Somerville to C.E. Trevelyan, 19 January 1848, PRO T64/368A.
5. C.E. Trevelyan to Earl of Clarendon, 26 January 1848, PRO T64/368A.
6. C.E. Trevelyan to Sir W.M. Somerville, 25 January 1848, PRO T64/368A.
7. ibid.
8. ibid.
9. Clarendon to C.E. Trevelyan, 27 January 1848, PRO T64/368A.
10. C.E. Trevelyan to Clarendon, 29 January 1848, PRO T64/368A.
11. Capt. Trevelyan to C.E. Trevelyan, 23 January 1848, PRO T64/368A.
12. La Trobe to Colonial Secretary, Sydney, 21 May 1850, Victoria PRO, VPRS 117, p94; Report of the Immigration Agent for 1848, Legislative Council, New South Wales, Votes & Proceedings, Vol 2, 1849, p.4.
13. Edward Senior to C.E. Trevelyan, 7 July 1848, PRO T64/368A. My italics.
14. "KEF," *Hints to Matrons*, quoted in Paula Hamilton, "'No Irish Need Apply': Prejudice as a factor in the development of immigration policy in New South Wales and Victoria, 1840–1870," PhD thesis, University of New South Wales, 1979, p.341.
15. "KEF," A *letter to young emigrants*, quoted in Hamilton, thesis, p.341
16. Inquiry into Misconduct abroad the Subraon, October 1849, CO 201/423.
17. Secretary to Marylebone Guardians, 11 May 1849, GLRO P89/MRY1/532.
18. ibid.
19. Report of Surgeon of the *Sophia*, 14 August 1850, Battye Library, CSR 192 f34.
20. La Trobe to Colonial Secretary, Sydney, 2 May 1850, VPRS 117, f86; Colonial Land & Emigration Commissioners to Merivale, 15 Sept. 1849, PRO CO 386/67.
21. Walcott to Colonial Secretary, Victoria, 20 July 1852, VPRS 117, 52/7553; W Stanley to Dr Mansfield, Lisnaskea Union, VPRS 1189, 52/7953.
22. Fitzroy to Grey, 1 Dec 1848, *Historical Records of Australia*, XXVI, p.722.

23. A.L. Elder to Colonial Secretary, 24 August 1848, South Australia Archives, GRG 24 Series 6/1848, 1299.

24. K. Melbourne to La Trobe, 19 January 1849. Enclosure No 2 in No 15 Fitzroy to Grey, 16 June 1849, British Parliamentary Papers, Colonies; Australia, Vol. 13, 50 (466).

25. Melbourne to La Trobe, 26 October 1849, sub-enclosure to Enclosure No 1, Fitzroy to Grey, 19 December 1849, NO 10, BPP, op.cit.

26. Fitzroy to Grey, 1 December 1849, HRA XXVI, p722.

27. Minute, Children's Apprenticeship Board, 4 September 1848, enclosed in Moorhouse to Colonial Secretary, 4 March 1850, SAA GRG 24/6/1850/518.

28. Secretary, Children's Apprenticeship Board, to Captain Young, 23 June 1849, SAA GRG 24/6/1849/1170.

29. Minutes of Children's Apprenticeship Board, 9 March 1849, enclosed in Adelaide to Colonial Secretary, 20 March 1849, SAA GRG 24/6/1849/601.

30. Moorhouse to Young, 5 October 1849, SAA GRG 24/6/1849/1839.

31. Moorhouse to Colonial Secretary, 28 February 1850, SAA GRG 24/6/1850/506.

32. Evidence of Daniel Egan, Minutes of Evidence before the Select Committee on Irish Female Immigration, Legislative Assembly of New South Wales Votes & Proceedings, Vol 2, 1858–9, p390, quoted in Hamilton, thesis.

33. Merewether to Wollongong Magistrates, 6 February 1850, NSW State Archives, 4/4638.

34. Water Police Magistrate to Orphan Committee, 11 July 1851, NSW SA, Reel 2648.

35. J D Lang, "Christian Colonization in Australia," British Banner, 15 November 1848, in M Kiddle (comp), The Letters of Dr Lang to the British Banner, No 36, quoted in Hamilton, thesis, p.356.

36. J D Lang, "Open Letter to Earl Grey on Leaving England," 21 November 1849, in ibid; J D Lang, Juvenile-Pauper Emigration—a letter to the members of the vestry of the parish of St Marylebone, London, London, 1848, pp.20–21.

37. ibid.

38. Memorandum of the Principal Correspondence between Dr Lang and the Colonial Land and Emigration Commissioners, Enclosure No 24 in Grey to Fitzroy, 15 December 1849, No 24, Legislative Council of NSW, V & P, Vol 2, 1850. Despatches re Emigration, pp. 104–105.

39. *Sydney Morning Herald*, 13 March 1850, quoted in Hamilton, thesis, p.359.
40. *Melbourne Argus*, 24 January 1850, quoted in Hamilton, thesis, p.360.
41. *Melbourne Argus*, 20 April 1850, quoted in Hamilton, thesis, p.360.
42. *Melbourne Argus*, 24 January 1850, quoted in Hamilton, thesis, p.362.
43. *Sydney Morning Herald*, 28 February 1850, quoted in Hamilton, thesis, p.362.
44. *People's Advocate*, 16 March 1850, quoted in Hamilton, thesis, p.363.
45. Votes & Proceedings of the Select Committee on Irish Female Immigration, 4 November 1858, Legislative Assembly of NSW, V & P, Vol 2, 1858–9.
46. Hamilton, thesis, p.368.

4.

The importance of being Irish in Colonial South Australia

ERIC RICHARDS*

South Australia was the least Irish part of nineteenth century Australia; it may follow therefore that it has least place in the study of the Irish-Australian migrant experience. On simple proportional terms fewer Irish came to Port Adelaide than to the other great immigrant cities of the continent. Moreover the Irish were late in the rush for initial colonisation; significant numbers of Irish did not arrive for more than a dozen years after the inception of the colony of South Australia in 1836. To borrow Oliver MacDonagh's phrase, the Irish in South Australia were not "a founding people"[1] and never became one third of the colonial population (though they did eventually exceed 10% of the immigrants). Few Irish therefore reaped the significant advantages available to the firstcomers. When they arrived they faced the established and unquestionable primacy of Anglo-Scottish Protestant colonisation.

Although there were substantial Scottish and German minorities within the colonial population, South Australia was overwhelmingly English in its origins. It was more than that: from the beginning South Australia was virtually a fragment of southern England, a Home Counties colony

*I wish to thank Philippa Fletcher, Robert Foster, Sally Richards, David Hilliard, Robin Haines, Sister Marie Foale, Leith MacGillivray and Ruth Schumann for their help in the preparation of this paper. More specifically I am greatly indebted to Susan Woodburn, who generously lent me notes relating to the preparation of her thesis.

specifically designed for superior expatriates. Add to this the
relentless advertising campaign which trumpeted the colony
as a haven for Protestant Dissenters, and it is small wonder
that South Australia seemed in Irish eyes the most alien
quarter of the new continent. Such an image was no
accident; the founders of South Australia lived almost
entirely by models of English society and mores. The first
Catholic priest in South Australia, the Rev. William Benson,
was hardly exaggerating when he described it in 1843 as "a
little Dissenting Colony, exclusively Protestant Evangelical."
He went further, saying that "when this colony was established no Catholic gentlemen of property were allowed to
join the Founders"—thereby implying that the planners
deliberately discouraged an Irish connection. Only when the
colonial population reached 14,000, asserted Benson, did
"our late Evangelical Governors" feel confident enough to
permit a minority of Catholics reasonable and equal entry.[2]
Another Catholic Irishman, Major Thomas O'Halloran, also
claimed that the early colonial planners had been anti-Irish,
wishing to restrict their numbers to less than 5 per cent of
the colonial population.[3]

The peculiarity of the foundation of South Australia has
one advantage for scholars of Irish Australia because it suggests a useful test for some of our conventional propositions
about the immigrant experience. South Australia was a
relatively inhospitable place: on the face of it there was little
room for the Irish in this society and little prospect for their
advancement. In the flood of Anglo-Scottish immigration
one might expect the Irish to be more marginalised than
elsewhere. They might expect to confront greater social and
economic rigidities, greater hostility, in comparison with their
country people in the rest of Australia. If our received generalisations are correct there should have been discernible
disadvantages in being Irish in South Australia.

To verify these sorts of propositions requires much more
systematic and comparative data than we at present possess,
least of all for South Australia. Ireland gave bone and sinew,
capital and skills to South Australia, but to specify a dis-

proportionate Irish effect is beyond our present levels of comparative calibration. Colonisation was often a powerful, homogenising process and the practical realities of migration in general transcended many of the local variations that one might have expected. The Irish were as much subject to this process as other elements in general colonisation.

In the noisy debate which announced the South Australia project to the world in the early 1830s—a debate which combined high theory with low propaganda—there were a number of specific attempts to connect Ireland with the new experimental colony. Edward Gibbon Wakefield had said in 1829 that one of the most important benefits of his plan of colonisation would be to divert the Irish exodus away from England towards her colonies. Simultaneously Irish landlords would be relieved of the surplus tenants who were depressing their rent rolls. Emigration, he argued, would provide a safety valve for the peasantry. With emigration the landlords of Ireland would avoid what otherwise was inevitable, that is, "yielding to the people's violence the land which was taken by violence from their fathers." Yet, in reality, there was nothing exclusively Irish about this proposition—we know that in 1831 Nassau Senior argued identically about the necessity of English emigration to diminish the appalling and worsening violence of class antagonism in England.[4]

As the Wakefieldian doctrines evolved towards their first practical operation in South Australia in 1836, there also emerged the influence of several men, including Wakefield himself, who had close knowledge of the land question in Ireland. Robert Torrens was one: he gave Wakefieldianism an Irish dimension, generally lacking in the ideas of the other colonial promoters. Torrens was instrumental in organising emigration and certainly harboured no prejudices against Ireland. Indeed he believed that Ireland presented the antipodean reciprocal of colonial conditions. Irish mass poverty, he hypothesised, was essentially the product of excessive labour applied to too little land. The surplus of labour should be drawn off so that "a less proportion of the population could be enabled to raise the subsistence of the whole." This of course was the factor-proportions argument embedded at the heart of the Wakefield theory. Torrens in the mid 1830s believed that the new plans for colonisation in Australia could well absorb 200,000 excess Irish without much difficulty.[5] He was Chairman of the Commissioners for South Australia and, in 1840, became one of the first Colonial Land and Emigration Commissioners.

Torrens developed his arguments further in 1839 by widening his range to attract Irish capital to the colony. He proposed "The Irish South Australian Emigration Society" which would raise one million pounds from Irish proprietors and capitalists to buy land in the colony. For each 80 acre section of land he purchased the investor would be entitled to the free passage of two adult labourers—thus eight hundred pounds of land purchase would allow the investor to send out "40 adult labourers from his over-peopled Irish estate to his uninhabited Australian estate."[6] The emigration of these cottier tenants would permit the landlord to consolidate their holdings into farms of adequate extent, which, in any other circumstances, "would be inhuman, would be dangerous, would be impracticable, and would lead to interminable predial war." But the true beauty of the scheme was that it created a double profit on the investment—in both Ireland and Australia:

> The removal of the redundant hands would increase the value of the Irish estate by facilitating the consolidation of farms, and the application of combined labour and capital to the land; and the influx of labour would bestow upon your Australian estate a value exceeding the minimum price of £1 per acre, at which waste land can be obtained in the colony.

Moreover the scheme was inherently humanitarian since "the transplanted tenantry would be placed in circumstances of comparative opulence." These half-pauperised families would eventually, through their own efforts, be in a position to become themselves capitalists and landed proprietors. Torrens saw this humanised version of emigration as a proper alternative to eviction and clearance.[7]

Ten years later, South Australia having since passed through a humiliating bankruptcy and then a recovery based mainly upon a copper boom, Robert Torrens remained undeterred in his convictions, as "the speculations of the closet had been made the lessons of experience." He reaffirmed his belief in "the practicability of defraying the cost of emigration by means of the marketable value which the influx of population confers upon the wild lands of a new country." The soundness of the theory, he claimed, was unaffected by the botching of the South Australian experiment in the collapse of 1841–2—indeed the remarkable recovery of the colony he attributed to the efficacy of the original theory since it was properly practised. Now, in 1849, he believed that the same process could save Ireland and rescue it from "the inveterate economical evils" under which it it continued to labour. He offered South Australia as a working model for an Irish colony in East Africa "upon a scale so extensive as to mitigate the existing alarm."[8]

The impact of Torrens' thinking in bringing Ireland and South Australia into a mutually beneficial connexion was to prove relatively small, partly because the determinants of emigration were far more complex than he allowed. Moreover there was opposition to his assumptions in both countries. In the parliamentary debate on the original South Australian Colonisation in 1834, while there was significant support from several Irish members, there was also vehement opposition from Feargus O'Connor who believed the idea of emigration diverted attention from the real solutions to Irish poverty and from the internal colonisation of Ireland itself.[9] And there were other critical contributions of substance: for instance the radical M.P. for Drogheda, Andrew Carew O'Dwyer, intervened to oppose the emigration of any married person unless his or her spouse went too, or unless it could be proved that adequate provision had been made for the children left behind—saying that in Ireland the families of emigrant pauper males would have no resource whatever and would be left in "a state of perfect destitution." Similarly the Irish Presbyterian, Edward Ruthven, initiated the clause in

the subsequent Act which required that the colony revert to
the Crown if it proved unsuccessful within a specified time.
He also demanded that the South Australian Commissioners
for Emigration despatch emigrants only under stringent
conditions, in sound and seaworthy ships approved by proper
officers—safeguards which reflected the recent catastrophes
which had overwhelmed emigrant vessels leaving the port of
Limerick.

Torrens, who sent his own son to Ireland to recruit
labourers and spoke of a New Erin in the South Seas, was
opposed by many elements in the colonial population who
turned up their noses at the principle of pauper immigration
and explicitly denounced the creation of a Catholic population. The Emigration Commissioners themselves, for several
years, rejected the applications of paupers, Irish or otherwise.
The distribution of emigration agents in the British Isles gave
less opportunity to the Irish than to anyone else.[10] Other
prominent colonies sought to encourage only the Protestant
Irish. George Fife Angas, perhaps the most influential of the
South Australian pioneers, canvassed the possibility of a
specifically Irish community in the new colony, comprising
righteous Protestant farmers with a certain amount of capital.
He was told however that there were no Protestant farmers
left in the south of Ireland and that the pool of suitable
migrants had been exhausted. Another project, to expatriate
100 families from Ulster to form an exclusive village in the
colony under the guidance of a minister and a Captain
Robertson, was too much even for Angas—"Their principles
are High Church Tory and I fear not so liberal nor tolerant as
we might desire the settlers of South Australia to be ... we
may hope that the benign influence of Christianity will
preponderate over uncharitable feelings."[11] The Ulster idea
came to nothing, otherwise Protestant extremism might well
have been transplanted at a critical moment in the genesis of
the new colony.

Not surprisingly, the proportion of Irish entering South
Australia in its first five years was small, probably less than 7
per cent. Yet, even by 1840, there were already indications of

increasing activity despite the relatively few agents recruiting for South Australia in Ireland. Indeed by July 1840 it was suggested that South Australia was stealing a march on the other colonies. In a report from New South Wales in July 1840 it was remarked that while their own representatives "were displaying their antipathy to Irish Immigrants, the agents of South Australia were perambulating the Green Isle, abusing New South Wales and establishing an extensive system of Emigration from Ireland to South Australia!"[12] Irish immigrants had been entering from various ports in England and Scotland, but the first direct voyage from Ireland was that of the *Mary Dugdale* which arrived at Port Adelaide in July 1840.

The flow of Irish to South Australia thus began modestly but widened considerably in the following decade. Perhaps the most surprising aspect of this immigration was its lack of any systematic bias towards the Ulster counties.[13] The influence of Robert Torrens and also of Bishop Murphy, who undertook a vigorous recruiting tour of Ireland in 1846, seems to have prevailed against the "Evangelical Governors." Between 1840 and 1866 assistance to South Australian Irish immigrants offered little evidence of under-representation from the Catholic districts.

In the 1840s it was common to emphasise the relative poverty of the Irish immigrants. In 1847 Bishop Murphy lamented that "our Catholics are all plain working people with the exception of perhaps a dozen families who are engaged in shopkeeping."[14] Indeed the embryonic Catholic Church depended mainly on the benevolent sponsorship of English-born Catholics, including William Phillips, Henry Johnson, W.H. Neale and William Leigh. The case, however is easily exaggerated; the poverty of the Church was partly a consequence of the smallness and dispersion of the Irish immigration; moreover Murphy's remarks ignored a handful of Catholic pastoralists who had entered the colony at its inception. In the 1850s a broader spectrum of Irish immigration changed the financial horizons of the colonial Church.

In the following four decades the Irish arrived in South Australia as a rising proportion of total immigration, increasing beyond 10 per cent to as much as 40 per cent in certain years. Thus Irish migrants responded first to the opportunities created by the colony's need for labour and its capacity to assist migration, and later by means of semi-subsidised chain migration in which they became more adept and experienced than other categories of immigrant. Some brought capital, some migrated as a means of recovering a family's fortunes, some out of desperation, others from a sense of adventure—the Irish were represented across the full spectrum of colony-making. On average they may have been poorer and more rural than the majority of immigrants. The least visible and least known element was the privately-financed component which did not pass through the usual bureaucracy to reach the colony. Paradoxically, we know most about the least well off of the newcomers—which is, of course, true of most Australian immigration. Indeed it is possible that much Irish immigration was similar to that of the rest of the British Isles.

The extent to which the South Australian Irish were products of Torrens' system of landlord investment, or victims of opportunist eviction and clearance, remains difficult to fathom. Certainly in the colony there were allegations that Irish landlords were clearing their estates and, like the parochial authorities, sending their worst tenants to South Australia. It was broadly alleged that "Irish landlords, in order to clear their estate, advance the necessary amount; they act, of course, in the same principle as the parochial authorities and very naturally retain their best people."[15] The only case that was ever cited to substantiate these allegations was that of 224 Catholic rural people from Clare who arrived by the *Birman* from Cork in late 1840. It was claimed that they had been evicted and emigrated (under implied compulsion) to South Australia at the behest of Sir Montagu Lowther Chapman, a large landowner of Killua Castle, Clonmellon in Westmeath, one of the Anglo-Irish establishment.[16] The evidence of the *Birman* emigrants does not confirm the allegations against Irish landlords—it does however vividly illustrate some of the early connections between Ireland and the new colony.

It is true that Chapman had purchased a large quantity of land in South Australia, for 4,000 pounds in a special survey, presumably as an investment. This, of course, entitled him to select land of his choice[17] and to send out a substantial number of migrants at no further cost. In order to select the land and the migrants, Chapman entered an arrangement with a manager, to accomplish both tasks. He chose Captain Charles Bagot,[18] whose own career illustrates a further migrant track out of Ireland. He was born at Nurney, Kildare, in 1788, youngest son and eleventh of 12 children of a small but prosperous landed proprietor and land agent. Unable to obtain a farm, Charles Bagot entered the army and served through the French Wars. He retired on half pay in 1819 and became land agent and farmer in Clare on behalf of his brother-in-law, Bundon Blood. Living at Rockfort, he recalled that he and his wife were "placed in a humble dwelling with very limited income, attended by a rude, uncultivated but exceedingly civil and amenable Irish peasantry." They were, he said, "a simple inoffensive people" in whose relief he assisted during the famine of 1821–2.

Bagot soon found his inoffensive tenantry radicalised under the influence of O'Connell and "the Romish Party." As land agent and magistrate he was now the target of outrages, secret societies and open violence (including the murder of William Blood). Bagot moved his family to Limerick in 1828, but he himself stayed on at Ennis and weathered the storm and, by 1833, was back to relative prosperity. But within four years he had decided to quit. He had become fearful of the consequences of the Poor Law in Ireland, and his children now needed careers: "The Australian colonies were now attracting a great deal of attention and both my boys were desirous to go there."

While exploring colonial prospects in London, Bagot met Sir Montagu Chapman who proposed that Bagot select and manage his large land grant in the new colony. It was a lucrative offer and Bagot set about the task with great efficiency; he provided the sort of managerial talent which was in severely short supply in the colonial economy. Land management in Australia was a ladder offering rapid returns to men of experience and energy—whether Ireland, and more especially Scotland, could afford to lose such men is another question.

The outcome of Bagot's arrangement with Chapman was phenomenally successful. Bagot bought land and sheep stock north of Adelaide at Koonunga Station, and more land at Kapunda on which his youngest son discovered important copper deposits in 1842. They were unlucky not to make an enormous fortune when the great Burra Burra mines were found a little while later. Nevertheless the Chapman connection, and the involvement in the great copper industry, were lucrative. Bagot himself became a major political figure in the colony, an advocate of Irish immigration and a world traveller, and his youngest son was knighted in England. He built a substantial dwelling in North Adelaide, called Nurney House, and he lived on until 1880.[19] Sir Montagu Chapman himself visited Australia in 1852 but lost his life in a shipwreck in the Tasman Sea.[20]

The migrants that Bagot brought from Clare had left Cork in August 1840 aboard a newly fitted barque, the *Birman*. There is no evidence that they were ever tenants of Chapman, still less that they were evicted. Bagot had selected "agricultural labourers" and their families, married couples and a substantial number of single males and females. They may have been the people whom the visiting priest Ullathorne described as "very poor but very good."[21] Bagot had travelled on the *Birman* with them—his own personal party was seven in number and he made elaborate arrangements for their comfort, especially in the provision of fresh meat—they took 10 sheep, 12 pigs, 12 poultry for eggs, 2 goats for milk, and 7 tons of baggage.[22] The assisted migrants travelled less comfortably, but, as a group, they seem to be too diversified to be described as hapless evicted tenants. Nor did they settle in a particular place in South Australia—they dispersed into the general population and have left little trace. Indeed there was nothing inherently Irish about the story and one can cite precise parallels from Scottish and English cases at much the same time. The main significance of the Chapman/Bagot episode is that it inaugurated an important and continuing connection between Ennis and County Clare and the colony of South Australia.

The main origins of assisted immigrants from Ireland to South Australia are quite clear. County Clare was repeatedly and consistently the greatest single source—25 per cent in 1840, 27 per cent in the 1850s, 45 per cent in 1864 and 38 per cent in 1866. Tipperary, Limerick and Cork came next but were some way behind. These four counties accounted for more than 50 per cent of assisted Irish immigrants in the third quarter of the century.[23] After 1867 assisted immigrants were no longer classified by counties of origin and it is impossible to be sure that the pattern continued, but the likelihood is high.

The stability of this pattern suggests the importance of family-based emigration and a chain formation—so much so the links became self-reinforcing, each migrant generating further migration from within his or her family. Individual family histories and genealogies, and other literary sources, tend to confirm the suggestion. For instance, many of the first members of the Sisters of St Joseph, 1867–72, were Irish-born—93 out of 146—but they were generally recruited from emigrant families already established in South Australia.[24]

The persistence of these connections was powerfully reinforced by the nomination system of immigration. This was a form of institutionalised chain migration whereby colonial residents nominated relatives or friends to gain partially or fully subsidised passages to South Australia. Here the evidence is quite clear—the Irish had extraordinarily disproportionate recourse to this device and brought out many such kinsfolk. In 1858 the Irish constituted 68 per cent of those nominated and 53 per cent in 1862, and in 1865 their nomination totally swamped those for English and Scots people. In 1873 to 1885 they were again the greatest single category amounting to 46 per cent of all nominations. However, unlike the Scots and the English, the Irish nominated a preponderance of single adults and rather more males than females. In part the success of Irish nominations reflected the colony's need for agricultural labour and domestic servants, categories which appeared more readily available in Ireland than in other parts of the United Kingdom. More particularly (especially since Clare and Cork continued to preponderate) it reflected the extraordinary solidarity of Irish connections and the remarkable climate of mobility in post-famine Ireland. There is some evidence that "groups from neighbouring villages in Killarney, Cavan or Cork often settled in the same region and intermarried,"[25] though, as I will suggest later, these may have acted primarily as staging posts for a further migration within a generation.

The fact that the Irish were by far the most effective users of the nomination system caused the colonial immigration authorities to take fright at the overbalance of the immigration towards the Irish. These political considerations were met in two ways—one was to re-assert the "home-proportions" policy and direct all "selected immigration" exclusively to Scotland and England; the other was to suspend, temporarily, the nomination system. Between 1872 and 1886 the South Australian government chose to send no travelling inspector of emigrants to Ireland and the selection of assisted migrants was virtually confined to the non-Irish parts of the British Isles.[26] Nevertheless the Irish component in government immigration rose to about 40 per cent at times in the 1850s, 60s and 70s, and the Catholic element in the population reached a plateau of about 14 per cent in the last quarter of the century.

The South Australian statistical data does not allow us to say much about the general composition of these migrants. Most of the assisted migrants were called "labourers" and "domestic servants" but these were labels of convenience necessary to satisfy the recruiting authorities. It is, however, clear that without subsidy these people would have had difficulty leaving Ireland, certainly by the expensive Australian passage, and this may have biassed their selection to the less depressed districts of Ireland. The fact that many, perhaps 50 per cent, were assisted rather than fully-subsidised, may also suggest that they derived from relatively well-heeled families who had already fared middlingly well in South Australia. The colonial statistics, unfortunately, do not help one way or another to test Dr Fitzpatrick's important proposition that the people were refugees from the spread of grazing in Midland Ireland, or that they were essentially ordinary folk from regions "remarkable neither for backwardness nor industrialisation."[27] It is difficult to deduce even this much from the colonial evidence, especially when we note that the counties whence the majority of the assisted immigrants came were also the most emigration-prone in Ireland during those years.[28]

There is indeed a statistical quicksand at the centre of the colonial evidence for immigration studies. Practically all the detailed information we possess about the origins and social characteristics of immigrants is strictly confined to the assisted and nominated portion of the immigrant population. The privately-financed immigrants were not recorded in this detail and sometimes remain entirely anonymous and beyond the reach of the statistics. Moreover private immigration constituted a changing proportion of the total, a "dark figure" in the Australian statistics. Sometimes efforts were made to determine the relativities. For instance in South Australia in 1851 there were 3,669 assisted immigrants as compared with 4,795 who travelled as private persons. At the time, however, even larger numbers of unspecified persons left the colony. In 1853 and 1854 assisted immigration totalled onlyt 34 per cent of registered immigrants and about these we know all their county origins and much more. But of the residual, that is those who made up two-thirds of the immigration figures for those years, we know virtually nothing. All this is depressing enough but rendered worse, especially for the Irish, by the high rate of mobility of migrants between the colonies and the fact that many Irish left the British Isles from non-Irish ports. These statistical problems subvert some of our best generalisations about the character of colonial immigration and suggest the need for complementary evidence from home sources.

At least one basic proposition about South Australian immigration remains intact—that the female component of assisted Irish immigration was unusually, even uniquely, high, and that it was in excess of males for certain years. The femininity of the Irish immigration into South Australia was the specific consequence of particular and atypical deluges of single Irish girls in three years (1848–9, 1855 and 1880), and was a response to special recruitment schemes engineered by the colonial authorities. These inflows, in effect, unbalanced the general average. In reality for most years the balance of the sexes was fairly even, and Irish males exceeded Irish females in 18 out of 31 years of assisted immigration to South Australia.[29]

The single Irish girls were introduced frankly to solve the labour, sexual and reproductive requirements of the colonial population. The *South Australian Register* in September 1848 spoke of "the delicate duty of equalising the sexes," and there were, of course, similar, though proportionately smaller, schemes in the other colonies. The first wave was in 1848 and then another in 1855, bringing a total of about 5,000 girls to the colony, many of them from severely disadvantaged backgrounds.[30] Their arrival, in numbers far greater than originally anticipated, produced a frenzy of comment and moralising. The episode stretched the limits of inter-communal tolerance in the colony and, temporarily, generated strong antipathies.

The main problem with the Irish girls was not their nationality. It was more to do with the sudden congestion of so many female juveniles, their lack of training and education, their religion (a relatively minor matter), and the fact that many of them arrived during the downturn in the colonial employment cycle. The arrangements governing the emigration were generally incompetent.

The facts of the episode are plain enough. South Australia, before and during the gold rushes, was desperate for labour; at one stage a scheme was mounted by pastoralists to import

large numbers of coolies through Hong Kong, and the need
for domestic servants was thought to be practically limitless.
Thus the introduction of girls from poor houses and elsewhere began in earnest in 1848, when 620 were brought from
Ireland as well as about 1,000 from England.[31] The colonial
expectations of these girls were difficult to satisfy—it was said
that "the Irish orphans are chiefly wanted for the Country
Settlers and are almost useless if they cannot milk cows and
wash clothes." In the towns, especially in Adelaide, domestic
servants needed a degree of familiarity with bourgeois living
beyond that of the graduates of poorhouses. The immigration officials described them generally as "a rough lot," yet
though "generally short and not at all well looking, they did
not appear weak or unhealthy; they seemed good humoured
and well disposed." An Anglican clergyman in Adelaide
remarked that the Irish orphans "from infancy [had] always
been ill fed" and could not be compared with English women
of the same age. But when another Anglican clergyman said
that South Australia wanted no Catholics and that the girls
would have to become Protestants, he was roundly
condemned in the Adelaide press.

Most of this cohort of immigration were quickly absorbed
into the workforce, though there were problems in 1849
when wages fell rapidly and unemployment developed. There
was evidence that some of the Irish girls were reduced to
prostitution, and that they contributed 42 per cent of
prostitutes in Adelaide in 1851. But there were identical
complaints about the English orphans, especially those from
Marylebone in London. By 1852 most of the girls had
become respectably married and many were employing their
own servants. The first experiment in mass female immigration had worked reasonably well, though we know little of
the response of the girls themselves.[32]

Severe labour shortages recurred during the gold rushes
and South Australia increased its demand for immigrants
throughout the British Isles. By 1853 the Irish comprised
more than 10 per cent and the local St Patrick's Society
advocated a renewal of the immigration of Irish pauper girls

"to replace the labourers lost to the diggings."[33] In the end the emigration authorities in England answered the call with a deluge of young females—in 1855 4,049 single girls arrived at Port Adelaide, of whom 74 per cent were Irish, mostly from the poorhouses. The scale of this immigration, the general inadequacy of the arrangements, the latent and growing hostility of the colonial population,[34] the rising unemployment in the colony, distress of the teenage girls—all this could easily have turned the episode into disaster.[35] The colony possessed only primitive reception facilities and the girls were shifted around in a despairing effort to find them work.

Consequently the migrant experiences of these girls looms large in the South Australian Irish story. It would be difficult to exaggerate the anxiety and distress of these young migrants. Many started their sagas with a long deck passage from Dublin to Plymouth aboard an inferior steamer in vile, cold and rough weather.[36] Many of them had friends and kin in Australia but were sent to the wrong destination. Many of the girls had never actually agreed to go to South Australia and only half of them had signed the necessary forms. Of a group of 464 interviewed in Adelaide in 1855, 72 had applied to go to Sydney, 159 to Melbourne, three to Geelong, and one had expected to go to America. The agents in Ireland had played fast and loose in their urgency to fill the ships; there had been re-selling of tickets and some of the girls had left without their parents' permission or under assumed names. There were credible allegations that the Poor Law officers and landlords had used the colonial scheme to get rid of those "whom they conceive encumbrances on their property, or who are supported by the rates in poor houses."[37] A government inquiry into these events condemned the gross laxity of procedure, the violation of instructions, and the misapplication of the public funds of South Australia. These were strong words and were, indeed, a prelude to an impending change of policy and the colony's subsequent rejection of London's control of its immigration monies and methods. The episode destroyed South Australia's confidence in the operations of the Land and Emigration Commissioners.

Once arrived in South Australia many of the girls applied to leave for other colonies and it is difficult to trace their subsequent movements. They had been treated like human flotsam and with little regard to their own feelings. It was noted of the passengers aboard the *Lord Raglan* in November 1856 that "the women must be very much under the sway of false promises to have their destination changed with so little trouble."[38] For several months after arrival the girls were constricted within an immigration depot in Adelaide and subjected to tight moral controls. They were overcrowded, overheated, overdisciplined and underpaid, and they came close to mutiny and riot. Subsequently many were arbitrarily dispersed to outlying rural areas in the distant outback—which itself caused fear and panic—and some returned to Adelaide with their hands stripped by the severity of the work they were required to perform.

There were endless complaints about the girls—for instance that a third of them were incapable of cooking, washing and indoor employment since they had received no training in domestic service. They were uneducated and at the same time not only resistant to rural employment but unequal to its simple requirements. It is not at all surprising that anti-pauper and anti-Irish feeling was generated. But it was not confined to the Irish; Scottish Highlanders faced the same uncomprehending and exasperating reaction and so too did some of the rural English immigrants. For instance, a colonial immigration official said of some Cornish folk arriving in 1857 that they were "the most ignorant and uncultivated race whom I found it difficult to subject to any rule and regulation."[39] Thus there was a certain equality of condemnation.

Originally however, there was little prejudice against the Irish girls, indeed there was a rush for their services. One report noted that "the respectable and superior demeanour of the better class of the Irish girl is something quite fascinating."[40] But their sheer numbers soon overwhelmed the local market and inevitably the immigrants became a substantial social problem. They generated the classic stereotypical antipathy among the servant-employing strata of Adelaide society—

that the girls were "a class utterly unfitted for domestic service of any kind." It took on an Irish dimension simply because the Irish proportion in assisted immigration had suddenly leapt from 9 per cent in 1853 to 43 per cent in 1855 and 47 per cent in 1858.

Yet the most remarkable aspect of the crisis was its brevity and swift evaporation. Within twelve months the deluge had been absorbed in the colony, mainly by dispersal into the country areas, most notable to the north of Adelaide at Clare and Kapunda, and to Willunga in the south. Soon indeed the South Australians were congratulating themselves for their tolerance and their herculean efforts at coping with the problem. Yet more remarkable, and significant in broader terms, is the fact that there was no folk memory of this invasion of Irish teenagers, no recollection in the community within Adelaide or beyond.

Of the girls themselves, of the migrant experiences, there are only glimpses. We know that they had left Ireland "full of hope for husbands, good wages and good food in South Australia—and found themselves unwelcome and unemployed, confused and friendless." *The Adelaide Times* in July 1855 described the arrival of one shipload:

> one hundred and forty of these young women . . . were yesterday brought up from the Port, and the blank look of despair, often ending in a flood of tears with which many a poor girl, as she was put down at the building with her small bundle, mutely regarded the crowd of fellow unfortunates, was most distressing.[41]

An Englishwoman employer, the leading Unitarian, Caroline Emily Clark, describing the arrival of an Irish servant girl, noted that she had to be taught everything, never having seen meat roasted and being ignorant of the names of the kitchen utensils. "I felt sorry for her, she was melancholy, she wished herself back home again with all her heart. It is indeed a dreary looking country now and especially for one from the emerald isle."[42]

The girls were sometimes humiliated by their employers and insulted by offers of employment at wages one-third only of the normal servant rates. Some of the girls who went to Gawler weren't even provided with mattresses and were expected to sleep on straw, just like pigs, according to one of their outraged countrymen. At Willunga they became mutinous, apparently out of fear of the bush and snakes, refusing to travel the rough country tracks, and complaining bitterly about the lack of letters from home, poor wages, and about being dispersed and thereby isolated from their friends. At Clare, 100 miles north of Adelaide and one of several temporary enclaves of Irish in the colony, their reception was more friendly and, under the leadership of P.D. Gleeson (Chairman of the District Council), employment was found for 40 girls and at least a quarter of them were married within three years, one to a local innkeeper and several to Protestant miners at the Burra Burra copper mines. Something like 120 girls were absorbed by Clare and district, but the great influx quietly passed out of popular recollection.[43] One hundred years later no one knew a thing about it.

The migrant experience is best seen through individual eyes though there is only slight testimony from the Irish girls.[44] Eliza Taafe, for instance, arrived aboard a shipful of orphans in 1849. We know that she had seen both her parents die in an Irish workhouse and had continued to live in the same workhouse until chosen as a migrant. Her behaviour aboard the ship was regarded as distinctly odd and it led to fears concerning her sanity, but the doctor thought that she was not incurably insane "but simply in need of kindness and care."[45] Her further fate is unknown. Mary Downey from Bantry in County Cork, arrived in the same year, aged 16—one of three in her family to survive the Famine—she had witnessed her parents and other members of her family buried in common graves. Her brother Eugene went to America and she never heard of him again, but her sister Julia was already in Australia. Mary Downey herself went to Mintaro, to Peter Brady's house—that of a well established Irish farmer. There she met George Faulkner, a self-educated labourer who had arrived in the colony, aged 15, in 1838 from Titchmarsh in England, and had saved

enough to buy a ten acre block in Mintaro. They married in
the Catholic church at Clare in June 1852 and soon after set
off by bullock dray for the Bendigo goldfields. After only
modest success they returned to farming at Mintaro where
during the following 21 years they had eleven children, of
whom two died in infancy. As settlement extended north in
the 1870s, their sons were part of the continuing colonisation
of the territory. Mary Faulkner lived on until 1904.[46]

In general most of the girls had no relatives or friends in
South Australia and many were disappointed on their arrival.
"They seem to think there is very little, if any, chance for
them, and I have found them in tears from this cause frequently," said the Matron of the Immigration Depot.[47]

Some of the voices of the girls in the Depot were heard
when interviewed by a Parliamentary Enquiry in 1856. For
instance Margaret Hanlon, who came from Naas in Co.
Kildare, was the daughter of a footman and groom. She was a
widow, accompanied by a 21 year old daughter. She came to
Australia "because I was in poverty at home, and my sister
sent for me, and paid one pound for me and the same for my
daughter." She had a crippled and smallpoxed arm—as she
said "I can work although I have the evil in my arm . . . I can
do a little washing; it is wonderful how much I can do
considering the extent of my affliction." But she could no
longer support herself.[48]

Frances McDowell had come from Dublin; she had been
a teacher in an industrial school and really could not
comprehend why she had emigrated: she had no friends or
income, and her family's property had been the subject of an
unresolved Chancery suit for the past 18 years. She, like
many of the other immigrants, had suffered poor health and
eye inflammation on arrival in Australia.[49] Bridget Carroll
entered the employment of George Sanders and his family in
1854–5, who owned rather poor land in Echunga Creek. Mrs
Jane Sanders recollected how "Bridget was in low spirits, and
when we got into the scrubby ranges, she broke down and
wept, contrasting the present with the pictures drawn. She
said the agents in Dublin, to persuade the girls to leave home,

said that women were so scarce in Australia that gentlemen would drive down to the wharf in their carriages when a ship came in, and would carry them off to be married." Bridget Carroll did however stay with the Sanders family for seven years and then married a blacksmith, prospering enough to be in a position to be able to send monies back to her mother in Ireland.[50]

Ellen Door came from Cork and had wanted to go to Sydney with her sister but they had been split up and she suffered terribly—"Yes, I cried a great deal, and said I would rather return home than be separated from my sister." She had been in domestic service in Cork and could do this work, but she refused to go into the outback. Her intention was to go to Sydney with financial help from her friends. This indeed was the fate of many of the girls—a further career of mobility. Some of them thought they could walk from Adelaide to Melbourne. This was a distance of over 500 miles through difficult country, yet they believed it only a day's walk.[51]

Many of the girls lacked family connections or friends either on board ship or in the colony. They were adrift in an alien world and vulnerable to destitution or worse. Others were more fortunate and the statistics of 1855 demonstrate that the single Irish women who arrived under the nomination scheme—named by landowners in the colony—fared overwhelmingly better than their assisted counterparts. One of the most striking impressions from contemporary reports is the remarkable network of kin and friends which supported Irish immigrants of all sorts—a network which frequently stretched across the colonies.[52] Irish networks naturally reinforced the existing patterns of immigration for perhaps five generations and were best seen in South Australia in places such as Clare and Virginia.

The story of the pauper girls tends to reinforce the stereotype of Irish immigration and there can be no doubt that among the single girls there were many pitiable refugees of the famine. In reality, South Australia attracted representatives from Ireland at all levels in the colonising society. It is possible to take soundings in each stratum of Irish South Australia and find these highly differentiated outflows of the Irish economy. Ireland provided capital and entrepreneurship as well as muscle and sinew, professional as well as labouring people. Nor were the Catholic Irish confined to the working classes, even though they were over-represented in the manual trades.

There is, for instance, the case of Michael O'Dea and his family, an independent farmer from Co. Clare. They were caught in the economic effects of the famine and faced the loss of their farm and the fall in social status that went with it. O'Dea's mother, whose husband died in 1845, appears to have made the critical decision to emigrate. In her son's words:

> she said if she was to be hard up she would rather be hard up
> in a strange land than where she would be known for she said
> it would break her heart to see any of the family as common
> servants and to have to work for the uncle and she would not
> stop in Ireland . . . whilst she had the means to get out of it.

Indeed their assets had been declining for several years and they had already thought of America. Their relatives told young Michael that they should never forget that "we belong to the middle class." Eventually in 1849 they obtained free passages to Port Adelaide. "When we landed the place looked dismal and huge to us . . . having no friends to meet us." O'Dea teamed up with some fellow Irish and took a job as a hutkeeper. He came into conflict with a German employer whom he refused to obey and was sacked; he refused work such as cleaning boots in Adelaide and, like so many others, took off for the gold diggings with a brother and a mate. He spent three years away, with a little success, returned to farm and married a woman from Co. Cavan. Ultimately he settled on land in Rutherglen in Victoria.[53] His was a modest story of the recovery of status by work, mobility and migration; a good Irish story but hardly exclusively Irish.

Another experience was that of the remarkably intrepid Isobel Alice Wyly who, at the age of 17, travelled alone to Adelaide in 1851. Her family, probably Quakers, had owned 2,000 acres in Co. Kildare and Co. Westmeath, but too many children and too little good fortune had caused their decline. Her father had 14 siblings and two uncles had emigrated, and her own family went to Bloomfield, Dublin. Isobel herself left for Adelaide, helped by Quaker connections. She became the forerunner of other Wyly migrants. Eight years after her arrival she married John Scott, a draper, in a Wesleyan chapel. She had done well as a migrant; according to her aunt she had found "a respectable, steady, sober young man without very much money to boast of, but he had a good business, and there is every prospect of happiness." Isobel herself had accumulated a fine stock of clothing, some furniture, and a share in a Building Society, and had been the object of three offers of marriage within three weeks.[54]

Against the grain of most of our generalisations about the South Australian Irish was the career of E.B. Gleeson, a Catholic squatter with capital who arrived in the first wave of colonisation in 1838. He migrated to the new colony under the auspices of the Australian Association of Bengal. He came to South Australia after a military career in India, described as "an Irish gentleman . . . from India with his lac of rupees, Arab horses, and Indian servants," not to mention his lady and two children. By 1840 he was already the second largest pastoralist in the Adelaide district, with 7,300 sheep, 550 cattle and 24 horses, much engaged in exploring possibilities to the north. He imported Indian coolies at this time but, in 1841, lost one of them in an Aboriginal attack. In the same year he was badly injured in the financial crisis which engulfed the colony. Selling off much of his property, he moved north, where he founded a township which he called Clare after his birthplace. He did well and by 1860 held 160 square miles in the district, was the first mayor of Clare in 1868, the Stipendiary Magistrate, and an extraordinarily popular and public-spirited figure—whimsically he was known as "Paddy Gleeson, King of Clare." He called his first house "Gleeville." When he died in 1870 the local Clare Freemasons obtained special dispensation to attend his funeral in full regalia. I can find no evidence to say that Gleeson was typical.[55]

From Rostrevor, near Newry in County Down, came John Reid, a merchant and shipowner who had suffered commercial losses in the depression of the early 1830s. His brother, a military man who served in N.S.W. in 1823–4, and later settled in the Hunter River with 2,000 acres, persuaded Reid to emigrate to Adelaide in 1838, encouraged by the know-ledge that there would be no convicts in the new colony. He paid his own passage and that of a considerable entourage, which included a nurse, a cook, a nursemaid and her hus-band. They were the first settlers at Gawler and attempted to establish a large farm helped by 12 families of labourers brought out from the family property in Ireland. But they failed badly—the Reids knew nothing of farming and their wage bills were far too high.

His daughter said of their labourers:

> a lazier and more unprovident set of people I never met with . . . our great trouble was our servants leaving us, after being years with us in Ireland. They could not stand the hardships . . . Even our old silver we had brought from Ireland went in wages.

In the outcome the Reids went back home to Ireland—though their brothers went off to the goldfields.[56]

Irish mobility was exemplified by another family, the Dempseys. Thomas Dempsey was born in Cootehill, Co. Cavan in 1792, a smallholder and weaver by trade with a seven acre holding. He married in 1818 and had produced eight children, all born in the same house, by 1840. They experienced considerable difficulties during the famine and it was sensible for the children to seek better subsistence beyond. Two sons went to Scotland to work on railway construction and saved thirty pounds, returned to Cavan in 1852 and re-emigrated soon thereafter. Meanwhile, in 1849 the fourth son, Andrew, described as a labourer, and two daughters, Bridget and Judith, both dairymaids, emigrated to South Australia. In 1851 Andrew Dempsey and three companions set out on foot for the Ballarat diggings. They did well, each making five hundred pounds within a few months. Dempsey returned and first built a public house at Dry Creek—called, of course, the "Cavan Arms." This was not lucrative and he later bought a team of bullocks and a block of land at Marrabel and married Catherine Doyle, who had arrived in the colony in 1850. Other brothers followed them out from Ireland and tried their luck, less successfully, at the goldfields, later to also join the bullock trade carrying Burra copper to the coast—in which the Irish had established a virtual monopoly.[57] In mid–1854 the rest of the family arrived from Ireland, including the aging parents. Andrew Dempsey died from a fall from a horse in March 1856 and two years later the family moved again. They gravitated northwards into another Irish district at Mintaro and Auburn with a section of 224 acres of virgin soil, and while they established themselves they supplemented their resources in ore carting at Burra and further forays to the goldfields and to the Snowy River. Felix Dempsey married Elizabeth Tully from Co. Cavan and there were other land purchases and more immigration of relatives. Members of the Dempsey family were still emigrating to join their kinfolk in South Australia 30 years after the original migration. Such continuity was not only a tribute to family solidarity, but also to the extraordinary effectiveness of their communication and organisation across the world. They became part of the internal migratory shifts of the colony in the 1870s, expanding and spreading far north of Adelaide.[58]

The Dempseys belonged to a broad band of Irish immigrants: adventurous, mobile and calculating, doing well as independent farmers in the internal expansion of the colony. Like many other Irish they seemed to take disproportionate advantage of new land legislation (associated with Strangway's Act in 1869) which gave them easier access to credit for agricultural expansion. In the 1870s they were highly enterprising farmers, well established on broad acres and surrounded by Irish Catholics with a vigorous church and school. They were rational and successful migrants who had recovered the fortunes, status and integrity of their families.[59]

A recurrent theme in these accounts is the widening connections within families. John Kelly, one of a family of 15 from Queen's County, seems to have emigrated to South Australia, by way of an interim sojourn in Scotland, at the age of 36 in 1839. He soon implored the rest of the Kellys to follow him: "I have no doubt that if you were here, you would do a great deal better than in Glasgow."

He warned them that they would have to work hard at the start:

> I am certain you would be a great deal healthier and stronger . . . if you could see Mary now I am sure you would not know her, she is as stout again as she was and has not had a day's sickness since she came out, and she many a time pities you when she thinks of you all confined in the Gallowgate up those stairs while we are all under a fine climate with plenty of parrots flying over.

Kelly had already bought land for forty-five pounds and was well established. He advised his kinfolk to club together to buy a colonial land order so that "four of you can get out as steerage passengers and by paying the difference you can get into the intermediate." Kelly himself had built a house but could not build another—he said they could use a tent while a house was built for them.[60]

There were occasions when Irish-born Australians were critical of the colony's immigration policy. In 1874 there was an ironic turning of the tables when the *Irish Harp* led an attack on the importation of unwanted urban tradesmen from London and girls "suffering from cutaneous and contagious diseases." Michael Kenny remarked that "one ship brings 19 painters from their comfortable homes in England to wander about our streets in the utterly vain hope of finding employment. . . . It is a monstrous injustice that we should be taxed for the purpose of importing labour to compete against ourselves."

Kenny himself was an interesting type—an intercolonial Irishman, born in Co. Clare in 1808, who had first emigrated to Van Diemen's Land in 1841. He claimed to have been instrumental in the campaign to elect Daniel O'Connell to the House of Commons in 1828–9. He had emigrated in a ship chartered specifically for agricultural labourers: that at least was how they all described themselves but, Kenny explained, they were mainly urban tradesmen, silversmiths, tailors, barbers, shoemakers, and so on, and only one in five "could tell which end of a plough went foremost." Kenny soon left Van Diemen's Land and settled in South Australia where he eventually married Bridgid Purtle, a widow from Co. Kerry who had first married on the docks in Dublin in 1840 in order to qualify for a passage to South Australia on the *Mary Dugdale*. Kenny was also joined by his brother Daniel in 1845. In February 1851 he told the South Australian government of his other relatives who would make "strong healthy useful farm servants and well adapted for the colony," but were presently destitute in Ireland. He said that he and his brother could give them employment on their 160 acres of wheat and it would be an act of "charity and brotherly affection." This indeed was the first of many arrangements by which he brought relatives and friends to South Australia.

Meanwhile however Kenny went to the Victorian goldfields, where he was said to have been involved in the Eureka Stockade episode. On his return, he confirmed his success in farming in various parts of the northern and western settled districts, and he also owned the Railway Hotel at Freeling. He was vocal in his support for greater access to cheap land and advocated a selective immigration policy restricted to genuine farm labourers who, unlike Cockney house painters, were in real demand in the north of the colony. For twenty years, he said, he had been a regular sponsor of parties of 20 Irish farm workers. In July 1866 he claimed "that there is not another house in South Australia from which as many new chums have started to look for employment as from mine, and not one came back without. If the government would give me 20 emigration forms I will find them 20 young men by the first ship. . . . They will take the bush, as their friends before them did, and find work for themselves." In 1874 Kenny proudly recollected that "I brought my friends to this colony to be farmers—and independent farmers if possible . . . I am most happy to be able to explain. . . . that I succeeded. I was up in the Northern Areas last week, and I called on half a dozen friends' places, each with a square mile, two or three teams of 2 furrow ploughs, and everything in proportion to make a farmer and his family happy and contented—no sign of starvation," he assured his readers and adversaries.[61] He indignantly rejected any idea that these people were nominated and introduced to become mere servants. They were independent farmers first and foremost.

Kenny's career was paralleled by that of another successful Irish farmer, Daniel Brady, born in Co. Cavan in 1797, married in 1828, and who arrived in Adelaide in 1840 with a family of seven children. In 1847 he was already sponsoring immigrants, assuring the government that "by my own and my family's industry I have been enabled purchase above 560 acres". He was settled at Virginia, north of Adelaide, but he also was drawn to the goldfields, returning with £500 in his pocket. Over the next 20 years he claimed to have brought out to the colony more than 500 people, including relatives from Co. Cavan.[62]

Michael Kenny and Daniel Brady expressed the values of agrarian Irish migration—the quest for independence on the land and some clear mark of economic success. In this, however, there was nothing that may be said to be exclusively Irish—exact parallels are to be found in other immigrant groups. Indeed a broader issue can hardly be avoided. The question of the emigrant experience entails some measures of collective success and failure (and criteria for each) and in this there may be some danger of an easy reinforcement of national stereotypes. Thus when Thomas Hogarth, a Scot from Ayrshire, referred to Kapunda, which was always a considerable centre for the Catholic Irish in South Australia, he remarked unequivocally that "the Catholics as usual are the poorer class, the Protestants the wealthy and fashionable."[63] Since there were relatively few large Irish capitalists in the initial settlement of the colony, and since a substantial proportion of the assisted immigrants from Ireland in the 1850s were poor teenage girls, it would not be surprising that the average Irish income was initially relatively low. The interesting question is whether the South Australian Irish were permanently disadvantaged in any measurable sense, whether their upward mobility was significantly impaired, bearing in mind, of course, their status on arrival.

The only systematic study of wealth in colonial South Australia does suggest that the Irish were very marginally under-represented. Only 6 per cent of the original "pastoral pioneers" in 1855 were Irish-born and among these Protestants (such as Oldham, Yeates, Torrens, Hope and Blood) outnumbered the Catholics (such as Gleeson, Coglin and Cudmore). But this is a trivial deficiency since the Irish were little more than 7 per cent of the first immigrants. The most salient finding of this study was the critical importance of making an early start in the business of pastoralism. The fact that the Irish were mostly latecomers obviously told against them. Indeed it was not so much a question of being Irish or not being Irish, it was much more a question of timing and with how much capital a landowner started and in this respect it is possible that the Irish migrants, on average, possessed less capital than other groups.[64]

We know less about the middle strata of urban and rural society, but it seems likely that the Irish were unusually prominent among the small independent farmers. Lower down the social strata crude measures of poverty appear to tell against the Irish. Assuming a close correlation between being Irish and being Catholic—despite the fact that the most illustrious Catholic in the colony, Sister Mary MacKillop, was a Scot—they were clearly over-represented in the ranks of the institutionalised destitute. For instance in the late 1850s they were disproportionately dependent on the Destitute Asylum, and between 1887 and 1892 28 per cent of child wards of state were Catholics, whereas they constituted only 15 per cent of the population. Too much should not hang on these figures—the same body of evidence shows that the Church of England children were also greatly over-represented among the destitute. The fact that Catholic families were 40 per cent larger than non-Catholic families has an obvious bearing upon the differentials.[65]

It is true that there were relatively few professionally-educated among the Irish immigrants and those who were, tended to be Protestant. Yet even this is easily overstated. In reality the Irish, both Catholic and Protestant, offered a broad range of colonial types. They were over-represented in the police force and amongst the magistracy in 1849. They provided 14 per cent of the immigrant Anglican clergy, an extraordinary number considering the smallness of Protestant Irish immigration. There were times when the Irish-born were statistically over-represented in the South Australian House of Assembly, though there were very few in the Legislative Council. There were two Irish-born Governors of the colony, one of them a practising Catholic. Irish-trained doctors were sometimes over-represented in the colonial profession, and if we consider both Catholic and state education, then Irish teachers were almost certainly likewise. In the creation of the United Labour Party the Irish were fully represented, and the grandson of one of the Irish orphan girls who arrived in 1856 became Chief Justice of the Supreme Court of South Australia.[66] Where evidence survives, the Irish-born were found in good proportions among the lawyers, land surveyors, hoteliers and landbrokers of the colony. The Irish were over-represented among the early professoriate at the University of Adelaide and there were more Irish than Scots among the founding members of the Adelaide Club, though almost all were Protestant.[67] None of this is especially surprising nor statistically significant except on two counts. First, it suggests that the Irish were not discernibly marginalised on the evidence of many of the basic indicators; second, it suggests that apart from religion, the Irish were more similar to, than different from, emigrants from the rest of the British Isles, and moreover that the differences tended to erode over time.

Differences between the Irish and the rest of the colonial community were further weakened by their pattern of settlement. The Irish in South Australia did not generally settle in tight concentrations either in town or country. They were distributed broadly and evenly across the population, though there were for short periods (probably little more than a single generation) higher densities in particular places, such as Kapunda, Clare, Virginia, Willunga and parts of Adelaide. "They avoided in the colony the extremes of national concentration that the *Register* criticised in the case of the Germans."[68] Even in working class districts they did not preponderate for any length of time. The evidence, impressionistic though it remains, is generally consistent with Dr Fitzpatrick's hypothesis about the "ordinariness and normality" of Irish immigration. In their continuing mobility, in their settlement patterns and in their broad social characteristics, they were not easily distinguishable from their British counterparts.

In religion, the greatest divide between the Irish and the rest of society, the differences were greater and more sustained. Moreover the colony of South Australia had attracted a substantial quota of religious zealots of all shades. In their midst the Catholics were undeniably a poor and relatively vulnerable minority. They certainly faced predictable assaults. In the late 1860s, for instance, Angas and his secretary, Henry Hussey, tried to rouse the forces of antipopery in the colony. They distributed 40,000 pamphlets denouncing the satanic origins of Roman Catholicism and did all they could to generate a full-blooded controversy. The *Irish Harp*, mouthpiece of the Catholic community, responded gamely and described the Protestant Association as "a clique of narrow-minded bigots." The entire episode was a disappointment to both sides; the exchanges were all rather anaemic and demonstrated mainly the fact that the old differences had not travelled well to South Australia.[69]

When Michael Davitt visited South Australia in 1895, he was much taken by various forms of social, economic and political experiment that he observed. Davitt indeed wrote one of the most penetrating and thoughtful accounts of contemporary South Australia. But he was unable to arouse the Irish South Australians to his own cause. As one of his fellow-countrymen commented: "We have had Davitt here, a straight forward and unselfish agitator, tho not an orator. The appeal hear for the [Election] Fund will fall flat, as the people are disheartened by the unseemly squabbles of home, and financially too low to render much assistance."[70] South Australia, it is true, was in depression, but the real message was that Irish political issues and values had not flourished in the colonial environment. Fenianism had not taken root in the colony,[71] and the Independence movement at the end of the First World War seemed too far away for involvement. When a cousin in Co. Cork was describing the mayhem and murder in the struggle against the Black and Tans, he told his South Australian kinsmen "not to be putting on airs and forgetting your native land." Yet this was close to the truth.[72] The emigrant experience of the Irish (as much as say the Scots) in South Australia was largely a matter of merging into a wider migrant world which created far fewer tensions than anyone had ever imagined.

There are great difficulties in attaching significance to being Scots or Irish or whatever, in terms of their specific impact on Australia. At a minimum, a statistical disproportion has to be demonstrated for a differential significance in colonial life. But even if we find Scots or Irish proportionately more prominent than, say, people from Cardigan or Yorkshire or Silesia, the critical variable need not have been Scottishness or Irishness but something else entirely—such as average age on arrival, or per capita wealth, or education. And it is plainly absurd anyway to cut an average through such populations as though they were homogeneous—for the Scots, for example, the Hebridean crofter had little in common, sometimes not even religion, with the Paisley weaver, the Edinburgh dominie or the Aberdonian pastoralist.

It is, of course, a nonsense to consider the Irish in isolation from possible control groups.[73] Ultimately such questions are comparative. The Irish, both Catholic and Protestant, penetrated all levels of South Australian society and were involved with all aspects of colony-making—and they responded to the needs of the times like other migrants. Even where the issue of Irishness obtruded into colonial public debate, the effects were temporary and became virtually unidentifiable after a few years.

The importance of being Irish in colonial South Australia is most readily accounted for in economic terms. It is evident, for example, that the colony absorbed some of the particular surpluses of the Irish economy—its excess female youth, its overproduction of Anglican clergy, some of the rural labour, and perhaps some of its displaced small or middling farmers. Especially clear, notwithstanding the original efforts of Colonel Torrens and despite exceptions such as Gleeson, Reid and Chapman, South Australia was not able to attract much capital from Ireland. The net flow of funds was most probably in the opposite direction. The colony imported some scarce managerial and technical skills from Ireland, but in most categories the Irish were statistically neutral, no more and no less significant than other groups of immigrants.

The Irish arrived later, in fewer numbers, and with smaller resources than much of the rest of the population; nevertheless there is little hint that they were systematically reduced to the margins of this society. They may have overcome their initial disadvantages by their greater mobility—their recourse to the goldfields and their enthusiastic acceptance of opportunities in the northern extension of settlement may suggest a disproportionate participation in new development. But perhaps the most striking aspect of this picture of the Irish in South Australia is their similarity with the rest of Irish Australia, at least in crude statistical terms. If we continue to believe that the Irish in Australian society generally owed their relative success to their status as family colonists and as a substantial percentage of the total population, then it must be surprising that the South Australian Irish conformed to this pattern. In terms of our received arguments the South Australian Irish were more successful than our explanations presently allow.

This does not, of course, trench upon other less mundane and measurable qualities—it is not to deny the peculiarities in the cultural baggage with which such groups as the Irish travelled. It may be argued, however, that on many criteria the Irish were not greatly different from other groups in the colony and that their main importance was as exemplars of the broad mechanisms of international migration in that great age of mobility.

This may seem a somewhat limp conclusion. But at least it possesses the virtue of avoiding the automatic assumption of Irish marginalisation, and removes us from the territory of national stereotypes. Some of the most fruitful work on Irish and other emigration in recent years has been devoted to the differential responses of the migrants from various social strata and geographical origins. It has become much clearer, by way of this disaggregated approach, that flows of people emerged in response to conditions at each end of the migrant chain. It diminishes the monolithic character of the Irish migrant host; it also liberates the migrants for purposes of comparison with other groups. Indeed, in a wider perspective, it may be that categories such as the Scots and the Welsh, even the Irish, are not the most useful as analytical devices in studying migration.[74] It may be better to develop a broader taxonomy or prosopography of migrants less dependent on nationality and less likely to reinforce national stereotypes. It is also more likely to expose the active variables in migrant history.

These suggestions may engender a more radical tendency, a more ambitious possibility. It may indeed be possible to transcend the matter of nationality and collective filial piety and to begin to see the Irish (and, of course, other groups of migrants) more fully as part of the early evolution of the international labour market and the mechanisms of the multinational world economy. Even better, we may see them in the perspective of the greater diaspora of the European peoples in the nineteenth and twentieth centuries. But this, it must be emphasised, is not designed to deny or to diminish the vitality of each of the national and regional components; rather it is to set them in a wider and more comparative framework. It does however take us far from the people with whom this paper has been engaged—the individual faces in the great migrant crowds, be they Irish or otherwise.

References

1. Oliver MacDonagh, "The Irish in Victoria 1851–91: a demographic essay," *A.N.U. Historical Journal* (1973–4), p. 76. Some of the statistics are summarised in Christopher Nance, "The Irish in South Australia during the colony's first four decades," *Journal of the Historical Society of South Australia* (hereafter J.H.S.S.A.), No. 5 (1978), pp.66–73 and in Geoffrey Sherrington, *Australia's Immigrants* (Sydney, 1980), p.82.

2. Letter of Benson, 18 February 1843, in Adelaide Archdiocesan Archives, quoted in Susan Pruul (subsequently Woodburn), "The Irish in N.S.W., Victoria and South Australia 1788–1880," M.A. Thesis, University of Adelaide, 1979, p. 203. The point had been made in June 1840 thus: "This province differs essentially from New South Wales and Van Diemen's Land in the particular that in it, Roman Catholics in number are an insignificant body, while in them they form a very large proportion of the population." Mortlock Library of South Australiana (hereafter MLSA) GRG/2/6/1, Despatches from Adelaide.

3. O'Halloran in *Adelaide Observer*, 14 July 1849, quoted in Pruul, thesis, p.198.

4. E.G. Wakefield, *Letter from Sydney* (London, 1829), p. 129; [Nassau Senior] *Remarks on Emigration* (unpublished printed manuscript MLSA PRG32/37).

5. Robert Torrens, *Emigration from Ireland to South Australia* (Dublin, 1839), pp.20–2. Comparable ideas were offered in the *Dublin University Magazine* 1839; see Margaret Press, *From Our Broken Toil. South Australian Catholics, 1836–1906* (Adelaide, 1986), p.91.

6. Torrens, *Emigration*, pp.20–2; *Plan of an Association in aid of the Irish Poor Law* (London, 1838), pp.24–6. In December 1839 Torrens issued a Prospectus for an "Irish South Australian Emigration Community" in which large profits were anticipated. Torrens mentioned profits on colonial lands of 1000 per cent in three years and an average gain of 80 per cent. As well as relief from overpopulation, and the diminution of "misery and destitution" among the labouring classes, he now also appealed directly to the guardians of the poor who could benefit from "a perpetually available Emigration Fund" with "the privilege of sending out free of cost a number of paupers." Mitchell Library, Sydney, A272 South Australian Papers, Prospectus of Irish South Australian Emigration Community.

7. On Torrens see S.A. Meenai, "Robert Torrens, 1780–1864", *Economica*, Vol. XXIII (1956); R.C.D. Black, *Economic Thought and the Irish question 1817–1870* (Cambridge, 1960); L. Robbins, *Robert Torrens and the Evolution of Classical Political Economy* (London,

1958). Note that, from as early as 1811, Torrens had been an advocate of Roman Catholic rights; he was, in effect, the perfect counterpoise to George Fife Angas, another founding father of the colony, who regarded the Catholic form of faith as "obnoxious error." See also D. Pike, *Paradise of Dissent* (Melbourne, 1957), p.128.

8. Robert Torrens, *Systematic Colonisation, Ireland Saved, Without Cost to the Imperial Treasury* (London, 1849). See also Maurice B. Keain, "The Catholic Church in South Australia—A Genealogist takes a look," in Andrew G. Peake (ed.), *Genealogical Papers—1980 Genealogy Congress* (Adelaide, 1981), p. 20.

9. O'Connor deplored selective emigration on the grounds that it was depriving the Mother Country of the workers it could least afford to lose: "it is not the idle and the indolent who emigrate, but the industrious." He said it would be dishonest for any Irish member to vote for the bill. See Peter Howell, "The South Australia Act," Dean Jaensch (ed.), *Flinders History of South Australia, Political History* (Adelaide, 1987), pp.43–8. The parliamentary debate is reported fully in B. Dickey and P. Howell, *South Australia's Foundation: Select Documents* (Adelaide, 1987), pp.32–42.

10. Initially thirteen in England, four in Scotland, one in Ireland: in 1865, sixteen in England, three in Scotland, one in Ireland. Pike, p.151, and Pruul, thesis, p.246.

11. Pike, *Paradise of Dissent*, p.140; PROSA, PRG174/1/801.

12. *Australian Chronicle*, 23 July 1840. Pace the remarks of Father Benson quoted in Press, *Broken Toil*, p.42, Bishop Murphy, on his tour of Ireland in 1846, did a great deal of recruiting telling potential migrants, including people with capital, to choose "this flourishing colony" which possessed "the finest climate in the world." Press, *Broken Toil*, p.78.

13. See Press, *Broken Toil*, pp.25, 31. There were already 300 Irish Catholics in South Australia in 1839. The 1840 voyagers were described as useful labourers likely to be of much service to the settlers, *South Australian Register*, 11 July 1840, but they were unlikely to be in a position to provide much financial help to the embryonic Catholic Church. See also *The Fitzgeralds. Irish Pioneers of South Australia*. (Adelaide, 1986), Chap. I.

14. See David Hilliard and Arnold D. Hunt, "Religion," in Eric Richards, *The Flinders History of South Australia: Social History (Adelaide, 1986)*, p.212; see also Press, *Broken Toil*, pp.31 and 51.

15. See Handasyde Duncan, June 1850, quoted in Pike, *op.cit.*, p.318; S.A.P.P. *Reports of the select committee of Legislative Council of South Australia . . . into the Excessive Female Immigration* (1856), Q9, 151; *Government Gazette*, 10 July 1851, pp.478–9.

16. See Pike, *Paradise*, pp.180–2; Eric Richards, "The Peopling of South Australia," in Richards, *Social History*, p.123.

17. PROSA GRG/35/584/31; GRG 48/5.

18. PROSA 839. A *Holograph Memoir of Capt Charles Hervey Bagot* (republished by Pioneer's Association, Adelaide 1960).

19. He wrote *The National Importance of Emigration* (London, 1863).

20. On Chapman's movements in Australia see *Adelaide Register*, 23 January 1852, 17 March 1852; *Adelaide Observer*, 20 March 1852; *Sydney Morning Herald*, 9 May 1852; *Annual Register* (1853), p.229.

21. Press, *Broken Toil*, p.146.

22. PROSA A939, Agreement between Archibald Adam Snr of Greenock and Chas. H. Bagot, 7 July 1840.

23. See Kenneth W.A. Bray, "Government Sponsored Immigration into South Australia 1872–86," M.A. thesis, University of Adelaide, 1961. PROSA GRG/35/46. Misc. Papers on Immigration.

24. Information from the work of Sister Marie Foale.

25. Press, *Broken Toil*, p.96; Pruul, thesis, p.246.

26. Bray, thesis, pp.154–6, App.C; PROSA, GRG 7/42 (3.v.).

27. See David Fitzpatrick, "Irish Emigration in the Later Nineteenth Century," *Irish Historical Studies*, XXII (1980), pp.134–7.

28. Clare was also the greatest source of immigrants for Victoria—see Chris McConville, "The Victorian Irish: emigrants and families 1831–91" in *Families in Colonial Australia*, edited by P. Grimshaw, C. McConville and E. McEwan, pp.6–7.

29. SAPP 1856 No. 183: despatches on Excessive Female Immigration During 1855, p.7.

30. The best source is C.V. Parkin, "Irish Female Immigration to South Australia," B.A. Honours thesis, University of Adelaide, 1964. The quotation from the *Register* is from p.20 of this thesis.

31. The Irish girls represented 37 per cent of the intake and of these only half were from the Catholic parts of Ireland.

32. Parkin, thesis, p.46.

33. Parkin, thesis, p.59.

34. Some of this common prejudice, temporary though it was, was regurgitated by Sir Charles Wentworth Dilke in *Greater Britain* (London, 1869), pp.372–4.

35. The select committee enquiry summarised it as the "shipment of unsuitable females, in most unusual numbers, without usual protection, and within a very limited period." SAPP *Reports of the Select Committee of the Legislative Council of South Australia . . . into the Excessive Female Immigration* (1856).

36. PROSA GRG35/48/1855 *Sea Park*. A Scottish journalist en route for Adelaide in 1858 described the embarkation scenes at

Birkenhead—notably "a group of Irish from the extreme west of Ireland, and having had a long and coarse voyage, having all lain down on the floor like as I have seen cattle after leaving a steamer."

37. *Report* Q51 et passim.

38. Parkin, thesis, p.74.

39. PROSA GRG 35/48/1857; Eric Richards, "The Highland Scots of South Australia in the 1850s," *J.H.S.S.A.*, Vol. 4 (1978).

40. PROSA GRG 35/48. On the whole the South Australian reaction was not so much anti-Irish as a fear of permanent pauperism. The governor of South Australia in these years was Sir Richard MacDonnell—himself a typical Anglo-Irish patrician oligarch in the colonial service. At the time of the crisis he much favoured compulsory outdoor work for the unemployed girls—"I confess that, as an Irishman, I infinitely prefer seeing my country women employed in any honest work, whether reaping, stacking or other outdoor farming occupations, to seeing them leading as at present, a life of forced idleness, demoralising to themselves and injurious to the best interests of the colony." Quoted in Parkin, thesis, p.110. The fear of pauperism diminished rapidly, partly because immigration ceased in the immediately following years.

41. Quoted in Parkin, thesis, p.109.

42. MLSA Crompton Papers, PRG 331, entries for 12/14 April 1851. See also PROSA A64 (A1) Letters of Catherine Hussey, and John Church's description, in 1853, of "a great rough Irish girl" who was innocent of the niceties of the English class system: MLSA D6440(C) Church Letters.

43. Parkin, thesis, pp.110 et seq.

44. Their subsequent careers are obscured by their married names and the loss of their original identities. Only a few faces in the crowds of migrants are retrievable.

45. Parkin, op.cit., pp.6–7. Report of surgeon to Moorhouse, 26 June 1849.

46. Report of Enquiry pp.358 et seq. George Faulkner, pamphlet *Our Ancestors* (Norton Summit, n.d.).

47. *Report, op. cit.*, p.358.

48. ibid, p. 650.

49. ibid, pp.31–41.

50. MLSA 1208, "Reminiscences of Jane Sanders".

51. Select Committee, pp.31–41. More than 250 left South Australia within ten months of arrival.

52. S.A.P.P. No.152, Assisted Immigration 1855, Appendix K, p.15.

53. MLSA, Memoirs of Michael O'Dea D5235, and "Memoirs of Michael O'Dea," edited by Susan Pruul, *South Australiana*, Vol.15, no.1 (1976), pp.3–35.

54. Based on Dorothy A.A. Wyly, *Irish Origins. A Family Settlement in Australia* (Launceston, 1976).

55. "A.A.L." "The First Settlers at Gawler," *Royal Geographical Society of Australia (S.A.) Proceedings*, Vol.XXVIII (1926–7), p.77; Rodney Cockburn, *Pastoral Pioneers of South Australia* (2 vols, Adelaide 1925), I, pp.86–7.

56. "A.A.L." "The First Settlers at Gawler," R.G.S.A. (S.A.) Proceedings, Vol.XXVIII (1926–7), pp.53–82.

57. See Pike, *Paradise*, p.337.

58. It is likely that the Irish were disproportionately influential in the northern extension of settlement, see Press, *Broken Toil*, pp.42, 46.

59. MLSA D5084 (T); *The Dempsey Family* (pamphlet 1933, republished by B. Condon, Adelaide, 1983).

60. MLSA PRG481 Papers of John Kelly and family. There were several requests for assisted passages for Kelly kinsfolk, possibly connected with John Kelly—see PROSA 1848/329, A6552/271–443.

61. *Irish Harp and Farmers' Herald*, 23 April 1874, 1 May, 8 May, 15 May, 21 May, 22 May, 29 May, 2 June, 12 June, 26 June 1874. Kenny's views on the superiority of Irish colonies echoed the remarks of the *Register* in 1850, that the Irish, being less affluent, went into the business of colonisation more directly—"the majority of them will become comfortable proprietors. Generally speaking the Irish peasant makes a more successful colonist than the English one." Quoted in Pruul, *op.cit.*, p.213.

62. MLSA, GRG 24/6A (1851) 437, 8 February 1851 Letter of Michael Kenny. Kenny's nomination activity is confirmed in part in MLSA, GRG 7/44 Index to free Colonial Nominations 1876–9; GRG 24/6A (1851) 437, 8 February 1851, GRG 24/6A (1851) 889, 17 March 1851, *Advertiser* 24 July 1886. See pamphlet Kevin Kenny, *The Descendants of Brigid Purtle . . .* (Adelaide, 1979). Press, *op.cit.*, p.150; Brady's progress is charted through his land purchases and applications for nominated migrants e.g. MLSA GRG 26/4 A (1847) 1223, GRG 24/4/P (1848) 390; "The Dempsey Family," MLSA Z Pam 929.902999423, p.4. See also Keain, *Catholic Church*, p.23.

63. MLSA D5747 (L) Reminiscences of Thomas Hogarth.

64. Sister Shirley F. Macklin, "Pastoral Pioneers in South Australia. A Quantitative Analysis," B.A. Hons. thesis, Flinders University, 1978.

65. See Margaret Barbalet, "State Children, Theory and Practice in South Australia, 1918–1928," M.A. Thesis, University of Adelaide, 1973; *Far from a Low Gutter Girl* (Melbourne, 1983)

pp.xvi–xv; Brian Dickey, "Dependence in South Australia," in *Australia 1888*, Bulletin No.8, Sept.1981; Pruul, thesis pp.224–5.

66. For example John Crawford Woods B.A., son of a farmer in Co.Down. An ordained Presbyterian minister, Woods was poor and his wife poorer and when he was offered a salary of 400 pounds p.a. for four years, plus two hundred pounds for his passage to Adelaide to serve as a minister of the Unitarian Church, he snapped up the opportunity, MLSA D5037/1/2, "Rambling Recollections of John Crawford Woods B.A." South Australia was led by an Irish Catholic Governor 1862–8. Sir Dominick Daly from Galway was "popular with all sections of the colony's population yet uncompromising in his Catholicism." The fact that the Governor openly attended Mass in Adelaide was regarded with some astonishment by local Catholics. See Press, *Broken Toil*, pp.168–9.

67. On doctors see *Proceedings of the South Australian Branch of the British Medical Association*, vol.1 (1880–83), vol.2 (1883–6), vol.3 (1887–92) and S.A. Medical Board Register and Minute Book, Vol.1, which indicates origins of doctor's first degree. At least one doctor, Dr David Mahony from Co. Kerry, was never registered formerly, see "A.A.L.," *op.cit.*, p.80. For teachers see Reports of the Education Board, printed in Government Gazettes and Parliamentary Papers. On the United Labor Party see Brian Dickey, "South Australia" in D.J. Murphy (ed.) *Labor in Politics* (St Lucia, 1975), and H. Coxon, J. Playford and R. Reid, *Biographical Register of the South Australian Parliament 1857–1957* (Adelaide 1985). On the conservative side of colonial politics there was also good Irish representation, notably from George Kingston and Rev. Charles Howard, often regarded as a red-hot Tory. See Press, op.cit., p.45. For clergymen see T.T. Reed, *Anglican Clergymen of South Australia in the Nineteenth Century* (Gumeracha, 1986). Other estimates are derived from *South Australian Year Books* (Adelaide, annually), and the *Biographical Register to South Australia* (4 volumes, Adelaide, 1986). It is worth noting that the Protestant bias among some of the professional groups reflected the fact that they were already professionally qualified before arrival in the colony. A more penetrating measure of relative welfare and social mobility would require a study of the second and third generation of migrants, Irish and non-Irish, Catholic and Protestant.

68. See Pruul, thesis, p.237. Clare was the most Irish place in South Australia yet even Clare had difficulty sustaining its particular character. In 1881, of a total population of 1,131 only 120 had been born in Ireland, 197 in England and Wales, 699 having been born in the colony. Without large transfusions from Ireland

local demography was bound to weaken the direct Irish influence.
S.A. *Census 1881 Part VII*. In 1891 of the S.A. population born in
the British Isles 30 per cent were from Ireland and 12 per cent from
Scotland, but Irish females counted only 23 per cent of total British
Isles-born females. Census 1891.

69. *Irish Harp*, 26 June 1874. When Irish servant girls were
described as "Jesuits in disguise," the *Harp*, 6 March 1874, said that
they "are good workers, notably honest and above all, deeply
imbued with a religious feeling, affording the surest guarantee of
their purity and character," and needed to be defended against the
nonsense of "Mrs Shoddy and Mrs Knickerbocker." On Angas see
D. Hilliard and Arnold Hunt, "Religion," in Richards, op.cit.,
pp.212–13 and H. Hussey, *More than Half a Century of Colonial Life
and Christian Experience* (Adelaide, 1897), chapter XVII.

70. Religious conflict was less than generally anticipated. In 1854
a ship's surgeon on the *Sir Allan McNab* remarked that it was
unwise to put Highlanders and Irish in the same ship—"the least
religious event tending to cause disturbance among them," P.P.
Tasmania, 1854. James John Evans, Hobart, 14 February 1854. See
also Ruth Schumann, "The Practice of Catholic Piety in Colonial
South Adelaide," *Flinders Journal of History and Politics*, vol. 9
(1983), pp.6–39.

71. Michael Davitt, *Life and Progress in Australia* (London, 1898);
Patrick McMahon Glynn, *Letters to his family 1874–1927* (Melbourne, 1974).

72. In 1868 there was a widespread and systematic police investigation into Fenianism in South Australia. It discovered that
while there had been open discussion of Fenian principles in public
houses in Clare, Kapunda and Adelaide, the Irish population was
well disposed to the "English" Government. Out of a total population of 170,000 "only" 88 people were known to be hostile.
PROSA GRG 5/2/1868/502, 395, 721; GRG 5/3; GRG 5/4. See
also Parliamentary Papers of N.S.W., 1868–9, "Attempted Assassination of H.R.H. The Duke of Edinburgh; Correspondence etc,"
pp.9–10.

73. Quoted in Eric Richards, "Immigrant Lives," Richards, *Social
History*, pp.163–4.

74. See, for example, Eric Richards, "Australia and the Scottish
Connection, 1788–1914," in R.A. Cage (ed.), *The Scots Abroad*
(London, 1985), pp.111–12.

5.

The Irish in Queensland:
an overview

M.E.R. MACGINLEY

Each overseas country to which the Irish have gone in numbers has its own unique history of Irish migration and settlement. This experience stems not only from the numbers and compositions of the Irish migratory stream, but also from circumstances in the receiving country, for example, its degree of white settlement and the presence of other ethnic groups, religious and social polarities and the character and extent of its economic development. As recent studies in social history demonstrate, these differences also influence Irish settlement within the one country. One cannot, for instance, safely extrapolate from one state to another within Australia without having undertaken the necessary research. However, a brief preliminary comment for Australia as a whole is in place here. Not only was Australia's indigenous population small and scattered on white arrival and soon dispersed from the major areas of settlement, but the white population, until the conclusion of the Second World War, was of predominantly British Isles origin, with their various pressures and interests, but with a very different geographical distribution.

To describe this predominant sector in the pre-war population—and still statistically the largest sector in the present Australian population—the term Anglo-Celtic has come into use. Among the Celtic component are classed the Irish, certainly the highland Scottish, and the Welsh. However, because of earlier migrations and transplantations, the classification is not fully accurate: among the Celtic group are also the Cornish and perhaps many of those hailing from Devon, while both Scotland and Ireland, as we know, have a population mix containing also Viking, Norman and Anglo-Saxon ancestry. The term Anglo-Celtic, however, remains useful and helps to situate the group which is the subject of this paper—the Irish in Queensland. It also serves to highlight a factor which has received little attention to date in Australian studies and which may be more typical of Queensland than other areas of Australia, namely the incorporation of the Irish within this Celtic context, with its pervasive contribution to the emergence of a recognisable Australianism. Much emphasis in Australian historical studies has been placed on the distinctiveness of the Irish, and understandably so, as the religion of the great majority of them provided the basis for the consolidated growth of the Australian Catholic church, while the leadership roles, especially in politics, of a number of Irish-Australians constituted a distinct and often countervailing voice in a country where the initial establishment influences were strongly in the British tradition. This emphasis on distinctiveness, however, can mask social integration at a more basic level, especially visible in Queensland. I am reminded of an observation of Professor T. N. Brown in his study of Irish-American nationalism: "Not uniqueness and magic, but the earthy ability to get along with people of diverse origins was the special quality of the Celt."[1] The sheer diffusion of the Irish in Queensland, among others equally struggling, assured a common intergration.

Irish migration to Queensland can be clearly traced statistically. Though some Irish were present from the first years of white settlement at the penal colony of Moreton Bay (established 1824), both as convicts and soldiers, and there were Irish convicts among the assigned workers of the Leslies and other early pastoralists, it remains true that the vast majority of Queensland's Irish population—as indeed its general population—arrived after the virtual dismantling of the penal establishment (1839) and the opening up of the Moreton Bay precincts to free settlement (1842).[2] Though most ships destined for New South Wales prior to Queensland's separation from the mother colony in December 1859, disembarked their passengers at Sydney, the Register of Migrants[3] records a number of ships arriving at the port of Brisbane from the late 1840s. Among the passengers on some of these was a high proportion of Irish. The *Rajah-Gopaul*, for example, which arrived in 1852 carried 324 passengers of whom 253 (almost 80 per cent) were Irish; the *Mangerton* in 1861 had 361 passengers of whom 261 (72 per cent) were Irish. These proportions reflect the high tide of emigration from Ireland during the decades 1841–1850 and 1851–1860, each period witnessing the emigration of well over a million people.[4] In its survey of immigrants over the years 1831– 1848, 1841 was recorded as the peak year in the *Votes and Proceedings* of the N.S.W. Legislative Council:[5] of 20,000 assisted labourers who came out, approximately 1,500 were Scotsmen, 4,500 were English and 14,000 were Irish. Of the latter, some 10,000 were listed as Roman Catholics (approximately 71 per cent), an early reminder, in the Australian case, of the by no means insignificant migration of Protestant Irish. These were the years which occasioned alarm in sectors of British opinion in the colony at the high percentage of Irish arriving. As seen in the 1861 case of the *Mangerton* above, the new self-governing colony of Queensland, at its inception, continued to share this high tide. However, this was counter-balanced by other ships whose passengers were predominantly English and Scottish.[6] In Queensland's first colonial census (1861) the percentage of Irish-born was 18.4 per cent, a figure which would grow in the next few decades.

When Queensland achieved separation from New South Wales, its population was about 25,000, almost all of whom were concentrated in the south-east corner, and most of whom had arrived in the previous dozen years.[7] Promotion of immigration, therefore, through a variety of incentives, such as assisted and free passages, was a primary concern of the first Queensland parliament and of subsequent governments until the outbreak of the First World War. This was to give a distinct complexion to Queensland as a colony of immigrants and had significant political consequences. Where the old, mainly English, squatter establishment had the political and economic influence to achieve separation from New South Wales, they were soon to find themselves confronted by the more egalitarian objectives of the newer migrants, among whom, as we have seen, were a considerable number of Irish.

Between 1861 and 1891, the Queensland population increased over fifteenfold, while significant port cities developed further north along the extensive coastline. The development of these resulted from government policy, as the Agent-General in London was instructed to dispatch immigrants, not only to Brisbane as a port of entry, but direct to the northern ports of the colony, in such proportions as the minister should from time to time direct.[8] As added inducement, the first Queensland parliament established a land order system, whereby immigrants who paid their own passages, or those who paid such passages for them, were entitled to receive a land order for £18, and after residence in the colony for two years the settler himself was entitled to a further land order for £12. This provision was soon utilised by Bishop James Quinn, the first Catholic bishop of Brisbane. Both to relieve famine conditions in County Offaly and to put his diocese on a firmer foundation, he launched his own Queensland Immigration Society, a bold entrepreneurial venture, financed chiefly through the land order system.[9] By realising on the initial land orders offered, Bishop Quinn was enabled to utilise some twelve ships which brought a total of 4,000 immigrants to Queensland before alarm at this volume of Irish migration, as well as a general trafficking in land orders, led to an adaptation of the government regulations which effectively terminated the scheme.[10] Alarm that Queensland might become Quinnsland is given point when his total of migrants is contrasted with the government total of 5,000 over the same interval, February 1862 to July 1865. With his vigorous promotion of land settlement, Quinn led many of his migrants to take up farming land in fertile areas of southern Queensland.

In the period 1860–1888, Queensland showed the greatest proportional increase in population due to immigration of all the Australian colonies, 71.3 per cent increase compared with an average of 32.7 per cent for the other colonies.[11] The two decades of the largest Irish intake were the 1860s—when some migration was deflected towards Australia by the unsettled conditions of the American Civil War—and the 1880s. This Irish migration was not part of the immediate post-Famine exodus and, in fact, came increasingly from an Ireland where a degree of social stability, and economic well-being, were already being achieved. As is well known, the Famine affected Irish society selectively. With the virtual elimination of the cottier class through Famine mortality and emigration, the practice of primogeniture in the passing on of land became increasingly the practice, leading younger sons and daughters of larger tenant farmers (and increasingly of farm owners) to emigrate in search of wider opportunity.[12] As M.E. Collins comments, "The virtual wiping out of the lowest groups changed the pattern of Irish society"[13]—it also altered the balance among those most likely to emigrate. Many of those who, by the 1870s and 1880s, had made the long trip to Australia—after meeting the criteria concerning health and suitability required in the Agent-General's instructions—came with some expectation of establishing themselves. The heyday of immigration in the 1880s was followed by severe recession in colonial Queensland, leading to an almost complete cessation of migration in the early 1890s. When migration picked up later in the decade there was a marked fall in the numbers of Irish—in fact, the census of 1901 shows a decrease of 2,535 in the Irish-born in the colony, due to deaths and inter-colonial migration. In the minor migration wave between 1894 and 1904, about two and a half thousand Irish came to Queensland, while in the larger wave, beginning in 1907 and reaching its peak in 1911, the Irish played a very minor role, forming fewer than 7 per cent of the total, where, earlier, they had regularly comprised 25 per cent to 30 per cent of Queensland's yearly immigrant intake.[14] People were still migrating in large numbers from Ireland, but Queensland, and indeed Australia as a whole, were no longer preferred destinations in comparison especially with North

America, but also Great Britain. In this first decade of the
new century, the Queensland government posted a special
agent in Ireland to encourage migration, but to little avail—
it would seem that Australia's distance was becoming more,
not less, of a deterrent, in the face of closer destinations and
more ready opportunity of return.

This falling off in Irish immigration is confirmed by census
data. In the 1886 census, the Irish-born comprised 31.6 per
cent of those born in the British Isles; in 1901, of the 25 per
cent of the Queensland population born in the British Isles,
the Irish represented 29.8 per cent. In 1911, there were 20
per cent born in the British Isles and of these 26.3 per cent
were Irish-born. Further analysis of this latter census reveals
that this was now an aging group, with approximately 80 per
cent over 40 years of age. By 1933, the Irish-born comprised
only 16 per cent of those born in the British Isles and only
2.1 per cent of the overall population. The largest age
concentration was now in the 65+ age-group.[15] The Irish, in
fact, made little contribution to inter-War immigration. By
this time the surviving Irish-born were seasoned veterans of
an earlier pioneering epoch, this having its corollary in the
fact that their descendants, the Irish ethnic sector in the
Queensland population, were more Australian-born than the
general population.

The nineteenth century migration so largely responsible
for the Queensland Irish was principally of young unmarried
adults; for example, in the 1880s, 90 per cent were in the 16–
30 age-group with some 40 per cent of these between 16 and
20. About 95 per cent were unmarried.

This pattern continued until 1904; from then on, more
family groups were represented, but, as we have seen, Irish
numbers as a whole had greatly fallen off by this time. This
earlier migration, however, possessed a definite familial
aspect, as can be noted from the shipping lists. While these
lists do not indicate family relationships, it is evident that
many of these young people were brothers and sisters and
cousins, judging by the groups with the same surname
coming from the same county. The familial aspect of Irish

migration is also indicated in the phenomenon of chain migration, where an Irish settler somewhere in Queensland soon began to bring out other relatives. In fact, as the Agent-General in London occasionally commented, the Irish made proportionately the most use of the category of "nominated passenger," whereby someone in the colony paid the amount required for others to come out.[16]

Another distinctive feature of Irish migration to Queensland is the fact that, overall, the numbers of women approximated those of men; in fact, over the years 1886–1891, the numbers of Irish female immigrants well exceeded the males. In the 1886 census, the male/female ratio for the Irish was 54.6:45.4; by 1891, it was 51.9:48.1. This is found for no other group; for example, for the English and Welsh, the corresponding ratio in this latter census was 59.3:40.7 and for the Scots, 60.3:39.7. The official statistics also reveal that many Irishmen did not marry, while a number of Irishwomen married outside their ethnic group. This latter fact, in particular, has led the demographer, Dr C.A. Price, to conclude that currently up to five million Australians, a third of the population, possess at least some Irish ancestry.[17]

Over four-fifths of the total Irish migration over the years 1885–1912, for which information is available, appear to have been Catholic. (Religion of full-payers is not given on the Queensland shipping lists, and religion is not given for any group of passengers from 1906 onwards). The proportion of Church of Ireland and Protestant increased to over 20 per cent of Irish in the 1894 to 1904 period, and may be assumed to have increased in the larger migration wave which followed. Actually, from 1907 to 1915, for Australia as a whole, immigration from Ulster exceeded that from the rest of Ireland.[18] Hence, the Catholic Irish migration is more predominantly nineteenth century than Irish migration as a whole—a fact substantiated in the 1933 census where, again for Australia as a whole, the Catholic population was only 9.7 per cent overseas-born, while the general population was 13.6 per cent overseas-born. In Queensland, more so than in the other Australian States, the Irish formed part of the free settled population from the beginning and the Catholic religion, if not always approved of by others, was never regarded as a minority religion of immigrants. In fact, in many inland and northern centres, it was the religion whose tangible presence was most obvious, in well-built churches, schools and convents—schools, in fact, which regularly took non-Catholic pupils, while the convents generally provided tuition in music and commercial subjects for the entire district.

An interesting feature of the government-sponsored migration to Queensland is that the ships on which the migrants travelled began disembarking their passengers, first of all at Thursday Island, and then at successive ports down the coasts, such as Cooktown, Townsville, Rockhampton, Bundaberg, Maryborough, before Brisbane, the final port of disembarkation, was reached. By then, a ship could have lost half its quota of passengers. Wherever the migrants landed, they tended to stay in or around the port town or to move into its hinterland. This gave the Irish in Queensland a considerable advantage as they came immediately to frontiers where they were among the first arrivals, as on the northern Queensland goldfields and in the developing railway settlements. R. B. Madgwick, in his study, *Immigration into Eastern Australia*, claims that the Irish shared in the development of the country in a way they did not do in America.[19] This, he says, was because "by the time of the great Irish emigration, the American economy was already well advanced. The Irish therefore came as foreigners who had to justify themselves in the eyes of the settled population." This did not hold for the Australian-Irish. It could be added that the Irish were that much more free to share in the development of Queensland than of the other colonies because of this factor of distribution and also because of the relatively small amount of industrialisation in Queensland. The shipping lists reveal that, among the Irish, there were relatively few with trades or skills compared with the number of English or Scots, Irish migration being predominantly from rural counties of what is now the Republic of Ireland.[20] The Irish in Queensland readily spread over goldfields, were employed in railroad construction and, in general, as bush workers. They were to produce influential leaders in the Australian Workers' Union, forged out of sectional strands on the northern Queensland goldfields and a major factor in the accession of Labor to power in the Queensland parliament in 1915. Irishmen and their descendants were to play a prominent role in the Queensland Labor Party until the late 1950s when a non-Labor coalition came to power, terminating some forty years of almost uninterrupted Labor rule.

The Irish in Queensland also had the ready opportunity of taking up land as this was thrown open for closer settlement under various governmental legislative provisions. The vigorous encouragement of land settlement by the early bishops, Quinn and Dunne, and by many Irish priests, led to the taking up of much good farming land on the Darling Downs, while Irish pastoralists, such as the Duracks,[21] appeared on the frontiers further west and north. Irish families were well represented among graziers in Central Queensland and among sugar farmers in the north, where Thomas Fitzgerald of Innisfail was a pioneer sugar planter. This leads us to consider the Irish support for non-Labor political alignments as they developed in Queensland. Before the advent of Labor-in-Politics, political power in Queensland was, in general, divided between a conservative constellation, having its chief support among the landed property owners, and a liberal party, of which the backbone was a growing urban business sector. Those Irish who were enfranchised and those who obtained seats in parliament in this era inclined to the conservative camp, especially as it took shape under the Scottish lawyer and property-owner, McIlwraith, who included four Catholic Irishmen in his cabinet. The first Queensland-born premier, the barrister T.J. Byrnes, son of Irish immigrant parents and strongly loyal to both Ireland and Catholicism, belonged in this constellation—as such, he found himself politically opposed to the emerging political conservatism. Many became supporters of the Country Party, a twentieth century development in Queensland politics which owed its origin to local farmers' groups. Irish names from the first years of settlement were prominent among those in local politics, especially in areas where they were closely settled as on the Darling Downs.

In the nineteenth century immigration into Queensland, as can be deduced from the Agent-General's reports, the great majority of all arrivals, whatever their country of origin, received government assistance for their passages, either wholly or in part. It was a frontier where physical strength and a degree of enterprise were the qualities which counted, rather than initial capital. As can be seen from the census, the Irish, both men and women, spread all over Queensland, with their numbers proportionally higher in inland and northern areas. They were soon to be found in a wide variety of occupations: as labourers and housemaids; as farmers and graziers; as hotel-keepers and shop-keepers; as teachers and policemen; as carriers and auctioneers; as newspaper editors and lawyers; and in growing numbers in the developing public service of the young colony.[22]

Interestingly, Irishwomen seem to have exhibited a marked degree of enterprise. In the 1921 census, in the section entitled Grades of Occupation, which stated religion not birthplace, although men as a whole fitted into the pattern of about 5 per cent employers, 10 per cent self-employed and 40 per cent salary- or wage-earners, Catholic women were proportionally highest among women who were employers or self-employed. This is also reflected in the overall Australian figures. In the 1933 census, the same grades of occupation are correlated against birthplace—here the Irish women were proportionally the highest among the employers and the self-employed. These two categories were, of course, very small for women as a whole.

However, the Catholic Irish were almost unrepresented as entrepreneurs in heavy industry such as shipbuilding and in banking and pastoral firms, where initial capital was necessary; on the other hand several became large retailers, both in Brisbane and in developing provincial centres. Burke's Shipping Company, founded in Brisbane, and the railway construction firm of O'Rourke and McSharry are but two nineteenth century examples of Catholic Irish enterprise, while in North Queensland several Catholic Irish families were involved in the early timber export trade. In Queensland there does not seem to have been any active or public discrimination such as the "No Irish Need Apply" riders to job advertisements which appeared in the older Australian settlements. Rather there seems here to have been a policy of keeping one's business within one's religious-social orientation—whether Orange, Protestant or Scots—to the exclusion or non-promotion of others, in this case Catholics. (Any discussion of this question requires careful definition: such discrimination was directed against Catholics, who were assumed to be Irish or of Irish descent—not against Protestant Irish). Similarly, large Irish retail firms and other businesses whose principals were Catholic, tended to employ Catholics. Lads of Irish Catholic background frequently found their first opening with a Catholic employer known to their parents.

The above is not to underplay the existence, and occasionally virulence, of religious and anti-Irish bigotry in Queensland, especially in the earlier decades of the colony. This can easily be seen in the colonial press, when almost every confessional group had its own mouthpiece and divisive issues arose in colonial politics. However, the reality lies at the everyday interface where, especially in rural areas, the solidarity of the settlers was more evident than doctrinaire divisions. We are reminded of Lawson's shearers, "whether Protestant or Roman" who,

> called no biped "Lord" or "Sir'
> and touched their hats to no man.

It is at this level that Queensland's ethos was forged by, amongst others, the Irish, both Protestant and Catholic, by miners from Wales and Cornwall, by pastoralists and stockmen from the Scottish Highlands, by humble tradesmen and industrial workers from the north of England, as they met and mixed in the course of daily business, at the entertainments in small country towns, and in supporting common causes, such as their political interests. For the Catholic Irish, however, there was the massive solidarity of their church: largely through their religious adherence, after the passing of the first generation, they retained few direct links with their areas of origin.

Much more needs to be done on a social analysis of the Irish in Queensland and an accurate picture will be built up only through careful area studies. From my own investigations it would seem that nineteenth century Irish migration to Queensland can be divided roughly into two strata or two ends of a spectrum. First of all, Irish society, like most European societies, was highly complex, with recognised hierarchies within each local social pyramid. As with other Western societies, the distinctions, in modern times, have tended to level out as a middle class who see themselves as such—often basing this on their occupational status—and a lower class whose members tend to have humbler occupations. Occupation, however, is not the sole criterion for such distinctions; among the Irish, as among other less industrialised peoples of the nineteenth century, family standing, dating from earlier concepts of social organisation, tended to persist as a primary indicator of social status. By the later nineteenth century, a middle class, in the modern Western sense, had also begun to emerge among the Catholic Irish.[23] These complexities in social understanding were part of the cultural heritage of Irish migrants to Queensland. Few may have brought money, a consequence of almost endemic depression in nineteenth century Ireland, but included among them were members of families of considerable standing in their local areas in Ireland. We find among this category of people in particular the desire to establish themselves, either by acquiring land or exploiting what avenues for enterprise were open to them. For whatever reason, before long, in whatever area the Irish settled in Queensland, we see a nexus of families arising who act as local leaders of their community, usually from both a civic and a religious point of view. They formed, for example, the core of Hibernian groups, which not only played a key role in raising money for the Irish Parliamentary Party in its struggle for Home Rule in Ireland,[24] but which supported the establishment of parishes and schools and placed a high premium on the education of their children.

At the other end of the spectrum were the more vulnerable, often the helpless end-product of a near century of economic depression and socially unsettled conditions. Accordingly, we find the Irish over-represented among those in gaols and asylums, and among the orphaned, while some came infected with the scourge of tuberculosis. In fact immigrants as a whole were more vulnerable socially in their colonial environment than the Queensland-born population, as the data on social institutions shows.[25] Also, the absolute figures both for the imprisoned and those in asylums were small, as Queensland society was, as a whole, noticeably law-abiding, a fact commented upon by the Comptroller-General of Prisons in his annual reports.[26] The Queensland frontier, with its space and relative openness, as well as its freedom from the starker aspects of want and cold, seems to have lessened the more difficult aspects of the migration experience for the Irish, as well as for others.

However, the greater vulnerability of the Irish in Queensland—and in Australian society in general—requires both further investigation and analysis rather than bare enumeration. Is it related, for example, to the pre-industrial culture prevailing in rural parts of Ireland prior to the Famine of the 1840s and the continuing alienation of such people when projected into industrial economies? Such alienation is many-faceted and is currently evidenced in the problems of indigenous peoples who find themselves stranded today amid commercially advanced cultures. In fact, the present social statistics of such peoples—the high incidence of imprisonment, especially for violent behaviour, drunkenness, social helplessness generally—bear great resemblance to the vulnerable stratum in nineteenth century Irish migration, given also the high level of conflict in Ireland at this time.

Moreover, the Irish ethnic community in Queensland developed a strong sense of solidarity at an early stage, as shown by the ubiquitous celebration of St Patrick's Day, with concerts, race-meetings and sports days. In country towns, for example, these were well-known annual events in which the local community generally shared. The first Queensland Irish association, the Queensland Hibernian Society, was founded in Brisbane in 1871 by Dr Kevin Izod O'Doherty, former Young Irelander and transportee to Van Diemen's Land. It made a particular appeal to Irishmen of all political and religious backgrounds and was also to include a benefit function.[27] It was subsequently eclipsed by the Hibernian Australasian Catholic Benefit society, established in Melbourne also in 1871, which after its introduction to Queensland (Rockhampton, 1874), spread rapidly throughout the colony. Branches were set up on a parish basis and members were familiarly known as the Hibernians. The present Queensland Irish Association, dating from 1898—though with some continuity with O'Doherty's Queensland Hibernian Society—has always been open to a broad spectrum of members.

It remains to raise the question: was Irish ethnic origin of any significance in Queensland as a host society? While more detailed studies need to be undertaken, the answer remains unequivocally *yes*: first of all, given the virtual non-recognition of Aboriginal society, the Irish, from the beginning, helped to form the white host society and, in doing so, unconsciously contributed their own composite of characteristics. They also consciously claimed a stake in the new society, a theme on which their press—the *Australian*, the *Age* and the *Catholic Advocate*, all published in Brisbane at different times from the 1870s into the 1930s[28]—was vocal and specific. Perhaps the most significant aspect of Irish migration to Queensland is its relative lateness, the fact that this migration so largely post-dates 1860, by which time circumstances in both Ireland and Australia were moving into a new historical and economic phase. A second aspect is that this migration had substantially terminated by 1900, indeed by 1890, so that persisting Irish influences were carried by an increasingly Australian-born Irish ethnic sector. For those in Queensland with Irish roots there is no mistaking the contribution made both to the local and the wider society, in both local and parliamentary politics, in the development of Australian unionism, in education through the sponsorship by the Catholic Irish of their separate and parallel system of schools, in sport (especially horse-racing) and, beyond these areas, in the indefinable, yet very real, attitudinal qualities brought to their social interactions. We may perhaps identify here a certain egalitarianism, whereby they expect to be accepted on their own merits, a ready sociability, a touch of fatalism and an often ironic type of humour. What remains unresearched is an overall Celtic contribution, in which the Irish remained the most distinguishable group, to that intangible yet recognisable thing, the ethos of present-day Queensland.

References
1. T.N. Brown, *Irish-American Nationalism, 1870–1890* (New York, 1966), p.32.
2. M. O'Keefe, *The Moreton Bay Penal Settlement* (Brisbane, 1974), pp.9–10.
3. Queensland State Archives.
4. *Commission on Emigration and other Population Problems: Report, 1948–54* (Dublin, 1954).
5. Quoted in G. Nadel, *Australia's Colonial Culture* (Harvard, 1957), p.243.
6. The first two ships listed in the Register, the *Artemesia* (1848) and the *Chasely* (1849) carried mainly English and Scottish passengers. The *William Miles* (1855) had a majority of Scottish passengers out of its total of 409.
7. The Government Census of 1846 gave the population of Brisbane as 829, while that of the whole Moreton Bay district was 2,257. Coglan gives the population of Queensland at the time of separation as 25,000, of whom 7,000 were in Brisbane. T.A. Coglan and T.T. Ewing, *The Progress of Australasia in the Nineteenth Century* (Toronto and Philadelphia, 1913), p.177. The 1861 census population was 30,115, with the surmised number of Aborigines being given separately as 15,000. (*Votes and Proceedings*, Queensland Legislative Assembly, 1861, p.35 of Statistical Register.)
8. *The Queensland Statutes*, Vol. 1 (Brisbane, 1889), p.874.

9. Summary based on T.P. Boland, "The Queensland Immigration Society—A Notable Experiment in Irish Settlement," in *The Royal Historical Society of Queensland Journal*, vii, no.2, 1962. A number of those who came to Queensland under this scheme paid their own fares. C.B. Lyons, writing to Archbishop Cullen, lists seven ships arriving between August 1862 and April 1863 which carried among them 456.5 paying statute adults. (Children were counted as half a statute adult.) Fares were paid at the rate of £17 steerage, £20 intermediate and £25 second cabin, somewhat above what was paid to the ship-owners in each category, to allow for commission to Quinn's agents. Also, according to Lyons, the Society bought land orders from some of these paying migrants. (C.B. Lyons to Drs Cullen and Murray, Cullen's secretary, Letters 1863, Dublin Diocesan Archives.)

10. In particular, the new requirement that an intending migrant had not signed away to another party his claim to a land order.

11. T.A. Coglan, *A Statistical Account of the Seven Colonies of Australia* (Sydney, 1890), p.9. A reason for this, undoubtedly, is that, during the thirty years 1861–91, the Queensland government, through a series of acts, maintained a system of free and assisted passages unequalled at the time elsewhere in Australia. Queensland was also beginning from a lower population base.

12. For factors in the transition of Irish society in the 19th century, see Joseph Lee, *The Modernisation of Irish Society* (Dublin, 1974).

13. M.E. Collins, *An Outline of Modern History, 1850–1951* (Dublin, 1974), p.2.

14. M.E.R. MacGinley, "A Study of Irish Migration to and Settlement in Queensland, 1885–1912" (unpublished M.A. thesis, University of Queensland, 1972), Ch.2. The chief references here are Queensland shipping lists (held in the Queensland State Archives), census returns, and the annual reports of the Agent-General in London. These latter are given in the *Votes and Proceedings* of the Queensland Legislative Assembly.

15. M.E.R. MacGinley, "Catholicism in Queensland, 1910–1935: A Social History" (unpublished Ph.D. thesis, University of Queensland, 1982). Ch.2.

16. "A Study of Irish Migration," p.10, fn.15.

17. C.A. Price. *The Ethnic Composition of the Australian People* (Melbourne, n.d.), p.6.

18. G.M. Tobin, *The Sea Divided Gael: A Study of the Irish Home Rule Movement in Victoria and New South Wales, 1880–1916* (unpublished M.A. thesis, Australian National University, 1969), pp. 16–17.

19. R.B. Madgwick, *Immigration into Eastern Australia, 1788–1851* (Sydney, 1969), p.236.
20. Every county was represented among the Irish immigrants, with the chief numbers coming from Clare, Tipperary, Cork, Kerry, Kilkenny and Galway. "A Study of Irish Migration," p.44.
21. Mary Durack's novel, *Kings in Grass Castles*, is a well-known account of this family.
22. Personal research in various areas of Queensland, with cross-reference to Queensland Government Gazettes, Queensland Blue Books, Post Office Directories and *Pugh's Almanac* (selected years).
23. An initial, and largely statistical, study on the Catholic middle class in Ireland is that of E.G.P. Brockie, "The Rise of the Catholic Middle Classes in Ireland. 1880–1922" (unpublished M.A. thesis, University College Cork 1980).
24. The first Land League groups in Australia were founded in Queensland when John Flood, former Fenian transportee to Western Australia, gathered a number of Davitt's former associates in Gympie to form the first support group. Similar groups soon emerged in Ipswich, Charters Towers, Warwick, Rockhampton and Brisbane. Queensland gave generous support to the various representatives of the Irish Parliamentary Party who toured Australia between 1883 and 1911. G. M. Tobin in his study of the Home Rule movement refers to Queensland's more tolerant acceptance of Home Rule promotion, which he attributes to the standing of its leading advocates in the general community and the leadership they were thus able to exercise. *Sea Divided Gael*, pp. 103, 196, 260.
25. "A Study of Irish Migration," p. 94.
26. ibid., pp. 88–91. "Statistically there was a greater degree of criminality in New South Wales, Victoria, and in particular West Australia, than there was in Queensland, which was somewhat on a level with Tasmania and New Zealand." (W. R. Johnston, "A Study of the Relationship between the Law, the State and the Community in Colonial Queensland" (unpublished M.A. thesis, University of Queensland, 1965), p. 168.
27. *Brisbane Courier*, 8 Sept. 1871.
28. Each of the papers mentioned reads more like an Irish national journal than a Catholic diocesan organ. It was only in the late 1920s that Archbishop Duhig bought the *Age* and converted it to a diocesan paper; its contemporary, the *Catholic Advocate*, ceased in the mid 1930s, leaving the field to this one Church-oriented publication.

6.
Stalwarts of the Garrison:
some Irish academics in Australia*

F. B. SMITH

Provincial scholars with ambitions lead strenuous lives. They have to think and read a lot to keep up with their scholarly metropolis, concern themselves with the business of their locality and strive to emulate the metropolis by maintaining a presentable acquaintance with other centres as well. Thus they gravitate towards pretentiousness. Their curiosity often atrophies under heavy teaching duties on wide-ranging subjects and the distracting obligations of being a sole big fish in a small pond. The lack of colleagues with similar scholarly interests, poor libraries and the insecurity generated by isolation, frequently mean that provincial scholars lag behind in the development of the theoretical concepts that nourish their subject and that often they plight their faith in far-off, well-publicised gurus whose time has in fact passed.

Academics of Irish origin in Australia, in so far as their linguistic and scholarly patria in London, Oxford and Cambridge are concerned, were doubly provincial.** From their

*I am indebted to members of the Ireland-Australia Conference for setting me right about nuances in the Irish ambiance, and especially to Geoffrey Serle who quietly corrected my blunders about the Melbourne scene. My other debts are to the *Australian Dictionary of Biography* and to Sam Goldberg, who made me redefine my questions.

** By Irish academics I mean persons who enjoyed emoluments as teachers in universities or in colleges associated with universities, or persons who actively participated in university affairs, who took their first degree at an Irish university, or who taught at one. I am not concerned with living persons or anyone recently deceased.

materially rich but culturally bare outpost of the Empire, they looked homeward to the unchallenged literature and progress of England and to the noble but embattled intellectual achievements of Ascendancy Ireland.

Melbourne University, founded in 1852, was predominantly an Irish foundation in colonial Australia. Its frankness imbued its proceedings with an earnest, self-scrutinising industry and pride which lasted until the student and staff rebellions of the 1960s.

Sydney University, by contrast, was a child of Oxford, although three of its founding fathers were from Trinity College Dublin. These, Henry Grattan Douglass, a medical man "of liberal and independent principles" and member of the Royal Irish Academy at 30 years of age, John Hubert Plunkett, legal acolyte to O'Connell and a courageous lawyer in colonial New South Wales, and Sir Roger Therry, Catholic barrister, apparently readily acquiesced in the decision to restrict the foundation professors at Sydney to graduates of Oxford or Cambridge. Their expectation was that such men would reproduce in the antipodes a suavely gentle college devoted to instilling "liberal and general knowledge" in crude colonial youths, barely liberated from the convict taint and tending to a crude mercantile materialism, knowledge which would make them into "civilised gentlemen" and thereby supply the coming democracy with models of disinterested civic virtue: Sir Charles Nicholson, an Edinburgh medical graduate, looked to the nascent university, which he richly endowed with Greek and Roman antiquities, to produce orators, poets, statesmen and philosophers. Sydney's coat of arms contains the Cambridge lion and the Oxford book pasted on the cross of St George. The chosen Latin motto was "the same under different stars." The founders spent a large part of their endowment on a magnificent Gothic revival great hall, more grand than any nineteenth century university building in Oxford or Cambridge, and filled its stained glass windows with English worthies and the crests of Oxford and Cambridge colleges. Another early acquisition was a mace, again emblazoned with Oxford and Cambridge arms.[1]

122

Melbourne's crest featured a rather matronly angel bearing an olive wreath, looking rather like Queen Victoria about 1850. Since then the angel has slimmed down to look like an ancient Greek intaglio goddess. She remains an heraldic eccentric. She was drawn by Ludwig Becker, a German artist who travelled with the Burke and Wills expedition. Melbourne's Latin motto, possibly chosen by chancellor Redmond Barry, another lawyer from Trinity College Dublin, also differs strikingly from Sydney's: "I shall grow in the esteem of future generations."[2]

Sydney's early appointments included major Oxford classicists and Liberals, such as Revd John Woolley, foundation headmaster of Rossall School and frustrated would-be rector of the University of Corfu, and Revd Charles Badham. Badham, Woolley's successor in 1867, when he was aged 53, was a major scholar. His contemporaries ranked him the greatest Greek scholar of the Victorian age. He edited Euripides and Plato: his *Philebus*, completed in Sydney in 1878, is his lasting achievement, yet he never prospered in England, partly perhaps because of his Tractarian leanings and close friendship with F. D. Maurice. Housman said that he was "the one English scholar of the mid-century whose reputation crossed the Channel ... but at home was excluded from academical preferment, set to teach boys at Birmingham, and finally transported to the Antipodes."[3]

As professor, at Sydney, he worked for public libraries and public examinations, made great public orations about liberal studies, and left a legacy of intellectual and political conservatism in Australian classical studies and no outstanding pupils. Sydney remained a glorious finishing school with a minute population. Not until the 1870s and 1880s did Sydney create the professional courses that might have bonded the university to the community and enabled it to grow in undergraduates and middle class support. In 1881 it had only 15 teachers and 150 students. Melbourne meanwhile had 28 teachers and around 500 students.[4]

Melbourne University itself was far from being an Oxford-Cambridge mule. Among its founders Sir William Stawell, who helped to draft its foundation statutes, and Sir Redmond Barry were both Trinity College Dublin barristers. Their instruction to the London selection committee left them free to consider candidates from any United Kingdom university. Melbourne, also following the pattern of the Queen's Colleges, began with four chairs in mathematics, classics and ancient history, natural science, modern history and political economy.[5] It is commonly said in Australia that the colonial universities were modelled upon a mixture of the Scottish universities and the University of London, but I think the closest exemplars of Sydney and Melbourne in time and in organisation and methods of coping with denominational hostilities were the Queen's Colleges of Ireland. Nicholson and Douglass had instructed their committee to choose "gentleman scholars" free of religious and political prejudices, who would lead young colonials to appreciate the "noblest creations of the human intellect." Denominational religion was confined to individual residential colleges at each university.

Sydney was vulnerable to charges from envious autodidactic politicians, such as Henry Parkes, that it was a mere extravagance isolated on its hill above Sydney town. Oxford and Cambridge, the sources of its professoriate, were, Parkes sneered in his newspaper, the *Empire*, "places famous for their lordliness in knowledge, in ignorance, in vice, and in antiquated statutes and sectarian illiberality." The *Empire* preferred a People's College, attuned to the "actual business of life." From the opposite side, the Anglican Bishop of Newcastle attacked the new university for being "Godless": this piece of stupidity happily switched Parkes and his allies around to defending the non-sectarian institution.[6]

Three of Melbourne's first four professors came from Ireland: William Parkinson Wilson, senior wrangler and first Smith's prizeman from Cambridge, foundation professor of mathematics at Queen's College Belfast, became professor of mathematics. Frederick McCoy, palaeontologist and zoologist, became professor of natural science. He had been professor of geology and curator of the museum at Queen's College Belfast. He said he was a son of a professor of medicine at Queen's

College Galway. Despite his pretensions, he seemingly was not a graduate of Trinity College Dublin or Cambridge or anywhere else. William Edward Hearn, classicist, historian, political economist and jurist, became Melbourne's first professor of modern history, literature, logic, and political economy. (Sydney had excluded modern history, regarding it as inflammatory). He had graduated as first senior moderator in classics, together with high distinctions in logic and ethics and law in 1847. He had been secretary of the Historical Society at Trinity College Dublin and had been admitted to the Irish bar in 1853. He came from the foundation chair of Greek at Queen's College Galway.

The Irish predominance was continued into the next generation. In the university colleges, the first two wardens of the Anglican college, Trinity, were Irish, as was the first vice-warden. The first acting principal was Revd George William Torrance, BA, Mus.B of Trinity College Dublin, in the 1860s, organist, choirmaster and composer of oratorios, whom McCoy and Stawell tried to install at Melbourne as Professor of Music. A charming, but apparently unworldly, man, he failed to farm the student fees of Trinity College productively and his connection with the University never developed. He finally returned to St Canice's Cathedral, Kilkenny.

His successor as principal was Alexander Leeper, son of the chaplain to the lord lieutenant and of the daughter of the president of the Royal College of Surgeons of Ireland. From Kingstown school, Leeper went to Trinity College Dublin—BA 1871—and thence to St John's College, Oxford. As a young man he had been an Irish nationalist, but after his first visit to Australia in 1871 he became a fanatical churchman and imperialist. As tutor in Sydney at 23 he fell in love with Adeline Allen, aged 16, the sister of his charges. Driven by tuberculosis and love for Adeline, he returned to Sydney in 1874 and married her. Leeper was described by a biographer wishing to be kind as "pertinaceous, anxious, bristly."'

Leeper's vice-principal was his friend John Withrop Hackett, yet another son of a Church of Ireland clergyman:

BA, TCD 1871, Irish Bar 1874. He came to Trinity College Melbourne in 1875 as tutor in law, political economy and logic, the standard Dublin University strengths. Hackett became a prominent Freemason. He went to West Australia in 1882 and made a fortune from newspapers. Within his little kingdom he controlled politicians, hindered Federation and like Hearn, Stawell and other Dublin University men in Australia, fought tenaciously to entrench the powers of upper houses against democracy. He led the royal commission that prepared the way for the University of Western Australia and, as chancellor, gave the casting vote against student fees, making the University of Western Australia possibly unique in the world. As his death the University received £425,000 and the Church of England £138,000 for St George's College. Hackett rapidly fell out with Leeper's concept of the centrality of the classics, as did the Trinity students. He wanted the University to offer technical subjects and the "whole practical sciences." "I believe," he added, "that the influence of Oxford, Cambridge and Dublin has been largely mischievous, as far as the new Churches of the Empire are concerned. . . ." They concentrated on "dead languages and the pursuit of what is called the higher mathematics."[8] Hackett wanted to see Australian universities as an integral part of their environment.

Hackett's liberalising contribution to university education in Australia is equalled by that of another graduate of Trinity College Dublin, William Barlow, BA 1855, gold medallist for oratory from the Historical Society. He was foundation registrar of the University of Adelaide and drafted and defended the statutes that would—but for asinine Imperial interference—have made Adelaide the first university in the Empire to admit women equally with men, and to have distinct degrees in science.[9] His name, like Hackett's and Thomas Rankin Lyle's, whom I shall mention later, does not feature in books about the Irish in Australia, Australia's debts to Irish nation-builders, or even "great Australians"; yet these men were the begetters of many of the arrangements and assumptions that are best in Australian life.[10]

Other Irishmen associated with Melbourne were Sir
Henry Wrixon, another Dublin University barrister, novelist
and politician; like Barry, Stawell, Hearn and Leeper, he was
prominent in the Historical Society while in Dublin, and was
Vice-Chancellor of Melbourne, 1897–1910. With the excep-
tion of the Englishman, and Catholic, Anthony Collings
Brownless, a founder of the medical school and later
Chancellor, nearly all the first generation of senior teachers
and governors of Melbourne University were Irish and
Protestants.[11] In the 1870s, of 156 active members of the
University Senate, 26, the largest single group, were Dublin
University men, followed by 24 Melbourne, 23 Edinburgh
and 19 Glasgow.[12] They set the university in a peculiarly Irish
legal, medical, clerical and political world that probably had
no equal outside Dublin.

From the 1880s the Irish influence was attenuated, but it
never disappeared. In the twentieth century its courtly high-
mindedness, versatility and scholarly excellence were continued by Thomas Rankin Lyle, Professor of Physics, and
W.A. Osborne, Professor of Physiology, amongst others.

The Irish professors had come to Melbourne because of
the opportunities in the law and education. Melbourne
University, like Sydney, offered professorial salaries of £1,000
a year for life appointments, with free housing and stabling.
They were possibly the highest academic salaries in the
Empire. Hearn and Wilson had been receiving £150 to £300
a year at the Queen's Colleges. They were worth their wage.
They were able scholars, devoted to their new university and
they left a profound impression on it.

Wilson, the mathematician and astronomer, started the
Melbourne Observatory in 1856 and urged the building of its
magnificently ambitious, huge four-foot reflector telescope.
Thereby he helped launch Australia's continuing distinction
in astronomy. Wilson lectured on Euclid, algebra, mechanics,
hydrostatics, pneumatics, heat, meteorology, optics, astronomy, electricity and magnetism. In 1858 he inaugurated the
first engineering course at an Australian university and, had
it kept to his high mathematical basis, engineering would

have been stronger in Australia than it subsequently became by following English "practical" engineering practice. He was a dapper man, a bachelor who supported two nephews, equipped with a valet and a butler. A devout Anglican, he helped to launch Trinity College Melbourne.

He joined Hearn in seeking to set aside classics as a prerequisite for mathematics and law, but failed. The courtly Redmond Barry, son of a major-general, and Stawell, son of a barrister and classical scholar, claiming descent from Henry III, saw Greek and Latin as the mechanism of gentility and would not surrender them, especially in a colony threatened by democracy and the ignorant, turbulent peasantry they had known at home.

The professors' attempt to remove the classical bar reflected the sheer shortage of matriculated students from a still rudimentary secondary school system, and the need to open up professional courses to non-matriculated students, aged 17–19, (rather than 16–17, the Oxford age), a development which happened willy-nilly, despite Stawell, Barry and Leeper.

Wilson was an eager practical researcher, who managed to buy a lot of expensive equipment, but he never developed a research programme among his pupils, although he taught W.C. Kernot, the engineering all-rounder and first professor of engineering at Melbourne. There were too few posts in the government and virtually none in the manufacturing industry for scientists. The Australian prejudice against trained specialists in industry was set early.

Like his colleagues, Wilson was innately politically and socially conservative and, scorched by his Irish experience, he was resolutely opposed to the merest manifestation of sectarian or political activity among the students. He carefully explained at the opening of Trinity College in 1870 that "I have heard people say that there was a great deal of thought and discussion amongst students, and that this might endanger the faith of theological students [who were to be taught separately in the college]. I deny that such free discussion exists at the University."[13]

Wilson's career points to some of the salient features of the Irish-Melbourne case. Like several of his colleagues, he was at once politically conservative and educationally innovative. At Belfast he had been trammelled by the pre-eminence of the classics and pure mathematics. He had begun to work in astronomy but had been hindered by want of funds and the opposition of his seniors, who preferred pure mathematics. He sought, and succeeded with Hearn's help, in making Melbourne more flexible in accepting new subjects, although he failed in promoting graduate studies and in limiting the stifling supremacy of the classics. But liberality in subject choice fortunately survived, at least until the 1960s and 1970s. Like his colleagues again, Wilson was astonishingly industrious, polymathic at a high level, and dedicated.

William Edward Hearn, son of a Church of Ireland clergyman, married to a Rose Sheridan le Fanu and then Isabel St Clair, daughter of a major, was a product of Portora Royal School, Enniskillen. Then came Trinity College Dublin and his brilliant record and his appointments in 1849 to Galway, and then Melbourne in 1854.

Like Wilson, he was a remarkable polymath. He acted twice as Professor of Classics, 1855–6 and again in 1871. In 1873 he became Dean of the Law Faculty. In his time he taught Greek, Latin, ancient and modern history, deductive and inductive logic, jurisprudence, history of the British Empire, political economy, Roman law, constitutional law, property, obligations, international law and procedure, and in between discoursed on the etymology of words, typically in an hour-long discussion during a law lecture on the history of the word "outlaw" or on another memorable occasion, "medieval." He constituted in himself a walking liberal education. His apartments adjoined his lecture theatre and he often lectured in slippers and dressing gown, under his academic gown.

He had a quick wit. Undergraduates loved and were awed by him. One day a young man entered flushed and wet, having hurried in from the rain of a cold Melbourne winter's day. Being late, he modestly slipped into a seat at the back.

Hearn immediately invited him to come nearer the fire to warm himself. The young man demurred, saying he would melt. "Yes, you're dripping already," Hearn remarked.[14]

He taught in a Socratic manner, and introduced acted trials, precursors to the modern moot. He educated a long line of lawyers and philosophers, including Samuel Alexander, Australia's first OM, and Isaac Isaacs, a great judge of the High Court and the First Australian Governor-General.

Hearn's beliefs about political economy, for which he is now remembered, were set in Ireland, while he was still in his 20s, as was his cunning in politics. His *Cassell Prize Essay on the Condition of Ireland* of 1851 already advocates an optimistic view of economics. "No one now says that Ireland is overpopulated . . . her distress arises, not from the number of her people, but from the fewness of her productions . . . no good reason can be shown why the legislature should interfere with land more than any other subject of commercial dealings. Land, if left perfectly free, would naturally fall into such arrangements as would be most profitable, and therefore best." Copious flattering references to the examiners, Jonathan Pim, Nelson Hancock and Montifort Longfield, must have helped him win the prize.

Two other passing comments in the *Essay* also reveal convictions that Hearn was to uphold in Melbourne. He proposed the assimilation of the law of real property to that of personal property, trusts and taxation, and he offered an outspoken defence of the Queen's Colleges against "Ultramontane" attacks on "infidel establishments."[15] Hearn was a devout Anglican with a strong sense of his denomination's role as the highest component of the liberal state. Obscurantist authoritarian Roman Catholicism offended everything he valued, not least his political optimism.

Similarly, Hearn's unpublished *Essay on Natural Religion* of 1853 or 1854 contains an optimistic, Paleyan view of the essential goodness of the Creation and of its progressive nature, not by transmutation of species, but in ascending sets of living creatures, each embodying a higher design. The essay vividly displays one of Hearn's most attractive qualities as a writer: his engrossing parade of diverse examples to embellish essentially simple and conventional central arguments. And yet, he did admit that Lamarckianism might occur. Progress might occur by intelligent adaptation by individuals in classes and the incorporation and transmission of that adaptation by the best.[16]

His *Plutology* (Melbourne, 1863) was his most famous book. Plutus was the god of wealth and abundant crops, the bosom companion of Mirth and Peace; once cured of blindness he recognizes and rewards only honest men—the present connotations of "economics," the noun Hearn sought to replace, are, alas, the opposite. Hearn defined Plutology as the satisfaction of demand occasioned by human wants. He argued that human ambitions, expectations and inventions must continually beget and enlarge the production and distribution of goods and services. Echoing his Cassell *Essay*, but set in a new context, he asserted that there was more than enough unutilised land in the world to negate the law of diminishing returns; this again was a major break with the early nineteenth century political economy of Malthus, Ricardo and J.S. Mill, particularly as Hearn guardedly appears to have condoned birth-control. He readily quoted Darwin, being the first political economist to do so, to argue that the incessant elaboration of human wants and competition to satisfy them by the application of even more complex science, technology and human ratiocination, would produce an even more productive and moral economy:

> The inter-dependence of the parts of any organism is a portion of its evolution. In the undeveloped state a simple organ performs a great variety of functions. These functions are essential to the life of the creature, and development does not supersede but improves their performance. Evolution implies the formation of definite and specific organs, and their subordination as well between each other to the whole. It follows therefore that the well-being of each part is essential to the well-being of the whole; that the general condition of the whole reacts upon the condition of each part . . . these consequences apply to social as well as to organic evolution . . . thus cooperation and exchange . . . not merely increase the

powers of industry, but form the very cement and bond of society itself. By their aid men's interests and their duties are inseparably intertwined. No class can entirely monopolise its gains; no class has exclusively to bear its losses."[17]

It is a splendidly readable book, although as Professor La Nauze demonstrated, some of the best arguments and illustrations were plagiarised, especially from the Canadian backwoods economist with similar ideas, John Rae.[18]

Given the free trade, optimistic view of free competition in the book, it is not surprising that economists of like persuasions should eulogise *Plutology*. W.S. Jevons and Alfred Marshall professed to have been deeply influenced by it. Von Hayek, in 1936, described Hearn as a "great economist with a singular gift for stating original and penetrating observations in the most apt and lucid language."[19]

Political economy, in Hearn's view, meant free trade. He was a prominent member of the Free Trade League in Victoria, a besieged cause in that fiercely, popularly protectionist colony. But Hearn was used to being a member of the righteous minority in a nation subject to the sway of the ignorant. His free trade opinions helped to isolate the university from the populace and the protectionist radical liberals, who might otherwise have been its best friends. On the other hand Hearn did win friends for the university from the squattocracy.

Government in Hearn's *Plutology* existed only to maintain domestic order and protect the nation against external threats. Superfluity of government in Ireland was his touchstone. He recalled Irish distress had been caused by Catholic disabilities imposed by improper governmental intervention. He also pointed to the suppression by the English government of the Irish wool trade, and the levying by the Irish parliament of irrational sectarian constraints on commercial and professional enterprise. He often returned to these points: clearly he was saddened by them, yet curiously his stance as a writer is that of a dispassionate English commentator and the great majority of "our" examples are English.[20] Apart from the occasional reference to the goldfields and Australian lands, one would never know the book had emanated from colonial Melbourne.

Hearn, like Wilson, was an educational innovator. He tried to establish a People's College, a kind of polytechnic, at the Melbourne Mechanics Institute and he sought to persuade the authorities to allow the use of state school buildings for adult education classes in the evenings, a sensible provision that is still only slowly coming about in Australia.

Hearn and Wilson tried again to open up Melbourne's course structures in 1888, by lowering the Latin and Greek barriers: they argued that

> the more closely colonial universities resemble those of the Mother Country, the greater is the probability of their failing.

> Shakespeare and Bunyan—not to mention the host of female authors—were not very distinguished Classical Scholars. Yet they had a sufficient command of English.

> In Victoria the inducements to enter active life at the earliest possible age are too strong to admit of the long study which the English system demands.[21]

Yet again the Irish courtly party, Barry, Stawell, McCoy, Leeper and their allies, defeated them.[22] This defeat was another forfeited opportunity to attract the less formally qualified "evening class" Irish Catholics, who, like other ambitious immigrants after them, when they did qualify, concentrated in a narrow, technical way upon law and medicine, to the impoverishment of the wider intellectual community and possibly also of the professions themselves.

Hearn was equally innovatory in his *Government of England* (1867), which ties with Bagehot's *English Constitution* (1865–67) as the first two studies of the impact of the cabinet system on English constitutional arrangements. Dicey said that "it taught me more than any other single work of the ways in which the labouring of lawyers established the basis of the constitution."[23]

At first glance, the strong Austinian, positive law cast of the book seems inconsistent with Hearn's views on limited government. But behind this emphasis lie Hearn's apprehensions about the fragility of the rule of law in rebellious colonies like Ireland, or in turbulently democratic ones like

Victoria, with its over-mighty workingmen and radical journalists. Hearn had parliamentary ambitions and made two attempts to enter the Legislative Assembly, the lower House, in 1874 and 1877, and finally gained election to the powerful Legislative Council, buttressed by a high property qualification, in 1878. He achieved this elevation despite Melbourne University statutes forbidding professors from meddling in party politics; Hearn simply changed his title to "Dean" of Law. Behind the scenes he was a prolific journalist for the conservative *Argus* and *Australasian*, and advisor to the reactionary Council, standing on its powers, created in the constitution by Sir William Stawell, to thwart the more democratically elected Assembly.

His known conservative politics, the necessity to defend civilisation, rank and civic virtue against the rule of the mob, makes it all the more odd that Charles Gavan Duffy, of the *Nation* and Young Ireland in 1848, and Minister for Lands in the ministry of John O'Shanassy, another Irish Catholic from Tipperary, should have asked Hearn to draft a new bill to extend small land holding on Crown lease lands. Hearn charged £500 for the job. And job it was: the Bill was hopelessly badly drafted, "and assigns" were omitted from the Act, together with other safeguards against personation and fraud, thereby permitting the leaseholding squatters and corrupt, blackmailing settlers to destroy the intention of the Act. It lasted only 9 weeks. It is a mystery why Duffy accepted the draft, especially after the weaknesses in land legislation were highlighted by its precursor of 1860 and Robertson's Act in New South Wales. Hearn was of course a glib parliamentary draftsman, as his other bills demonstrate. His involvement with the slippery R.D. Ireland on the Duffy bill suggests a conspiracy to wreck Duffy's intentions. Ireland was yet another barrister from Trinity College Dublin. He had been a supporter of Irish confederation in 1848 and after his arrival in Victoria in 1852 served on a committee to welcome Smith O'Brien. He successfully defended the Eureka Stockade prisoners in 1855 and thereafter became a leader at the Irish/Victorian Bar. In 1863 he is said to have made £140,000 in fees. Ireland secretly consulted with at least one influential squatter about Duffy's bill and predicted its failure.[24]

Duffy never forgave Hearn. The episode rehearsed so many of the contests and deceits of home. David Syme's radical Melbourne *Age* called Hearn "the Professor of Political Dodgery." "His mind," Syme remarked, and Syme was also an able political economist, "is very sharp but very small."[25]

In 1878 Hearn produced *The Aryan Household*, arguing a similar line to Henry Maine's *Ancient Law* of 1861, and *Village Communities* of 1871. Then appeared *The Theory of Legal Rights and Duties* (1883). Both these books display a strong notion of positive law together with the faith that the state can be diminished to its true role if the true symbiosis between private and public law is achieved. To this end Hearn, that rare thing, an academic Queen's Counsel, and a team of brilliant pupils, laboured for over a decade to produce what would have been the first codified legal system in a common-law country.[26] The Victorian government took fright and never implemented it. Hearn never completed his great design. One tantalising speculation is that it might have moved Australia towards becoming a unitary state with positive rights.

Frederick McCoy, like Hearn, is a remarkable example of that last generation of commanding generalists. His formal education is a mystery, but in 1844, aged 27, he published *A Synopsis of the Carboniferous Fossils of Ireland* and then a *Synopsis of the Silurian Fossils*. In 1846, at £100 a year, he began to work for Adam Sedgwick, the professor of Geology at Cambridge, classifying 30 years' accumulation of bits of rock and fossils, hopelessly jumbled. Gentlemen collected, servants classified. McCoy fell foul of the mighty Samuel Woodward at the British Museum, on the leverage of the adductive muscle in the Brachiopoda. It appears that McCoy first had the idea, but it got to Woodward who, as befitted a gentleman scientist and not a mere technical assistant, published it. McCoy was also employed on the British geological survey, again, it seems, as an indispensable menial.[27] In 1850 he was appointed to the chair of geology and mineralogy at Queen's College Belfast. He alternated between this post and Cambridge. After prodigious labour he produced, under Sedgwick's name as principal author, A *Detailed Systematic Description of the British Palaeozoic Fossils*..., dated 1849–54. This is a huge compilation of beautifully classified and arranged fossils. McCoy attributed the identification of about half of them to himself, a high-handed, but probably justified proceeding, which roused the envy of the gentlemen scientists. In 1854 he left for Melbourne. Like his founding colleagues, McCoy was a polymath. As Professor of Natural Science he taught geology, mineralogy, palaeontology, botany, physiology, comparative anatomy, elementary chemistry. He was a dandy, whose gingery Dundreary whiskers became lemon-tinted through the years. Socially, he was a cut below his fellows, and perhaps the more dandyish and empire-building because of it. He spoke with a brogue, which the students mocked. His colleagues spoke with a clipped Ascendancy accent. Student hearsay had it that he was a Catholic, but he mixed with Anglicans from the 1860s and buried his wife with Church of England rites. He was avid for international recognition and achieved his ambitions: Cambridge DSc in 1860, FRS in 1880, honorary member of learned societies in Cambridge, London, Edinburgh, Manchester, Moscow, New Zealand and Sydney and royal honours from Italy and Austria. Significantly perhaps, unlike his colleagues he received no honours from Ireland. But he outdid them by becoming the first Australian professor to be knighted in 1891, and he also was avenged by receiving the Murchison Medal of the Geological Society in 1879. Like Barry, he loved to wear court dress at university functions, draped with his decorations.[28]

Underneath the charm lay an iron will. Against the odds he built an astonishing museum in Melbourne. He scrounged and purchased and begged over 510,000 specimens of snakes, dolphins, the world's largest whale skeleton, endless flasks of microscopic sea life, together with the Curtis collection of British insects—a major collection of 33,000 specimens—the Lovell-Reeve collection of shells, another major collection, a set of gorilla skins—gorillas had only been captured since 1847—and a set of Gould's birds.[29] But McCoy's museum admitted no Aborigines or aboriginal material. They presented too many problems about linear human evolution.[30] He never mentioned them, except to discuss materials they ate and used.

McCoy worked on a world scale, with easy references to Europe, Asia and the USA. He carefully assimilated Australian geology to European time horizons and fossil assemblages and much of his dating still stands, as, for instance, the Mesozoic coal measures.

He was also a patriot, glorying in his new colonial power. He fought Baron Ferdinand von Mueller, who in a typical colonial gesture, sought to give *two* large meteorites to the British Museum. One was already dispatched and the other sawn in half—at one ton—ready to go. McCoy, as usual, charmed, nagged and bullied government to stop it, "if there be no relenting on the part of those [von Mueller] who contemplate the more than ostrich-like gluttony of the British Museum swallowing up our two Victorian meteoritic iron masses when one alone would form fit food for all their philosophic speculations and leave us to feast on one as well." It stayed and is still in the Victorian Museum.[31]

Like his colleagues, McCoy was politically conservative, but he was also reactionary in his teaching. Once he was attacked by a radical lower class politician, at a meeting during which McCoy sought more funds for his museum. He replied with beautiful evasion of the main point that "as the constituents of Mr X did not expect him to understand or conform to the standard of manners which was customary among gentlemen" he would forgive him.[32]

He was essentially a taxonomist, exhibiting the glories of the Creator's design. He never had a laboratory and never took students on geological field trips. He now left the collecting to other gentlemen. He had no concept of a research programme. His world of unspecialised science teaching and busy, random collecting passed away long before he died, still in office.[33]

Yet the rancour of his old Cambridge slights persisted. He once confided to an otherwise completely new, young acquaintance at the Melbourne Cup in 1898, Charles Trevelyan, travelling with Sidney and Beatrice Webb, that he, McCoy, rather than Darwin, should have sailed on the *Beagle*.[34] His lectures were full of quips against Robert Chambers's linear evolutionary and immensely popular *Vestiges of the Natural History of Creation* (1844) and against Charles Darwin.

He appreciated that Darwinian natural selection meant the total upset of his careful taxonomies, and that "God's provision of complete suites of plants and animals, separated in time and place" was endangered. Within the system, God, by a version of the law of conservation of energy, through creation, birth, life and death, controlled the whole universe of life. If the materialists were right, McCoy explained, there could be no death and no discernible laws or limits to existence. Moreover, there was no warrant in scripture for the transmutation of species.

McCoy also produced, in the absence of any notion of palaeoclimatology, more subtle arguments against Darwin. Darwin, he said, posited the powerful influence of external circumstances upon the transmutation of species, but if he was right, Australia and South Africa, with similar climatic landscapes, should have produced similar sorts of animals, yet South Africa had cloven-foot herbivores and the cat family of carnivores, while Australia had marsupials. Each animal economy was *complete* as God ordained it, yet each was utterly distinct. Moreover, Australian evidence proved that evolution did not proceed from simpler to more elaborate forms. Trigonia, a fossil bivalve, existed in Australia from the Mesozoic to the present, unchanged. Older fossil forms of marsupial were closer in structure to modern forms than the extinct Diprotodons and Nototheriums.[35]

These lectures against Darwin, of three hours each without notes, were delivered to the Early Closing Association, a reformist body sponsored by liberal Anglican clergymen. McCoy, like his university colleagues, had no real scholarly audience. Colonial Australia, like colonial Ireland, provided insufficient students, research pupils or posts in the slow developing universities, as well as a civil service resistant to recruitment and promotion by merit, to be able to build networks on the Oxford, Cambridge model. He and his colleagues lost contact with Ireland, except to get honorary degrees in absentia, 20–30 years later. These were poor recompense for the almost total neglect of their work in the metropolises, and appropriation into larger theoretical schemata of their taxonomic descriptions, whether in zoology, anthropology or botany, by metropolitan bigwigs at the price of an acknowledgement in small print. Unlike their Oxford and Cambridge confreres, they never developed the student following and control that would have enabled them to build specialist honours schools of the 1860s to 1880s and research laboratories and libraries. These did not emerge in Science until the 1920s and in Arts until the 1940s.

In these conditions McCoy atrophied. Following his mentor Sedgwick, he never accepted the Ordovician epoch as a break with the Silurian. He also sought, like Sedgwick, to explain new suites of fossils by positing submergences of the continent at the breaks between the Palaeozoic and Meseozoic and Tertiary.[36] Each new suite represented a new creation: that is, a series of catastrophies marking discontinuous sequences, each accompanied by a miraculous creation to be ultimately realised by man humbly realising the mind of God. Now that catastrophe theory, especially at the ending of the Mesozoic, and hypotheses about short-term variations in species are back in fashion, McCoy's views do not look as quaint as they did ten years ago. But, nonetheless, while he encouraged independent gentlemanly collectors, he did not fire his pupils' curiosity and seems to have produced no notable successors.

Ireland continued to supply outstanding professors to Melbourne until the 1940s. William Alexander Osborne (1873–1967) was born in County Down, the son of a Presbyterian clergyman. He was trained at Queen's College, Belfast, London and Tübingen. He was elected Professor of Physiology and Histology at Melbourne in 1903 and became Dean of the Medical School between 1929 to 1938. He, too, was an extraordinary polymath, helping at various stages to teach agriculture, pharmacology, nutrition and biochemistry, and he was widely read in English, German and classical literature and philosophy. He also published poetry and biographies. In his retirement he became a celebrated radio quiz-man and sage.

Osborne's confident intellectual versatility rested upon a confident professional and political conservatism. He imbued his students with a strong sense of their professional superiority, their obligations to patients and their unreflecting opposition to any attempt by the state to redistribute access to medical attention.

He was a member of the Melbourne Club (Wilson had been excluded and became a founder of the rival, less select Australian Club), as had been Barry, Stawell, Hearn and others before him (Barry was three times President), and was a leading light in the Imperial Federation Movement and the Round Table group, a pro-Imperial, Protestant masonry, devoted to pressing British leadership of the world. Osborne has been described as tolerant, except that he could not stand "South of Ireland men"—he boasted that he had never voted for a candidate with a Catholic Irish name—"Asiatics, negroes and lawyers."[37] And yet, like Barry, McCoy, Hearn and the others, Osborne was a visionary, resolved to seize his chance to build enduring institutions in his adopted country. He backed the National Library of Australia from the outset and, in his late 80s, he materially encouraged the new university at Townsville.

Ireland's greatest scientific gift to Australia was Sir Thomas Lyle, born 1860 in Coleraine, the son of a farmer. He graduated from Trinity College Dublin with gold medals in mathematics and experimental science. He soon made his mark by devising ways of measuring the light outputs of Irish lighthouses. He was also an Irish rugby international, but for reasons that I do not know, he failed to win a post at Dublin University and instead lectured, with great éclat, at University College Dublin in the mid 1880s. In 1888 he was elected

Professor of Natural Philosophy at Melbourne. While a knee injury had ended his footballing career, in Melbourne he became a keen follower and administrator of Australian Rules Football.

Lyle's arrival at Melbourne closely followed that of David Masson, the chemist, and Baldwin Spencer, the zoologist and anthropologist, and Melbourne entered a golden period. Lyle was Melbourne's greatest scientist before the Nobel laureate, Macfarlane Burnet. Together with Spencer and Masson, Lyle created a new science faculty and began a graduate research programme which was to produce a stream of distinguished Fellows of the Royal Society and men who were to play crucial scientific roles, especially in optics, in both wars.

Lyle was a world leader in theorising about alternating currents and their measurement and control. He, along with W.A. Osborne, helped to found the Commonwealth Scientific and Industrial Research Organisation. Moreover, with Sir John Monash, he helped to devise some of the world's best long distance high tension electricity power lines from Yallourn 100 miles to Melbourne. He was President of the Melbourne Club in 1928, after marrying into the Western District squattocracy. Politically, he was conservative. He left nearly £80,000.[38]

Outside the busy professoriate, the heads of the Presbyterian and Anglican Colleges, as glorified headmasters with *ex officio* places in university government, also had leisure to make money and become prominent in the community.

John McFarland, the first master of Ormond College, the Presbyterian foundation at Melbourne University, was also a brilliant product of Queen's College Belfast, winning every possible prize, having proceeded there from the Royal Academical Institution in Omagh. MacFarland's mother was the daughter of a notable Covenanting minister, his father a linen draper. MacFarland then went on to St John's College Cambridge, and a first in mathematics in 1876. But he had no patronage and thus went as master to Repton School. He came to Ormond College as its first master in 1881. At Ormond, he was unostentatiously devout, but refused to implement compulsory prayers. His association with Melbourne University lasted 56 years and ended in the 1930s.

Outside Ormond and the university, he was a founder of the Universal Service League to press conscription in 1916, against the Catholic Archbishop Mannix (Osborne used to call him the "hooligan of Maynooth") and the Labor Party. MacFarland also became a prominent member of the Royal Colonial Institute and the Round Table. He was a liberal imperialist, but not a rabid anti-Catholic like his colleague and rival Alexander Leeper of Trinity, although he did speak at the Loyalist Counter Demonstration on St Patrick's Day 1917 in the midst of the turmoil about Irish disloyalty and the defeat of the first Australian conscription plebiscite. He later, in 1930–31, chaired the inaugural meetings of the All for Australia League, which developed into the United Australia Party which evolved into the present conservative, business-orientated Liberal Party, although he took no part in the UAP.

MacFarland, mistakenly and approvingly thought by many, including Sidney and Beatrice Webb, to be a Scot, made a fortune as a director of National Mutual Life and the Trustees Executors Agency Co. McCoy also appears to have made money out of the latter company. MacFarland remained a bachelor and gave at least £75,000 to Ormond and the Presbyterian Church.[39]

Alexander Leeper, MacFarland's rival, became principal of Trinity College Melbourne in 1876. He was an overbearing man, who believed in the supremacy of the classics as a training for gentlemen and as an introduction to the obligations of Empire. He ran his college strictly and tried to run the university on the same lines. He led the campaigns against the reinstatement of the Professor of Music, George Marshall Hall, who had been sacked after writing some weakly *fin de siècle* erotic verse, and who did not respect the Sabbath. In 1915 Leeper successfully bullied the university into dismissing two apolitical Germans, to prove its loyalty. He tabled his motion for their dismissal on Empire Day.[40] His whole disturbed emotional and imaginative life lay with

England; disloyal Ireland and its disloyal offspring, Australia, were only to be saved by endless secret and public work by the garrison. He denounced and never used the first Commonwealth Australian stamps, depicting a kangaroo rather than the king. In 1912 he led the Melbourne Ulster and Loyal Irish Association in opposing the Liberals' Home Rule bill. He strongly supported conscription and, unlike MacFarland, expelled young men whom he thought should join the colours. The No case in the plebiscite was promoted, he declared, by "the shirkers, the pro-Germans, the Sinn Feiners, the Mannixites, the IWW traitors, the pacifists and the cranks."[41] He regularly organized loyalist meetings on St Patrick's Day. Like MacFarland, Hearn and Lyle, he held ostentatiously aloof from the Celtic revival or the various Irish literary and social clubs in Australia.

Leeper's most recent library idols were Browning and George Eliot. He never accommodated to modernism, or to Australian writing, behaviour or politics. A true provincial, he was uneasy in his local setting, convinced that the best always lay elsewhere, and in the past. He was committed to imposing a literary tradition that smothered local time-scales and fixed as archetypes human relationships, landscapes and events which had no resonance in the local context. He thereby helped to misplace the colonial imagination and render his Melbourne students even more marginal and insular in relation to their linguistic patria. The outcome was a cast of mind, notably evident among the Melbourne educated classes, which was insecure and by turns brashly dismissive or crassly deferential to out-of-date cultural forms from the metropolis and ill at ease with its younger poets, novelists and painters.

This dislocation had repercussions in one notably important public institution where Leeper had a major influence. Like MacFarland, Leeper, by virtue of his connections with the Melbourne imperial squatting, mercantile, professional network, was a trustee of the National Gallery of Victoria and the Felton Bequest. The Bequest was, in its time, a fairly rich endowment for the purchase of works of art and for various charitable trusts. Leeper was resolved to build "a great gallery" and that he helped to do: during his time several magnificent paintings were acquired. (Incidentally the National Gallery is contemporaneous with the National Gallery of Ireland. Wilson had been a prime mover in its creation, backed by Gavan Duffy and George Higinbotham. Wilson's original remit was very similar to that for the Dublin gallery. The influences would be worth tracing. The more obvious case of influence is the Dublin Four Courts and the Melbourne Supreme Court building). But Leeper's and his colleagues' tastes were highly conservative. They backed safe eighteenth century British works, Dutch seventeenth century pieces and some great masterpieces from the Italian fifteenth and sixteenth centuries. Some major French impressionist pieces were rejected. Australian painting was bought sparingly. Modernist works were spurned. Leeper also agreed to the purchase of several overpriced minor and workshop pieces. He and his fellows showed remarkable faith in their generally unadventurous London advisers, and apparently never considered buying direct from Paris, Rome or Madrid. They also proved suspicious of the one adviser, Frank Rinder, who sought, but failed, to widen their horizons.[42]

Ultimately, the Melbourne Irish professors were garrison men, staunch, well-trained, upright and alien. They set standards of faith in learning as a way to virtue, rationality and civilised society that is an invaluable legacy. But they also isolated Melbourne University more than it perhaps need have been from the needs of a colonial society in a difficult new environment: agricultural science, soil science, mining and mechanical engineering, anthropology and Asian studies were all neglected. (Sydney University on the other hand established chairs in anthropology and Asian studies a generation ahead of Melbourne.) The founding fathers came from a university system utterly dependent upon government subsidy and left Melbourne in particular still dependent upon it. They never looked to American land grant colleges as a model. Even now, our rulers launch "universities" without endowments, and their founding councillors apparently never

demand them. The Irish professoriate's links, through the
Melbourne Club, the Anglican and Presbyterian churches,
the church secondary schools, their marriages and the marriages of their children, were among that other garrison, the
squattocracy, who lived their imaginative lives and indeed
much of their physical lives remote from Australia and gave
too little of their wealth to Australian institutions. The
technically well-equipped, narrow, self-serving professionals
Hearn and Osborne educated, returned, and return, little
affection or material help to the institution that licensed
them to farm the community. Melbourne and, I think, other
Australian universities, have no chairs endowed by class-
mates, unlike their American counterparts. Melbourne, like
other Australian universities, only came belatedly in the late
1880s to embody some of the values and conserving beliefs
that public institutions, to be vital, must express. And then
the Depression and financial scandal of 1901 intervened to
slow that development until the late 1930s. Radicals and
Catholics, who could have formed a rich source of support,
turned to building conformist, stultifying elementary school
systems, with entrenched resistance to high technical and
university preparatory education.

Yet the garrison helped to make Melbourne, the manifestation of the talented gold-rush generation, what Charles
Trevelyan, the worldly-wise Cambridge man accompanying
the Webbs, valued as "the most intellectual society I have
been in outside England, whether in America or the
Colonies ... there is far less provincialism than elsewhere."
But he also noted of Melbourne University that "the people
at large do not regard it as their institution as in America.
The state pays only a small sum to supplement the
endowment and reduced it by two-thirds in the bad times."[43]

Beatrice Webb's private verdict was similar:

> Melbourne University has more energy and is served by a far
> superior class of English and Scotch [read Irish] Professors,
> than Sydney University. But it is divorced from the life of the
> nation; the University exists "on sufferance" being always
> attacked by the democratic party.[44]

Melbourne, like the Queen's Colleges, its true originals in my view, was a plantation university. It had no integral connections with its community. It had and has no municipal support on the pattern of say, Manchester or Birmingham, nor was it an autonomous institution of masters and students, richly endowed by its Church and State origins, wholly integrated with the ruling classes, on the Oxford or Paris model. Melbourne lacked, and lacks, political, municipal and business and professional support, religious backing and popular comprehension of its purposes. Despite its isolation, or perhaps because of it, superlative quality of its Irish founding fathers gave it good standards, but these standards were not shared by the community, which saw it as a training convenience which should process their sons and daughters into the professions as cheaply and quickly as possible. By comparison with Oxford and Cambridge, and the universities of North America, Melbourne and its sister universities enjoy little loyalty from their graduates. But then it is the nature of garrison institutions to be unpopular creatures of remote governments, necessarily aloof from the people whose civility is at once their self-appointed charge and source of income and dignity.

References
1. G.L. Fischer, *The University of Sydney 1850–1975* (Sydney, 1975), p.16.
2. Ernest Scott, *A History of the University of Melbourne* (Melbourne, 1936), pp. 9–10.
3. Hugh Lloyd Jones, (ed.) U. von Wilamowitz-Moellendorff, *History of Classical Scholarship* (London, 1982), p.137.
4. Fischer, *Sydney*, pp.44–5; D.J. Mulvaney and J.H. Calaby "So Much That is New", *Baldwin Spencer, 1860–1929* (Melbourne, 1985) p.76.
5. The committee comprised G.B. Airy and Sir John Herschel, the astronomers, Henry Maldon, Professor of Greek at University College London, Robert Lowe, the Oxford ex-colonial, and Sir William a'Beckett, a colonial lawyer in London. Most of these men also acted for Sydney.
6. A.W. Martin, *Henry Parkes* (Melbourne, 1980), pp.91–3.
7. Quoted by J.R. Poynter, "Alexander Leeper," *Australian Dictionary of Biography*, vol.10, p.55.

8. Fred Alexander, *Campus at Crawley* (Melbourne 1963), p.20.

9. W.G.K. Duncan and Roger Ashley Leonard, *The University of Adelaide 1874–1974* (Adelaide 1973), pp.13–14.

10. The most generous of these compilations remains P.S. Cleary, *Australia's Debt to Irish Nation-Builders* (Sydney, 1933). There is also a lively unpublished survey, by the late J.J. Auchmuty. I have deposited a copy in the ANU library.

11. It is worth adding two other creative Irish pioneers: John Kirkland, first Professor of Chemistry at Melbourne was from TCD, while Richard Tracy, the first teacher of obstetrics, came from the Dublin School of Medicine.

12. Noted from a memorandum in the Hearn Papers, by Ruth Campbell, *A History Of The Melbourne Law School* (Melbourne, 1977), p.72. Eric Richards has pointed out to me that Conan Doyle had noticed the Irish presence at Melbourne University. Doyle appointed James McMurdo O'Brien, "The first and most distinguished pupil" of the great Ainslie Grey, to the physiological chair at Melbourne. "A Physiologist's Wife," in *Round the Red Lamp* (1894).

13. Geoffrey Blainey, *A Centenary History of the University of Melbourne* (Melbourne, 1957), p.47.

14. Campbell, *Law School*, p.48.

15. William Edward Hearn, *The Cassell Prize Essay on the Condition of Ireland* (London and Dublin, 1851), pp. 105–8, 112, 117.

16. J.A. La Nauze, "Hearn on Natural Religion: An Unpublished Manuscript," *Historical Studies*, vol.12, no.45, Oct. 1965, pp. 119–22.

17. Quoted by J.A. La Nauze in *Political Economy in Australia* (Melbourne, 1949), pp.64–5.

18. La Nauze, *Political Economy*, pp.69–71, 76–7.

19. ibid, p.52.

20. William Edward Hearn, *Plutology or the Theory of the Efforts to Satisfy Human Wants* (Melbourne, 1863), pp.49, 156–7, 345, 403.

21. Scott, *University of Melbourne*, p.24.

22. The defenders of the old regime, incidentally, included Dr Richard Eades, TCD–MB–1836 FRCSI 1844, who migrated to Adelaide in 1849. Later, as Lord Mayor of Melbourne in 1860, he courageously confronted a very excited crowd, including many Irish, outside the parliament building, read the Riot Act and dispersed them. They were demanding land distribution for small farms, while inside the parliament their champion, Wilson Moses Grey, TCD 1835, Irish Bar 1838, editor of the *Freeman's Journal*, who arrived with Gavan Duffy in 1855, was demanding a land bill. Sometimes the Melbourne intellectual and political arena appears

like a tiny, rich Pacific atoll, peopled by a standard Irish theatrical party, endlessly rehearsing old lines.

23. Scott, *University of Melbourne*, p.24.

24. Hearn, Memorandum, 25 April 1863, Melbourne University Archives, 2/1/6–7; *Victorian Parliamentary Debates*, vol.3, March 1867, (R.D. Ireland); Charles Gavan Duffy, *My Life in Two Hemispheres* (2 vols, London, 1878), vol.II, pp.229–33.

25. Scott, *University of Melbourne*, p.26.

26. W.E. Hearn, *Address on Amendment of the Law* (Melbourne, ND [early 1880s?]).

27. Adam Sedgwick, *A Detailed Systematic Description of the British Palaeozoic Fossils* . . . (Cambridge, 1849–54), pp.X–XIII.

28. G.C. Fendley, "Sir Frederick McCoy," *Australian Dictionary of Biography*, vol.5,pp.134–36.

29. R.T.M. Pescott, *Collections of a Century* (Melbourne, 1954), pp.23–69.

30. I owe this observation to Professor John Mulvaney.

31. Pescott, *Collections*, p.49.

32. ibid, pp.86–7.

33. Mulvaney and Calaby, *Baldwin Spencer*, p.79

34. Charles Philips Trevelyan, *Letters From North America And The Pacific 1898* (London, 1969), p.211.

35. Professor McCoy, *The Order And Plan Of Creation* (Melbourne, 1870), 1871; Frederick McCoy, *Prodromus to the Palaeontology of Victoria* (Decade I, Melbourne, 1874), p.21; "Microzoan" [McCoy], *Australasian*, 17 September 1870.

36. Frederick McCoy, *On The Recent Zoology and Palaeontology of Victoria* (Melbourne, 1867), pp.19,24.

37. K.F. Russell, *The Melbourne Medical School 1862–1962* (Melbourne, 1977), p.168.

38. R.W. Home, "Sir Thomas Ranken Lyle," *Australian Dictionary of Biography*, vol.10, pp.172–74.

39. Geoffrey Serle, "Sir John MacFarland," in Stuart Macintyre, (ed.), *Ormond College* (Melbourne, 1984). Probate of McCoy's will in *The Australasian*, 20 May 1899.

40. Blainey, *University of Melbourne*, p.137.

41. Quoted by Poynter, "Leeper," *Australian Dictionary of Biography*, vol.10, p.56.

42. Leonard B. Cox, *The National Gallery of Victoria 1861 to 1968* (Melbourne [1969?]), pp.73, 121–30.

43. Trevelyan, *Letters*, p.202, 206.

44. A.G. Austin, (ed), *The Webbs' Australian Diary 1898* (Melbourne, 1965), p.88.

7.

'Der mary this is fine cuntry is there is in the would': Irish-English and Irish in late eighteenth century Australia

JAKELIN TROY

In this article, I propose to examine the possible Irish contribution to the Australian sociolinguistic context and especially to the development of NSW[1] Pidgin in the late eighteenth and nineteenth centuries. From 1788 onward there were Irish people in Australia and for most of the nineteenth century at least a quarter of the population was Irish or of Irish parentage. The Irish were prominent in the earliest establishment of frontier settlements, first as convicts working for the government and later as assigned convict servants, free servants and free settlers on small land-holdings. Given their significant numbers, it would be remarkable if the Irish had made no contribution to the Australian linguistic context in that period.

It would be particularly surprising if they had made no contribution to the development of NSW Pidgin, as most of the Irish were located in the urban and rural working-class sectors of the Australian population, placing them in direct and extended contact with Aborigines who were also moving into these sectors. The populating of frontier settlements by the Irish increased their importance in the incipient stages of NSW Pidgin development and in spreading the Pidgin among Aborigines. No attempt has been made by linguists working on pidgin and creole languages in Australia to assess the

148

possible Irish contribution to the development of these languages, let alone to examine their data for elements contributed by the Irish. I have written this article with both these goals in mind: assessment of possible contributions and a limited examination of data for NSW Pidgin.

A major problem I have encountered in discussing the languages of the Irish has been the absence of statistical analysis of "county of origin" for the Irish in Australia. Such statistics would facilitate more accurate assumptions about the languages they spoke than are possible here. It is also unfortunate that musters and censuses in Australia for the period did not have a field for languages. However, I have made some tentative assumptions based on other statistical information I have available for Ireland and Australia. Fortunately, textual linguistic evidence is available for analysis, examples of which are included.

To facilitate the discussions in this article a few linguistic terms need to be defined. The result of contact between groups of people with no common language is in the very first stages "jargon" and if the contact continues "pidgin" language will develop. The difference between jargon and pidgin is that pidgin is not idiosyncratic. It has a stable, although simple, grammar and a basic set of lexical items. Therefore, a pidgin is a language with a community of speakers, while jargon is an *ad hoc* response to a communication problem, fabricated by an individual. If a pidgin gains a community of speakers for whom it is a first language, or one of a group of first languages, it becomes a "creole" and its syntax and lexicon will expand accordingly.[2] NSW Pidgin is the most demonstrable linguistic response by the Aborigines to their contact with the languages of the non-Aborigines settling in NSW in the period under discussion.[3] NSW Pidgin is not a dialect of English. No pidgin is a dialect of another language.

Thus NSW Pidgin was a language in its own right used by Aborigines and non-Aborigines who had some knowledge of it. It contained input from Aboriginal languages and from other languages spoken in the colony of NSW to which Aborigines had access. English was a major input to NSW

Pidgin, a fact which is evident from the quantity of English lexical forms it contained. However, it was not necessarily English of England. In many cases the Irish were the most numerous in terms of early contact with Aborigines and it was their Irish-English which must have provided the input to NSW Pidgin. Evidence of direct Irish Gaelic (hereafter "Irish") input to NSW Pidgin is rare. However, Irish-English contained Irish substratum influence (as it still does) and it was through that Irish substratum content that Irish provided its input to NSW Pidgin. A "substratum language" is one which in the creation of pidgin and creole languages provides most of the input to the grammar and phonology. It is usually the language of the socially inferior people in the sociolinguistic context. A "superstratum" language then provides most of the lexicon, and it is usually the language of the socially superior.[4] Consider the case of Irish-English. English was imposed on the speakers of Irish by successful invaders who became socially dominant over the Irish from the sixteenth century onwards. Their language became the language of dominance, the "superstratum," and Irish became the language of the subordinates, the "substratum." In order to communicate with the dominators the subordinates attempted to acquire English. However, for the majority of the substratum speakers the superstratum was not available through formal education until the mid-nineteenth century, so they acquired a little knowledge through random contact. As English became more widely and regularly accessible, Irish elements in the English dialects and pidgin speech of the Irish (pidgins were very likely spoken too) were gradually replaced by English ones. However, some Irish elements were never eradicated, hence the contemporary dialects of Irish-English with their varying degrees of substratum elements. Irish-English dialects are not pidgins, but dialects of English, and cannot be regarded as comparable in form to NSW Pidgin. It therefore follows that, if any elements from Irish-English can be recognised in NSW Pidgin, it is because Irish-English was the source of input. In the same way, if any elements of English-English are recognisable in NSW Pidgin it does not mean that English-English is a pidgin. Dialects of Irish-English have been the first language or one of a group of Irish languages for Irish people for centuries, a claim no pidgin could ever make.

The Irish and Australian-English

The only discussions I have found for the languages of the Irish in Australia have gone no further than to recognise the potential Irish contribution to Australian-English given the large numbers of Irish people in Australia, and to conclude that the contribution was negligible. That conclusion was reached because no basic research was carried out with the specific purpose of looking for features contributed from the linguistic output of the Irish to Australian-English. The tendency has been to focus on the output from the London criminals and the working-class of southern England who were sent or who emigrated to Australia.

Having analysed the lexicon in sources of written Australian-English, W.S. Ramson wrote that in spite of the large numbers of Irish in the colonies of Australia in the late eighteenth and nineteenth centuries, the Irish "have made no separate and distinctly Irish contribution to the Australian vocabulary, those words used in Australia which are recorded by Wright [1898–1905] as current in Ireland being recorded also in English dialects, particularly that of Lancashire."[5] He goes on to explain his claim in terms of the heterogeneity of early New South Wales society in which "no one dialect group would have remained isolated enough to preserve its individuality."[6] In addition he noted that "it is perhaps more important that the most significant population movement in Britain in the early nineteenth century was of impoverished Irish workers to the new factory areas of Lancashire, Yorkshire, and Scotland. Many of these must have subsequently been transported to Sydney as convicts,[7] or come out as assisted immigrants, and their speech, as that of a minority group in the English towns, would have already been modified."[8] This statement ignores the fact that many Irish people came direct from Ireland to Australia and that even those who were from "a minority group in the English towns" still spoke dialects of English that were conditioned by Irish-English.

In discussing "the Australian accent," A.G. Mitchell wrote: "It was in its origins a working-class speech, the language of people who were poor and for the most part unskilled. It had a large component of southeastern English city speech and of Irish. It included ways of speech characteristic of many parts of England, Scotland, and Wales, but everyone of these pretty certainly small in comparison with the southeast English and Irish component. The proportion of Irish in the years before 1850 seems to have been higher than in the years after 1850."[9] Unfortunately, Mitchell did not expand on the Irish component he identified and thereby reinforced the generally held notion that the only significant input to Australian-English was from dialects of south-east England.

R. Langker researched the language of convictism and Flash [the thieves' cant of England] in NSW and stated that the Irish had a "disproportionately small influence on Australian-English."[10] This statement is misleading, as it is based only on a limited study of lexicon and does not allow for any other kind of substratum influence in Australian-English from Irish-English. Langker later remarked that the vocabulary of Flash "was derived from English dialects, Old and Middle English, Celtic (Gaelic, Erse, Welsh, Cornish and Manx), Latin, most of the accessible contemporary modern European languages, Yiddish and Romany. The immediate source of many Celtic terms in cant was Shelta, a language spoken by provincial tinkers and vagabonds, especially those of Irish extraction." Given that Shelta (which contains solid Irish substratum input[11]) was "the immediate source of many Celtic items in cant," input to Australian-English from cant carried that lexical base with it. Therefore, many cant items in Australian-English were derived from Irish through cant. In other words, some of the Irish input to Australian-English and contact languages was present in the speech of non-Irish immigrants, and was no doubt reinforced if the Irish brought identical usages with them to Australia.

Statistical Information on the Irish in the Australian Population

One of the most useful sources for statistics on Irish emigration to Australia is unfortunately not yet available for general use. It is a database currently being compiled by Richard Reid using data from Irish archives.[12] It includes data for the place of origin within counties for each immigrant. In the absence of such a resource, I have relied upon the statistics available from the major sources for statistics relating to the Irish in Australia.

The majority of the Australian population were convicts during the first fifty or so years of settlement and the Irish were a major sector of the convict population. There were Irish people in Australia from 1788 on[13] but the first large group of Irish convicts arrived on the *Queen* in 1791.[14] At that time they comprised 3.5 per cent of the total population.[15] From 1791 to 1800 Irish convicts were 16 per cent of the total of convict arrivals at a time when at least 98 per cent of the population was convict.[16] In 1821 the population of NSW was approximately 45 per cent convict and 12 per cent of the population were Irish convicts.[17] Looking at free in proportion to bond people in NSW, the proportions increased from 116 free to 100 bond in 1821, to 377 free to 100 bond in 1841.[18] The Irish convict element in the population diminished accordingly by approximately 35 per cent over the same 20 years to reach the figure of 7 per cent of the total Australian population in 1841.[19] Irishmen counted for 23 per cent of the total number of convict males in Australia for the period of transportation from 1788 to 1867.[20] Lucas used native place as an indicator of nationality to discover that more Irish women were transported to Australia than from any other ethnic group, including the English.[21]

Statistics for the total population reveal that from 1861 to 1891 nearly 26 per cent of the Australian population was identified as "Irish."[22] However, available census figures demonstrate that the proportion of the Australian population born in Ireland dropped from 15 per cent in 1861, to 12.7 per cent in 1871, 9.4 per cent in 1881, 7.2 per cent in

1891 and 4.9 per cent by 1901.[23] O'Farrell[24] quotes the statistics of R.B. Madgwick who calculated "that 48 per cent of assisted immigrants, from 1829, when schemes started, to 1851, were Irish and that there were relatively few who came unassisted. O'Farrell further states that "precise figures for there Irish immigration have always been uncertain."[25] However, he notes that Margaret Kiddle estimated that over 35 per cent of the immigrants who came to Australia in the period under discussion were Irish, a figure which could be raised if it was possible to assess the number of Irish classified as English because they travelled from English ports.[26]

These figures demonstrate that the sector of the Australian population identified as Irish-born ranged from 16 per cent in the late eighteenth century to 26 per cent in the late nineteenth century. For the purposes of this paper such generalisations are enough to give some idea of the large number of people in Australia who were classified as "Irish." The point is that they were not an insignificant sector of the population and that their presence added an Irish dimension to Australian society. O'Farrell has demonstrated that the Irish contributed in a multitude of ways to the development of the Australian economy, political system, social systems and "national character."

The Irish and the Aborigines

In order to demonstrate that the Irish were in contact with the Aborigines it is necessary to place the Irish and the Aborigines within the socio-economic structure of Australian society and within the geographical boundaries of settlement. The first is because from 1788 forward there were Aborigines beginning to participate in the socio-economic structures of the British settlement. At an early stage some Aborigines discovered ways in which to exploit the colonists, just as some colonists were finding ways in which to exploit the Aborigines. Such interactions were the subject for many lengthy descriptions in early accounts of the colony.[27] By 1800, when the Irish sector of the Australian population was about 16 per cent of the total, there were Aborigines living in and around the settlement of Sydney and interacting with the non-Aboriginal inhabitants. They worked on a casual basis for the colonists, following their own needs, and were very much in evidence around the streets of Sydney. Communication was carried out between Aborigines and colonists in incipient NSW Pidgin, which had its beginnings in such early interactions, in the capture of adult Aborigines and in the nurturing by colonists of adult and child victims of the smallpox plagues of the early 1790s.[28] Aborigines were moving into the working-class of the colonial Australian population, although not as a stable part of the workforce. They interacted regularly with convict labourers and domestics and with the working-class among the emancipated and free minority. A few favoured local Aborigines were *au fait* with the society of the governors and their officers. Bennelong, captured in 1789 for Governor Arthur Phillip, was one of the most famous.[29] However, as was the case throughout the nineteenth century, the wealthier middle and upper-classes of urban Australia never interacted with Aborigines unless in the attempt to "civilise" chosen individuals—especially those who were the offspring of a non-Aboriginal parent. It was only in rural areas that regular, casual interactions occurred between Aborigines and the middle and upper-classes of colonial society, and such interactions were between the few pastoralists and farmers who lived on their land.[30] The majority of Aborigines who lived in and around towns and cities interacted solely with the working-class with whom they occasionally worked and socialised. Aboriginal women entered into some of the earliest and most sustained social relationships with non-Aborigines as the sexual partners, companions and servants of non-Aboriginal men. From the earliest years of settlement Aboriginal men exploited the potential of relationships between Aboriginal women and non-Aboriginal men by hiring out women, sometimes for months at a time, in exchange for goods and to establish social connections.[31]

O'Farrell[32] has written a major reference work which diachronically places the Irish within Australian society. His work provides convincing evidence which demonstrates his contention that for most of the late eighteenth century and the nineteenth century "Australian-Irish were poor . . . their poverty was a way of life."[33] The fact of their persistent poverty locates the Irish in Australia within the working-class; "the Parliamentary Select Committee which investigated the condition of the Sydney working class in 1860" found "a high Irish component."[34] The assisted immigrant population in Australia also had a large Irish component. Unable to induce large numbers of English and Scots to emigrate and satisfy the Australian demand for immigrants, "the emigration commissioners in the British Isles were compelled to send Irish, mainly the poor and destitute, particularly from Cork, Clare, and Tipperary: the typical Irish emigrants to Australia in the 1830s and 1840s tended to be semi-skilled farm workers forced off the land by the contraction of tillage in those areas."[35] The Irish provided unskilled and semi-skilled labour for Australia, and in the middle of the century also populated the goldfields.[36]

Among the convicts O'Farrell claims four-fifths were genuine criminals—although concurring with L.L. Robson[37] that they were "a better type of convict, less criminally inclined . . . less likely to turn to crime in Australia," and most of the Irish convicts were peasants, one-third of whom possessed skills of some kind.[38] Therefore, most of the Irish convicts were equipped to join the urban and rural working-class in Australia. Rubenstein has carried out research into the wealthy of New South Wales in the middle of the nineteenth century and has found that almost none were Irish Catholics.[39] Emancipated Irish convicts often took advantage of the availability of land grants, and later of small selections of 100 acres or so, to set themselves up as farmers and graziers. Many who did so had worked for free settlers as assigned servants or for the government on farms and later on the large pastoral properties being developed from the 1820s onward. The Irish did not generally become large landholders, they remained within the rural working-class.[40] Irish people were often the innkeepers and carters in rural areas.[41] In 1832 one of the two inns in the major settlement of Bathurst was run by an Irish woman, Mrs Dillon.[42] Emancipists also took labouring and domestic positions in the towns or on farms and pastoral properties. In rural areas Aborigines were frequently employed to do menial tasks around the properties and were especially valued for stock-work on the large pastoral holdings. Such positions were also filled by Irish who were assigned or free servants. In the Bathurst district, NSW, the 1828 census revealed that three hundred of one thousand non-Aborigines in the district were male Irish convicts, working as assigned servants on local pastoral properties. They were principally employed as stockmen, hutkeepers and shepherds[43]—positions which put them in frequent and sustained contact with local Aborigines. Most of them achieved harmonious relations with the Aborigines for their own safety, if not for social or economic reasons, and some had Aboriginal women living with them.

O'Farrell emphasizes that the Irish tended to remain together, creating pockets of Irish settlement throughout Australia,[44] both in the towns and cities and in the country.[45] "The initial Irish population concentrations reflected an Irish gravitation towards rural areas and pursuits. In Victoria, for instance, the Irish-born and Catholic population of the towns and cities were, to the end of the century, below the average for the colony."[46] In the pockets of Irish rural settlement, the Irish were the only non-Aborigines with whom local Aborigines were in regular and sustained contact. Porter's Retreat, NSW, provides an excellent example of a concentrated Irish settlement. In the early 1820s the district was settled almost exclusively by emancipated Irish convicts, and their free-born children. For example, there was the Cosgrave family, started by an emancipated convict Irishman and his free wife who had followed him to Australia from Ireland. They moved to Porter's Retreat, lived as servants from 1825, squatters from 1829 and selectors from 1837.[47] "Like the Cosgraves, many settlers in Porter's Retreat district such as Hogans, Behans, Hanrahans and Kirwans originally came from St. Mary's-South Creek area between Parramatta and

Penrith."[48] Irish people and people of Irish descent continued to settle there throughout the nineteenth century.

Bathurst, west of Sydney, was the first inland settlement in Australia and for the first fifteen years of its existence the population was predominantly convict and working-class. The convicts were nearly all Irishmen.[49] The first settlement was a convict garrison set up in 1815 which was followed, in 1818, by a farming settlement, populated with working-class free settlers and emancipated convicts.[50] The population in 1820 was one hundred and fourteen, seventy-five of whom were convicts and in 1821 two hundred and eighty-seven, of whom two hundred and ten were convicts. The population was predominantly male; only one of the two hundred and ten convicts of 1821 was female and there were few free women.[51] In the early 1820s the first of the large pastoral grants were made to wealthy middle and upper-class colonists. J.P.M. Long (son of a former Anglican Archbishop of Bathurst) comments that at that stage "the gentry who grazed their stock there understandably had no wish to take themselves and their families to live at this frontier post, so remote from the comparatively civilised life of Sydney. The resident population, therefore, belonged almost entirely to one class, for the small settler, whether an Emancipist or not, had more in common with his convict servant and the neighbouring shepherds and stockmen, than with the owners of stock who occasionally visited their stations."[52] Therefore, Aborigines in the Bathurst area had their earliest sustained contacts with convicts and their keepers and with working-class free and emancipated settlers, many of whom were Irish.

Following the settlement of Bathurst, the next major settlement outside Sydney was north, in the Lake Macquarie district. The earliest settlement in the area was a penal colony established at Newcastle near Port Macquarie. It was set up in 1804 and large numbers of Irish prisoners were sent there during the twenty years of its occupation.[53] Lake Macquarie was settled by the 1820s and the official history of the district points out that "the convict population of the Lake Macquarie and Brisbane Water districts belonged to the assigned servant

class, and the majority of these were of Irish blood."[54] Revd
Lancelot Threlkeld took some of the first assignees to the
area to help him set up his mission to the Awaba Aborigines.
In 1829, forty-two of eighty-nine people in the area were
assigned convicts,[55] and in 1831 the numbers of convicts had
increased to four-fifths of the population.[56] In 1840, the
Brisbane Water census counted one hundred and ninety-
eight convicts in a total district population of one thousand
and ninety.[57] Therefore, Irishmen were again pro-minent
among the first non-Aborigines in sustained contact with
Aborigines in the Lake Macquarie district. Local Aborigines, not surprisingly, are recorded as having Irish names
such as Paddy, Molly Morgan and Old Jackey.

The earliest major settlement at Port Stephens, near Lake
Macquarie, was established by Robert Dawson, the first Chief
Agent for the Australian Agricultural Company. In 1825, he
took forty English settlers to the area and soon after received
an assignment of seventeen convicts who were to be shepherds
on the more remote stations he had selected for the company.
Dawson received many convicts as assigned servants and
they were "chiefly Irishmen."[58] He chose one convict who
had been an assistant in a school in Dublin to be the school-
master for the settlement's children.[59] Dawson reported that
the Aborigines of Port Stephens and district became very
friendly with him and with the settlers and convicts under
his care. They did casual work in exchange for clothes and
food, working alongside convict servants. On many occasions
they helped Dawson apprehend runaway convicts. The Aborigines Dawson knew habitually spoke NSW Pidgin to the
non-Aborigines—some of them had learnt it at the penal
settlement of Newcastle or on Revd Threlkeld's mission. The
NSW Pidgin reported by Dawson contains evidence of input
from Irish-English and is discussed below.

Bathurst, Port Macquarie, and Port Stephens are important
to the concerns of this article, because they were the first
areas of major settlement after Sydney. Their histories follow
the pattern of most early settlements in Australia, being first
penal settlements with convicts paving the way for free

settlers to follow (literally and metaphorically as convicts built the first Australian roads). Aborigines and Irish convicts often worked with each other during the pioneering and road-building stages of settlements, because "civilised" Aborigines were employed by the government to act as guides to such parties. For example, the road party that built Cox's link between Sydney and Bathurst in 1814–15 consisted of a chain-gang (including Irish convicts), six soldiers (at least two of them Irish) and two Aborigines from Richmond.[60] Given that the Irish featured prominently among convicts, emancipists, free and assigned servants and small-time land-holders, and that those were the groups of people who populated the first settlements outside Sydney, it therefore follows that the Irish were a major group in the earliest period in which sustained contacts between Aborigines and non-Aborigines occurred. It was in those sustained contacts that NSW Pidgin had its inception, early development and dissemination.

The Languages of the Irish in Australia
In order to determine what the Irish were speaking when they arrived in Australia it is necessary to know where in Ireland they came from and when they came to Australia. I have discussed above the lack of available statistical material relevant to such an enquiry, which leaves the researcher with the impressionistic generalisations of authorities in the field and the limited statistics that are available. Drawing on these resources, my comments are merely generalisations. However, they are powerful generalisations, in the sense that they make clear the fact that, broadly speaking, the Irish were a linguistic group distinct from those of other ethnic groups. Within the general category of "the Irish linguistic group" there are of course many linguistic sub-categories according to places of origin within Ireland. Such detailed categorisation, while being briefly dealt with here, is the subject for further linguistic research, which will rely heavily on the results of further demographic studies. What the Irish spoke in Australia can only be ascertained from documents which provide

evidence of Irish speech, such as letters, court records, diaries and novels or books of reminiscences. I feel justified in using such documents as they are the same range of materials successfully used by Hogan in his seminal work on English in Ireland.[61] In formulating his diachronic grammatical and phonological descriptions, he has even used the language presented in plays written by people with firsthand knowledge of Irish-English, as documentary evidence for Irish-English, comparing it where possible with other evidence. There are no studies of the languages of the Irish in Australia. Therefore, one can only rely upon research into the languages of the Irish in Ireland to provide clues about the languages of emigrants and convicts on arrival and then, using Australian documentary sources, speculate about the survival, transformation and disappearance of such languages in Australia.

O'Farrell maintains that the majority of Irish emigrants to Australia for the period 1840s to 1880s hailed from the South West, particularly Munster, Cork, Clare, Limerick and Tipperary, and from border areas of Ulster, and that they were mostly poor, rural people.[62] He also notes the same period as the "period of the greatest number of arrivals"[63] of Irish immigrants in Australia. When assisted passage emigration ceased in the 1880s the numbers of emigrants from South West Ireland declined and there was a swing to emigration by richer people from the East, particularly Leinster and especially around Dublin, with some even later emigration from counties of Ulster.[64] Referring to the samples presented by Robson, it appears that Dublin, Cork, Tipperary and Limerick were in that order the principal Irish counties of trial for male Irish convicts, followed by Antrim, Galway, King's, Meath, Waterford, Westmeath, Roscommon, Kilkenny, Kerry, Cavan, Clare, Mayo, Queen's, Down, Longford, with a few from Wexford, Wicklow, Carlow, Louth, Sligo, Londonderry, Monaghan, Fermanagh, Donegal and Leitrim.[65] The sample for women is different: the principal counties of trial were Dublin and Cork, followed by Limerick, Galway, Antrim, Tipperary, Down, Tyrone, Armagh, Mayo, Kerry, Clare, Wexford, Wicklow, Monaghan, with fewest from Meath,

Cavan, Roscommon, Kildare, Fermanagh, Kilkenny, Waterford, Carlow, Westmeath, Queen's, Longford, Londonderry, Donegal, Louth, Leitrim, Sligo, and King's.[66] 47 per cent of both the men and the women were tried in Dublin and Cork. Of those tried in Ireland approximately 63 per cent of the men[67] and approximately 50 per cent of the women[68] were born in their county of trial. Therefore, according to Robson's sample about 30 per cent of the men and 23.5 per cent of the women transported to Australia were from Dublin and Cork, the remainder being from the other counties listed. Most of the Irish convicts tried in Dublin and Cork were poor, working-class and under twenty years old, while those tried in other counties tended to be over the age of twenty and working in rural pursuits.[69] Robson cautions that it is difficult to know whether the convicts from "non-industrialised counties" were town or village dwellers or lived in isolated places deep in the country.[70] Peter Cunningham commented that the Irish convicts classified themselves regionally and he was probably referring to the under twenty-year-old convicts, because the categories he noted were Cork, Dublin and Ulster: "the Irish divide themselves into three, namely, the 'Cork boys,' the 'Dublin boys,' and the 'North boys,' ... The 'North boys' are commonly called *Scotchmen* by the others, and indeed many spoke the Scotch dialect so broadly as almost to puzzle *me* to unravel it."[71]

Throughout the period under discussion the principle languages spoken in Ireland were Irish and English, with Irish gradually losing its ascendancy to English by the mid-nineteenth century. Irish existed in many dialectal variations and during this period its community of speakers decreased to the point of extinction in many areas of Ireland. English in Ireland also existed in dialectal variations, the majority of which belonged to the broad dialect category "Irish-English," which includes all kinds of English peculiar to Ireland. Irish scholars often spoke French, as a long tradition of scholarly exchange had existed between France and Ireland. In Australia the French complained that they were often mistaken for Irishmen.[72] However, the majority of Irish people who came to Australia were not scholars and therefore they were likely to have spoken Irish and/or Irish-English. Certainly, the majority of convicts and emigrants were poor people of rural Ireland, and those who were not came from the poor of the urban working-class, groups among whom English-English was an unattainable luxury. Without the benefit of extended education in English, which was available to wealthier Irish, it was among the poor of Ireland that English spread most slowly. Their English was also most likely to be learnt from other Irish people and therefore contain a great deal of Irish substratum input.

The numbers who were monolingual or bilingual in Irish on arrival in Australia can only be guessed at. However, in speaking of the convicts, O'Farrell contends that "many of the Irish did not speak English amongst themselves, but Gaelic."[73] He acknowledges that Irish was spoken by many Irish (both free and bond) on arrival in Australia, but claims that by the end of the eighteenth century in Ireland speaking Irish had become "a clear liability for getting on in the world." He says this was a sentiment which was also held by the Irish in Australia and which led to their abandoning Irish as quickly as possible—"little wonder that the language, already dying in Ireland, promptly vanished in Australia."[74] O'Farrell is writing as a social historian whose ideas are valid within his framework. From the point of view of O'Farrell's social history of Australia what is important is that monolingual speakers of Irish arriving in Australia desired to acquire English—that was the social reality. However, the linguistic reality was different. No matter how much a person desires to acquire another language, it is a slow process and many emigrants to Australia, even now with the benefit of specially designed language programmes, never acquire full control of English. Certainly, most of the Irish who arrived as monolingual Irish-speakers would have retained vestiges of their first language throughout their lifetime. Those who were bilingual may well have ceased using Irish and relied upon their Irish-English. However, O'Farrell has also made it quite clear that in Australia, Irish became an "in-group" community language (as it was in Ireland at various times[75]) for Irish Australians. So, for example, he states that "there is ample suggestion that many of the pioneer Irish in Victoria's western districts spoke Gaelic amongst themselves."[76] O'Farrell quotes Ryan, who recalled Irish community gatherings of the 1840s and 1850s—"the weddings, wakes and christenings of local clans were all district occasions, lasting three days and nights, the young courting, the old talking and drinking, the talking, even the courting, in Gaelic."[77]

"The earliest reference to the use of the Irish language in Australia was made in 1800, when the authorities suspected a conspiracy because convicts were speaking earnestly among themselves in Irish."[78] This evidence was given at the enquiry into the "Irish conspiracy" by the witness Hester Stroud, who said that "from what she saw of the Irishmen being in small parties in the camp at Toongabby and by their walking about together and talking very earnestly in Irish, deponent verily believes they were intent upon something that was improper."[79] The Irish speaking in a way unintelligible to the authorities was regarded with great suspicion. It is possible that even if what was spoken was "heavy" Irish-English, it may have been regarded as Irish because it sounded so foreign to other English-speaking people. The officials of the colony feared an Irish uprising and it has been recorded that the Irish were persecuted for speaking Irish because it was invariably regarded as plotting to rebel. For example, in 1833 Father Ullathorne praised Governor Bourke's lenient attitude towards Catholics in NSW and wrote: "The old people here who remember when fifty lashes was the price of refusing to go to Church, or of speaking one word in Irish, see all these changes with astonishment and gratitude."[80]

A letter, written in 1833, from Father Conolly to Right Revd Dr Morris provides evidence of monolingualism in Irish among Irish Catholics in NSW: "nothing ever surprised me more than the appointment of so young a man to be Vicar General in N.S. Wales, unacquainted as he is with the habits and manners of the Irish who chiefly constitute the Catholic population of the colony. When the British Government had, in the first instance, sanctioned the appointment of R.C. Chaplains in N.S. Wales and Van Diemen's Land, Ireland was the place where missionaries were sought for. Many persons in N.S. Wales cannot make their confessions but in Irish."[81] According to J. Kenny,[82] Conolly was literate in, and spoke, Irish and used his knowledge in dealing with many Irish Catholics, including the convict Alexander Pierce. In an account distorted by Birt's confusion about details of Australian history and possibly by the nature of the evidence, Kenny quoted the oral evidence of C. Fitzpatrick: "Father Conolly attended him and got from him the details of his life, which he wrote down in Irish . . . [he] read it on the scaffold, folding up the paper and putting it in his pocket . . . then Governor Phillip [Birt is obviously confused here; the governor must have been Arthur, the presiding Governor of Tasmania, because Pierce was executed in Tasmania in 1824], who thought Father Conolly rather a simple kind of man, sent his orderly with the request to favour him with the account of Pierce's life. The priest sent it, but neither the Governor nor any of the officials 'could make it out.' They thought it was Hebrew, and had to send for Father Conolly to translate it. This was a standing joke afterwards against the Governor, who had thought very little of the attainments of the humble priest."[83] O'Farrell cites two instances where interpreters were required in court for Irish speakers[84] and Robson mentions the case of Michael Tierney from Co. Galway, sent to Van Diemen's land, who was unable to speak English.[85]

The only account of Aborigines using Irish that I have found, so far, is a fragment in an account of a corroboree near Bathurst attended by two young Irishmen who evidently taught the Aborigines a song in Gaelic which became pidginised into "Irish-Warregara."[86] Therefore, I focus on Irish-English as of much greater significance to the development of NSW Pidgin. The Irish who did not speak English on arrival where possible acquired it in Australia. Unless they received sustained and lengthy formal instruction in English— English, their English retained elements of Irishness that placed it within the dialect group Irish-English. In fact, monolingual Irish-speakers would have experienced some of the processes of pidginisation, which are induced by language acquisition without formal training and which were also experienced by Aborigines in their contact with English.

Hogan, an authority on the linguistic situation in Ireland in the late eighteenth and nineteenth centuries, maintains that English "did not begin to spread among the people until the end of the eighteenth century, nor did it emerge victorious from the struggle with Irish until the middle of the nineteenth. Immediately after the final destruction of the old Ireland the gap between planter and native was too wide for the language of the former to spread among the latter. The gentry seem to have learned a little Irish, rather than the peasants English."[87] Bliss explains that "it is remarkably difficult to determine the number of English speakers in Ireland at any date before the first language census in 1851."[88] Seán de Fréine mapped the spread of English in Ireland in 1800 and found that Irish was dominant over most of the country, and certainly all the South West.[89] Aside from Dublin, the areas from which the Irish in Australia, up to 1800, had come, were still Irish-speaking. In discussing the spread of English in the early nineteenth century, Bliss cites Richard Edgeworth's 1811 comment that the Irish peasantry "have within these few years made a greater progress in learning English, than the Welsh have made since the time of Edward the First, in acquiring the language."[90] He then quotes "rough figures compiled by Christopher Anderson in 1828," which "suggest that in the eastern half of the country more than 50 per cent of the people were indeed English-speaking; but in the western half less than 50 per cent and in most of Connacht less than 10 per cent were English-speaking."[91] Most of the Irish going to Australia at that time came from the South West and therefore fall within the less than 50 per cent English-speaking group. Bliss and de Fréine agree on the middle of the century as the period in which English became ascendant in Ireland, de Fréine claiming that the final demise of Irish was caused by the Great Famine, which caused the death or emigration of most of the remaining Irish speakers, leaving only the tiny Gaeltacht pockets which still exist in Ireland today.[92] Thus most of the Irish who emigrated to Australia before the mid-nineteenth century were from the Irish-speaking areas of South West Ireland, as outlined by Hogan and de Fréine. This is not to say they were not bilingual to some degree, but that Irish was at least one of their first languages. The 1851 census found only one quarter of the population of Ireland speaking Irish, with just 5 per cent monolingual Irish speakers (these figures are however debated by twentieth century linguists).[93] The decline of Irish from a majority to a minority language has, as previously stated, been blamed on the Famine, which from 1845 to 1850 raged among the poor of Ireland, killing about a million and forcing another million to emigrate.[94] However, many of the poor Irish for whom education was still a luxury and who emigrated because of the famine had Irish as at least a functioning second language. O'Farrell has found that the numbers of Irish who emigrated to Australia in the middle of the nineteenth century as a result of the Famine were low, compared to those who came for the gold-rushes although those people were also from the poorer classes of rural and urban Ireland. The conclusion can be drawn that Irish was not a completely dead language for most of the Irish emigrating to Australia, even in the middle of the nineteenth century. As the end of the century drew near and English increased its dominance in Ireland, so the numbers of Irish-speakers emigrating to Australia decreased accordingly.

Bliss makes the important point that even among the Irish who could speak English, the language was acquired from teachers or other Irishmen whose own English was very different from the "standard English" of England, "so that there was nothing to check the progressive influence of the Irish language." The Irish who attended school (hedge schools and, after 1831, the national schools) were taught English by teachers whose speech "was already strongly influenced by Irish." Hence the speech of the pupils was even more so.[95] The process of the Irish learning English from Irish-English speakers has perpetuated to the present and explains the strong influence still exerted by Irish in areas where it has long been a dead language.[96] Hogan explains that the "English of the Protestant Irish nation [which he defines as having begun in the seventeenth century with the English plantations] is the form of English which, mixed with older Anglo-Irish and learned by a population with an Irish speech-basis, is the language of Ireland today."[97] It follows that this English with Irish substratum influence was also the English taken to Australia and perpetuated there by the Irish. Using the dialect divisions identified by authorities on Irish-English, it is possible to further classify the Irish-English brought to Australia. As most of the Irish came from Munster with a few from Leinster, particularly Dublin, the dialects of those areas figured most prominently among the Irish in Australia during the period under discussion. Bliss notes that the dialects of the three southern provinces of Ireland are quite uniform having "fewer basic differences than one might expect."[98]

Irish-English was just as distinctly an Irish mode of speech as was Irish, and it was recognised in Australia as the "brogue" (speech which mixed Irish with English[99]). O'Farrell found that one of the things which marked the Irish out from other Australians was their "immediately recognisable" brogue.[100] So recognisable was the brogue that other colonists were even able to recognise dialect variations. For example, the novelist Alexander Harris used a character called "Dubbo" (which referred to his Dublin origins), who had a "voice of that mixed accent which distinguishes the offspring of Dublin parents of the lowest class born in one of our great English cities."[101] Through their tendency to form communities in Australia, the Irish perpetuated their brogue among themselves and it was acquired by their children: "especially in its rural form, the Irish world of early New South Wales was a hierarchical and clannish one, handing on its customs, and even its brogue to succeeding native-born generations."[102] The "inherited brogue long lingered in the children of Irish areas; it was common in the Catholic schools of the western districts of Victoria into the 1930s, in children of the third or fourth Australian generation."[103]

The fact that some of the Australian-Irish maintained their brogue at least until the 1930s is in itself very significant to the Australian linguistic context. The significance lies in the conclusion which can be drawn from this information—that the Australian Irish were a linguistic group of their own, well into the twentieth century. They formed their own dialect group with the complex of varieties of English spoken in Australian by native-born Australians. The Australian-Irish were Australians, born in Australia and therefore their English can be regarded as Australian-English. No contradictions arise from such a statement because Australian-English has long been recognised to be a cover term for many varieties of English spoken by Australians who acquired English in Australia as at least one of their first languages. Recent basic research into Australian-English has been directed at finding regional and social variation and the results have shown that such variation does exist. Ethnic origin and social class have been found to be important variables in the distinction of varieties. Examples include the project at the University of Queensland on linguistic diversity in the speech of schoolchildren; Barbara Horvath of the University of Sydney's work on variation in Sydney speech; and the Bradleys, of La Trobe University, who have been working on phonological variables in Australian-English. The Bradleys have found a variation in schwaful versus non-schwaful endings (for example, "growan" versus "grown'), which may be attributable to the perpetuation of an Irish-English feature in Australian English.[104] The Australian Dictionary Project[105] has identified lexicon with Irish origins in Australian-English. Oral evidence and the Macquarie Dictionary provide many examples of Irish lexical items common in nineteenth century Australian literature which have persisted into the twentieth century, such as "spalpeen," "shanty," "sheila," "pannikin" and "pampootees." "Pampooties" (in Irish "pamputa"), which is an Irish word for a kind of foot covering made quickly by lacing untanned hide,[106] has also entered the vocabulary of Aborigines in western NSW as a word for shoes.[107] Common in the speech of working-class

Australians is the now rare use of "which" for the relators "these" and "this" and which the OED notes as a feature of Irish-English. Another feature of Australian speech, not necessarily restricted to the working-class, is the use of "yous" as the second person plural "you." This is likely to have been an input to Australian-English from the Irish-English second person plural form "ye's."[108]

Documentary evidence for Irish-English in nineteenth century Australia

Samples of the documentary evidence for the use of Irish-English in nineteenth century Australia are here presented with a brief discussion of their features. The sources are necessarily scattered, but form a corpus which can be analysed in much the same way that Hogan analysed historical documents for Irish-English.[109] All the records were produced by people with first-hand knowledge of Irish-English, either as speakers or people who had mixed with the Irish in Australia. Court records are problematic in the sense that court reporters in the nineteenth century did not necessarily write exactly what they heard. It is apparent on perusal of such records that while some reporters adhered as closely as possible to syntax and attempted to represent some of the phonology expressed in the different kinds of speech they heard in the courtroom, others "corrected" speech in terms of their own standard. One might expect novelists to create literary styles which did not reflect the real speech of Irish people; however, it is far more difficult to invent language than it is to use language with which one is familiar. Therefore, while exaggeration is likely to have been employed, the forms of Irish-English used in novels written by authors familiar with the Irish in Australia do reflect general features of Irish-English in Australia. Consistency is the key to reliability, just as Hogan[110] found in his research. Those authors who were inconsistent and strayed dramatically from what would be predictable for Irish-English of the period are, of course, not to be relied upon.

The novelist Alexander Harris created several fictional Irish colonial characters. In order to represent their speech in his books he drew upon his first-hand experience of the Irish in Australia. For example, the character Biddy, an Irish houseservant on a pastoral property, uttered the following: "Fait, Miss, I don't know if I'll go there at all: I shall always be thinkin' the devil 'll fetch me out of it,—sure 'twas one of his imps that built it. Musha! bad luck to him every day he rises";[111] and, "Don't none of ye's take it for him, boys,...Let the spalpeen go wid it himself. Anamondyoul!"[112] Within these short quotes are lexical, phonological and syntactic information about Irish-English in mid-nineteenth century Australia. Typical lexicon, all of which can still be heard at least in Co. Kerry,[113] are "fait" from "in faith," a common general exclamation;[114] "sure," of which Joyce commented that this "is one of our commonest opening words for a sentence,"[115] "musha" which is Harris's version of "mossa" or "wisha," both variants of Irish "maseadh," all of which are a "sort of assertive particle used at the opening of a sentence";[116] "ye's," Irish-English for the second plural pronoun "you," "spalpeen" or a "low rascal," from the Irish "spailpin," which originally meant labouring men; "anamondyoul," definitely an oath, but more difficult to gloss, it appears to be an Irish form and could be "the name of God" from the Irish "ainm an dia" or perhaps "mannam on ye"—"my soul on you" (although Joyce believes it to be an affectionate exclamation[117]). The only noteworthy phonological information in the quotes is the absence of word final interdental fricatives, a feature typical of Southern Irish-English[118]—evidenced in "fait" and "wid." An inconsistency with Irish-English appears in Harris's retention of the English interdental fricatives word initially—so Biddy says "the," "that" and "there." The sentence "sure 'twas one of his imps that built it," demonstrates clefting which is a typical syntactic feature of Southern Irish-English. Bliss explains clefting thus: "In Irish, as in other Celtic languages, the verb normally stands first in the sentence. For the sake of emphasis, however, some other part of the sentence may stand there. In this case the word or phrase to be emphasised is moved forward [this is known as clefting] and is preceded by the form of the verb 'to be' known as the copula, either in the present tense . . . , or in the past tense . . . , the rest of the sentence is cast into the form of a relative clause."[119]

Michael Cosgrove stood trial at Sydney Supreme Court on 12 May, 1835, for horse stealing, and extracts from his trial record him as uttering the following sentence: "It was my father's mare I was riding."[120] Here again is an example of clefting typical of Southern Irish-English. However, this is the speech of a nineteen-year-old man who arrived in Australia as a six-year-old child brought by his mother who was joining her convict husband. Both parents were natives of Galway (villages unknown) and they settled first in an Irish part of Sydney and later among other Irish settlers at Porter's Retreat.[121] Therefore, although their son Michael had spent most of his life in Australia, his English exhibited elements that are demonstrably from Irish-English.

Moreover Cunningham reports an Irish convict, on his passage out to Australia, as having said: "Mr. Reedy's parlour was never half so *clane*."[122] His emphasis of "clane" for "clean," indicates that this was an accent difference he perceived in at least that Irishman's speech. I believe it was a plausible observation as it is consistent with Sheridan's note that the Irish pronounced words such as "tea, sea, please, as, tay, say, plays," confirmed by Bliss "as still common enough in rural areas today."[123]

William Henry Suttor was an Australian-born grazier who "acting in accordance with the unexpected . . . solicitations of many friends . . . consented to collect in a small volume"[124] articles he had originally written for charity and published in a Sydney newspaper. Amongst his reminiscences are records of the way in which Irish people he had encountered spoke. For example, when writing about his experiences as a hospital collector: ". . . a woman's voice behind the door asked in [sic] strong Irish accent, 'what do ye want? Who's there? . . . I've nothing for ye,'[125] and 'what do ye want making all that noise? Are ye police wid a warrant, or what are ye, at all at all?"[126] Here again is the Irish-English "ye" (second person singular "you"), and absence of the word final interdental fricative in "wid" ("with"). "At all at all" was described by Joyce as "so prevalent amongst us that in a very good English grammar . . . speakers and writers are warned against it." He explained its origins in the Irish word "idir" which means "at all," and which was often reduplicated, "idir, idir" for emphasis.[127]

Letters written by Irish people also supply linguistic evidence. For example the following, which is a section of the convict Thomas Fallon's letter home to his wife in 1835: ". . . dere mary I receivd you loveing letter which wish for long time. . . . Der mary, I never work one day but fourteen days for myselfe since I been in this cuntry because it is not allowed by Government but if I wonst got my liberty I cud. . . . Der mary this is fine cuntry is there is in the wourld for ateing and drinking Der mary if you wor in this cuntry you cud be worth pound per week but by owne labour . . . ".[128] Phonological information is supplied in some of the spellings such as "cuntry" for "country"; "cud" for "could"; "ateing" or "eating," which is similar to the item "clane" in Cunningham discussed above. As regards "wor," Joyce noted that this was a very common Southern Irish pronunciation of "were."[129] "You" ("your") in "receivd you loveing . . ." is the Irish-English second person possessive form "ye."[130]

Evidence of phonological conditioning from Irish-English in New South Wales pidgin

Notwithstanding the problems of orthography,[131] I claim that some of the data I use as evidence for NSW Pidgin seem to contain input from Irish-English. Most notable is the absence of interdental fricatives in some NSW Pidgin data, while they appear in other data. It seems that one of the determining factors is the concentration of Irish people in areas where NSW Pidgin does not show evidence of interdental fricatives. It could be argued that the absence of interdental fricatives is the result of substratum input from Aboriginal languages as they do not generally contain those sounds.[132]

However, this would not explain the data which contain interdental fricatives. Further, there are Aboriginal languages in which interdental fricatives do occur,[133] and it was observed in 1828 that Aborigines did not have trouble pronouncing such sounds: "several of them can speak English fluently, and pronounce the 'the', which more polished foreigners find so difficult."[134] It is more logical to explain the variation in terms of sociolinguistic contexts. In situations where Aborigines heard Irish-English they would have found that the lack of interdental fricatives was a feature in common with the phonological systems of their own languages. Therefore, they would have been able to imitate that feature of Irish-English with ease. Where they heard English containing interdental fricatives they attempted to imitate the unfamiliar sound with varying degrees of success.

"Ah Massa William, who shoot de redbill? I tell you fader!"[135] was said by an Aboriginal woman in the west of Sydney, where there were many Irish farmers and labourers. Here "de" and "fader" lack the interdental fricative word initially and word medially respectively. In the Port Stephens district the NSW Pidgin reported by Dawson consistently employs an Irish-English-like treatment of English interdental fricatives. Throughout Dawson's text the following items appear in the NSW Pidgin of Port Stephens: "dere" for "there"—it very occasionally appears as "there," which may have been used by Aborigines who had acquired another variety of NSW Pidgin; "dat" for "that," "tings" and "thousand," for example, "murray tousand tings" or "many thousand things';[136] "tinky" for "think," "-y" is the NSW Pidgin transitive marker usually represented as "it" or "im";[137] "udder" for "other'; "dey" for "they." That the Aborigines had a great deal to do with Irish convicts in the Port Stephens area is evidenced by the fact that they called all runaway convicts "croppy."[138] This item became the NSW Pidgin word used by Aborigines as a generic term for convicts, even though it was used by non-Aborigines only in referring to Irish convicts.[139]

Conclusion

In this article it has been demonstrated that the Irish were a large segment of the Australian population and that they were linguistically distinguishable from the rest of the population. It has also been demonstrated that the Irish were in a position to provide some of the earliest and most sustained input to NSW Pidgin. Further research will facilitate a full description of the ways in which the Irish adapted linguistically and the contribution they made to the development of languages in their new country. The social contributions of the Irish to Australia have long been acknowledged while their linguistic contributions have been ignored or dismissed as inconsequential. To ignore the Irish contribution to the development of linguistic diversity in Australia is to ignore one of the major sources of sociolinguistic input for which evidence still exists.

References

1. New South Wales.
2. For a detailed discussion of pidgin and creole languages see Peter Muhlhausler, *Pidgin and Creole Linguistics*, (Oxford, 1986).
3. For a full introduction to NSW Pidgin see Jakelin Troy "Australian Aboriginal Contact with the English Language in New South Wales, 1788 to 1845," BA Hons. thesis, 1985.
4. See Muhlhausler, *Pidgin*, pp.119–33, for a more elaborate discussion of superstratum and substratum.
5. W.S. Ramson, *Australian English: An Historical Study of the Vocabulary 1788–1895* (Canberra, 1966).
6. He is now planning a dictionary of regional Australian English which will illuminate the preservation of dialectal varieties in Australian English. W.S. Ramson personal communication.
7. See L.L. Robson on the Irish convicts in England, in L.L. Robson, *The Convict Settlers of Australia*, (Melbourne, 1965).
8. Ramson, *Australian English*, p. 51.
9. A.G. Mitchell, "The Pronunciation of English in Australia," in W.S. Ramson (ed.), *English Transported: Essays on Australasian English* (Canberra, 1970), p.9.
10. R. Langker, "The Vocabulary of Convictism and Flash in New South Wales 1788–1850," MA Hons thesis, 1979. Patrick O'Farrell, *The Irish in Australia* (Sydney, 1986) p.27.

11. Ian Hancock, "Shelta and Polari," in Peter Trudgill (ed.), *Language in the British Isles* (Cambridge, 1984), pp.384–403.

12. Richard Reid, personal communication.

13. David Lucas, *The Welsh, Irish, Scots and English in Australia*, (Canberra, 1987), p.13.

14. O'Farrell, *Irish in Australia*, p.23.

15. Calculated from ibid., p.222, & *The Australian Encyclopedia*, vol. 1, (Sydney, 1928).

16. Calculated from figures in G.B. Barton, *History of New South Wales from the Records* (Sydney, 1889–94), quoted in P.E. Leroy, "The Emancipists from Prison to Freedom: the Story of the Australian Convicts and their Descendants," 2 vols, PhD thesis, 1960, vol II, p.507.

17. *Historical Records of Australia*, series 1, X, p.575, quoted in P.E. Leroy, *The Emancipists*, p.509.

18. ibid.

19. ibid.

20. Lucas, *The Welsh*, p.13.

21. ibid.

22. Charles Price, *Australian Immigration*, ms, 1987.

23. Lucas, *The Welsh*, p.94.

24. O'Farrell, *Irish in Australia*, p.69.

25. ibid.

26. ibid.

27. For references to such accounts see the annotated bibliography of Victor Crittenden, *A Bibliography of the First Fleet* (Canberra, 1981).

28. Discussed in Troy, thesis.

29. ibid.

30. The interactions of the Suttor family of Bathurst with Aborigines, and those of other rural upper-class colonial families, are written about in various nineteenth century sources such as: William Henry Suttor, *Australian Stories Retold and Sketches of Country Life* (1887, Bathurst).

31. Jakelin Troy, "The role of Aboriginal women in the development of contact languages in New South Wales from the late eighteenth to the early twentieth century" in Anne Pauwels (ed), *Women and language in Australian and New Zealand society.* (Sydney, 1987) pp. 155–69.

32. O'Farrell, *Irish in Australia*.

33. ibid., p.20.

34. ibid., p.82.

35. ibid., p.71.

36. ibid., p.84.

37. Robson, *Convict Settlers*, pp.24–8.
38. Patrick O'Farrell, *Irish in Australia*, p.24.
39. Bill Rubenstein, "The Top Wealth-holders of New South Wales in 1830–44," *The Push from the Bush*, no. 8, December, 1980, pp. 34–5.
40. O'Farrell, *Irish in Australia*, p.88.
41. ibid.
42. Bernard Greaves, (ed.), *The Story of Bathurst*, p.18.
43. Robin Maclachlan, compiler of the Michell College of Advanced Education Bathurst Database, personal communication.
44. O'Farrell, *Irish in Australia* pp. 85–6.
45. ibid., pp.81–88.
46. ibid., p.88.
47. Brian Johnston, *Cecily Cosgrove, a Bush Pioneer. A History of the Cosgrove family of Porter's Retreat, N.S.W.* (Belfield, 1983), pp.36,42.
48. ibid., p.19.
49. Robin Maclachlan, personal communication.
50. Greaves, *Bathurst*, p.5.
51. ibid., p.17.
52. ibid., p.115.
53. Keith H. Clouten, *Reid's Mistake* (Lake Macquarie, 1967), p.12.
54. ibid., p.57.
55. ibid.
56. ibid., p.59.
57. ibid., p.57.
58. Robert Dawson, *The Present State of Australia* (London, 1831, 2nd edition), p.37.
59. ibid.
60. J.C. Taussing in Greaves, *Bathurst*, pp.4–5.
61. Jeremiah J. Hogan, *The English Language in Ireland* (Dublin, 1927).
62. O'Farrell, *Irish in Australia*, pp.71, 85 & 93.
63. ibid., p.93.
64. ibid.
65. Robson, *Convict Settlers*, p.178.
66. ibid., p.186.
67. ibid., p.191.
68. ibid., p.202.
69. ibid., pp.21–8.
70. Robson, *Convict Settlers*, p.25.
71. He emphasised his difficulty in understanding them because he was from Scotland and was accustomed to the Scots accents including those of Ireland. Peter Cunningham, *Two Years in New South Wales* (London, 1872), vol.11, p.247.

72. Colin Thorton-Smith (University of Melbourne, who is researching French impressions of colonial Australia), personal communication.

73. O'Farrell, *Irish in Australia*, p.25.

74. ibid., p.27.

75. For example, Jeremiah J. Hogan explains that the English-speaking citizens of medieval Waterford and Cork used Irish as an in-group language. Hogan, *English in Ireland* p.30.

76. O'Farrell, *Irish in Australia* p.26.

77. P.G. Ryan, *Reminiscences of Australia* (Sydney, 1895), in O'Farrell, *Irish in Australia*, p.124.

78. *Tir Na Nog*, May, 1984, p.4, in Lucas, *The Welsh*, p.41.

79. *Historical Records of Australia*, vol 11. p.641, in T.J. Kiernan, *The Irish Exiles in Australia* (1954, Dublin) p.19.

80. In H.N. Birt, *Benedictine Pioneers in Australia*, vol. 1, (London 1911) p.162.

81. ibid., p.90.

82. J.Kenny, *A History of the Commencement and Progress of Catholicity in Australia up to the year 1840* (Sydney, 1887), p.67, in ibid., p.86–7.

83. ibid.

84. O'Farrell, *Irish in Australia*, p.26.

85. Robson, *Convict Settlers*, p.50.

86. To be written up in Jakelin Troy, forthcoming, "New South Wales Pidgin from the late eighteenth century to the early twentieth century," PhD thesis.

87. Hogan, English in Ireland, p.54.

88. Alan J. Bliss, "The emergence of modern English dialects in Ireland," in Diarmaid O Muirithe (ed), *The English Language in Ireland*, (Cork, 1977), p.16.

89. Seán de Fréine, "The Dominance of the English language in the Nineteenth Century," in O Muirithe, *English Language in Ireland*, pp.71–87.

90. Bliss, *English Dialects* p.16.

91. Christopher Anderson, *Historical Sketches of the Ancient Native Irish* (1828), pp. 143–64, in Bliss, *English Dialects* p.16.

92. De Fréine, *Dominance of English Language*, pp. 71–87.

93. ibid. Frank Murphy, *The Bog Irish: Who they were and How they Lived*, (Ringwood, 1987), pp 9–10, & John Edwards, "Irish and English in Ireland," in Peter Trudgill (ed), *Language in the British Isles*, (Cambridge, 1984), p. 481.

94. ibid.

95. Bliss, *English Dialects*, p.17.

96. ibid., p.19.

97. Hogan, English in Ireland, p.54.

98. Bliss, English Dialects, p.19.

99. Bliss, cites 1689 as the date of the first use of the word "brogue" and the Thomas Sheridan, *Dictionary of the English Language*, (Dublin, 1780) has an early description of this usage. P.W. Joyce asserts the "brogue" was from the Irish word "*bróg*" which was the characteristically Irish thong-stitched shoe and which was considered so typical of Ireland, that its name was applied to what was seen as typically Irish speech, in P.W. Joyce, *English as we speak it in Ireland*, (London, 1910), p.225.

100. O'Farrell, *Irish in Australia*, p.80.

101. Alexander Harris, *The Immigrant Family*, Canberra, 1967, 1st published 1849), p.65.

102. ibid., p.89.

103. O'Farrell, *Irish in Australia*, p.28.

104. David Bradley, personal communication.

105. Directed by Bill Ramson, at the Australian Nation University.

106. P.W. Joyce, *English As We Speak It*, p.300 & David Shaw-Smith, *Ireland's Traditional Crafts*, (London, 1984), pp. 186–7.

107. Tamsin Donaldson, personal communication.

108. P.W. Joyce comments that the Irish avoid the "obscurity" in English of "you" being both singular and plural by always using "ye" in the plural whenever possible and creating new forms for the plural such as "*yous, yez, yiz.*" *English As We Speak It*, p.88.

109. Hogan, *English in Ireland*.

110. ibid. Citing works of Dekker, Shakespeare, Johson, and Randolph he remarks that "the dialect in these is pretty regular" p.56.

111. Harris, Immigrant Family, p.90.

112. ibid., p.109.

113. Padraig O'Leary, a native of Killarney, Co. Kerry (aged 24) assures me that while he does not use these items (aside from "ye's" and "sure') he has often heard them used by older members of his family and he understands the sense in which they are used; personal communication.

114. Joyce, *English As We Speak It*, pp.70–1.

115. ibid., pp.338–9.

116. ibid., pp.296 & 351.

117. ibid., p. 291.

118. Alan J. Bliss, "English in the south of Ireland," in Peter Trudgill (ed), *Language in the British Isles* (Cambridge, 1984), p.137.

119. ibid., p.146.

120. Johnston, *Cecily Cosgrove*, p.31.

121. ibid., pp. 1& 16ff.
122. Cunningham, *Two Years*, p.242.
123. Sheridan & Bliss, in Bliss, *English Dialects*, p.15.
124. William Henry Suttor, *Australian Stories*, preface.
125. ibid., p.165.
126. ibid., p.166.
127. P.W. Joyce, *English As We Speak It*, p.48., Padraig O'Leary says it is still common to hear "at all at all" and he would be comfortable using it. Personal communication.
128. In O'Farrell, *Letters from Irish Australia 1825–1929*, (Sydney, 1984), pp. 13–14.
129. P.W. Joyce, *English As We Speak It*, p78.
130. ibid., p.88.
131. The data I use for my analyses were recorded in the nineteenth century and the orthographies used in the data were chosen by the individuals recording the material.
132. R.M.W. Dixon, *The Language of Australia* (Cambridge, 1980) p.125.
133. L.A. Hercus, "Victorian Languages: a Late Survey," *Pacific Linguistics* B:77 (Canberra, 1986).
134. Roger Oldfield, in Niel Gunson (ed)., *Australian Reminiscences and Papers of L.E. Trelkeld, Missionary to the Aborigines 1824–1859* (Canberra, 1974), vol. 11, p. 363.
135. Cunningham, *Two Years*, p.31.
136. Dawson, *Present State of Australia*, p.62.
137. Troy, thesis, p.201.
138. Dawson, *Present State of Australia*, p.299.
139. Troy, thesis, p.128.

8.
H.B. Higgins: 'One of those wild and irreconcilable Irishmen'[1]

JOHN RICKARD

When Higgins was a child his family lived for a time at Killarney, in a house with a large garret, to which, as he recalled in old age, "we noisy boys were consigned on wet days, to play handball with our father or to amuse ourselves. Being so remote from the street level it was called 'Australia'".[2] The Higgins family knew little of Australia then. Botany Bay was the only place in Australia they had heard of, and was associated with the transportation of convicts. It would seem that the garret was called "Australia," not only because of its distance from the centre of the house, but also because it was a suitable place to which "noisy boys," like convicts, could be consigned, so that life down below could proceed unhindered. Yet the garret called "Australia' suggests the subtle means by which the idea of emigration could enter a people's consciousness: as if in the house of Ireland there was always a notional garret, to which the difficult or surplus could be despatched. Yet from the children's perspective to climb those rickety stairs was to escape into their own world. Remote and rudimentary as it may have been, the garret in the roof also offered the best prospect.

But first a word about Higgins's career. Arriving in Australia in 1870, aged eighteen, he went on to a career in law and politics which culminated in twenty-three years on the bench of the High Court, and fourteen years as president of the Commonwealth Arbitration Court. A recent publica-

tion—one of the many stimulated by the Bicentenary—
nominated Higgins as one of the fifty men and women who
had done most to shape Australian society. The title of this
somewhat dubious enterprise (to which I contributed) was
The Greats[3]—a title which, it could be said, grates too. There
were many criticisms which could have been made of the
selection (only three of the fifty were women), but of the
Irish-Australians in the book, which include bushranger Ned
Kelly and painter Sidney Nolan (both, in a sense, dependent
on each other), Higgins's place might be considered fairly
secure. Indeed the recent polemics of the New Right in
Australia have, in a back-handed fashion, confirmed his
importance, for the New Right has fixed on Higgins as the
historical villain responsible for many of Australia's current
economic woes. They have even named their society, said to
be a think-tank, after an obscure Tasmanian newspaper editor
who was unsuccessfully prosecuted for a contempt of court in
respect of Higgins. This H.R. Nicholls[4] is held up as a hero for
having assailed the arbitration system which Higgins did so
much to create. The New Right has thus identified industrial
arbitration, and the social justice ideology which underpins
it, as a crucial element in Australian society, though one, of
course, which they seek to abolish.

Higgins was one of a small band of middle-class radicals
who, in the period 1890–1914, did much to provide the inspiration for a Lib-Lab programme of social reform. This programme has been characterised as "le socialisme sans doctrines,"[5]
but it had more ideological coherence than this soubriquet
suggests. It was a programme which sought to ameliorate the
tensions of class warfare and in doing so had little compunc-
tion in mobilising the State to this end. Thus Higgins
visualised himself, as president of the Arbitration Court, as
representing the public interest, but not so much with a view
to disciplining labour, as to giving it the "fair and reasonable"
wages and conditions which the free market could not guarantee. In the period before the Great War, Higgin's Court became
a kind of minor international show-piece, an integral part of
"the social laboratory of the world," as Australasia was dubbed.

When he died in 1929, after almost sixty years in his adopted country, he was hailed as a great Australian. Yet his will, to the surprise and dismay of many, was dominated by a £20,000 bequest to the Royal Irish Academy for the study of Irish language and literature, buttressed by a £4,000 legacy to the Royal Dublin Society, to provide scholarships or prizes for young art students. In 1975, when I visited the Academy, this was still its largest bequest.

Higgins's Irish background was an unusual one, and helped to give his later "Irishness" in the colonial setting a distinctive character. He could claim, looking back, that the Higgins clan had once been Catholics, but that towards the end of the eighteenth century a son married a Huguenot, and that this section of the family defected to the Church of Ireland. Higgins's grandfather, James Higgins, had hoped that his son, John, would enter the Church of Ireland, but instead he felt the call of Wesleyanism and displeased James by becoming a preacher. In 1848, at the height of the Famine, John Higgins married Anne Bournes, their first son James arriving in 1849; Henry Bournes Higgins, the second son, was born in 1851 at Newtownards, County Down. Six other children followed.

In my biography of Higgins I have attempted to sketch in the psychological dynamics of the family, particularly the dichotomy between the two eldest brothers, James, the incorrigible n'er-do-well charmer, and Henry, the dutiful and "delicate" favourite of his parents. It was a tightly-knit family, characterised by strong emotional relationships. But in the context of this article it is more appropriate to focus on the social atmosphere of the Higginses' world. The Wesleyan community was a small one—at its height in 1844 there was a recorded membership of 44,000—and circuits were large. Every three years the minister and his family moved on. Hence although the Higgins family mixed with the dispersed Wesleyan communities—shopkeepers, a few farmers, soldiers in garrison—they put down few roots. The family world was an enclosed one, in which the mother, Anne, was particularly important, given John's frequent absences ministering to the circuit. This Wesleyan world was symbolised by the small, austere chapel and the minister's house often adjoining it. Although "chapel" might still be ten o'clock on Sundays, to allow members to go to "church" at twelve, there was little dialogue between the Wesleyans and the Church of Ireland. When the Higgins boys were sent to school they went, as ministers' sons, to the Wesleyan Connexional School in Dublin.

The result was that Higgins grew up in a world very much segregated from the social reality of Catholic Ireland. The fact that he was "delicate" and afflicted with a paralysing stammer heightened his dependence on family and immediate surroundings, and tended to give to the outside world the allure of the unattainable. At the same time, he had little sense of identity with the Anglo-Irish ascendancy of the Church of Ireland: this was a world which the Higgins family would tend to characterise as stiff, formal and unfeeling (the world John Higgins had rebelled against). There was also a marked economic gap between the comfortable circumstances of the Anglo-Irish gentry and the cheerful frugality and shabby genteel values which the Higginses embraced. Similarly Higgins had little reason to feel any affinity with the Protestantism of Ulster. Newry was the only circuit in the North where John Higgins ministered, and it had for his son few of the pleasant memories associated with Killarney, Clonmel and Fermoy. And when Higgins briefly worked as a youth in Belfast he disliked the place; at the warehouse where he was employed he found the life of his fellow workers characterised by a joyless dissipation. In a broad sense, then, while Protestant Ireland formed Higgin's cultural context—and was, in terms of contacts and relationships, to remain important for him in Australia—it was an Ireland to which he felt no particular loyalty, in the political sense.

His Wesleyanism thus gave Higgins an unusual perspective on Irish life, distanced from Catholic Ireland, but also, in some measure, alienated from Protestant Ireland. In later years Higgins shed his Wesleyanism. (Indeed, most of his brothers and sisters, if they remained religiously inclined, tended to shift to other denominations—one was a devout Baptist, another a Quaker, a third a Christian Scientist.) Although he retained an affection for the simplicity and joyfulness of his father's religion, Higgins's familiarity with, yet at the same time sense of separation from, the Protestant mainstream, afforded him the opportunity to reject its values in later life. Catholic Ireland remained an enigma, possessed of a mystery and even enchantment which were enhanced by distance. So, in remote Victoria, he gradually set about coming to terms with the unknown Ireland.

From Higgins's birth in 1851, the idea of emigration was in a sense always there, even if John Higgins had given it scant consideration for his own family. John had a brother, Charley, who seems to have been a bit of a problem, and father James several times considered emigration to be the solution. "There are a great many young persons going to New South Wales to earn their bread," he writes to John in 1854, "and I am thinking of making up what would bring [Charley] there and provide for himself." Some years later Charley was in fact packed off to the United States. Also in 1854 a relative writes to John from Cardiff where, he says, "The people are very cold and distant." "Poor old Ireland, people complain of you, but such folk should come to Cardiff and never fear they'd be cured."[6]

Higgins recalled the scenes at the Killarney railway station, when young men and women were leaving, bound for the steamer for America at Cork—"old fathers realizing that they now saw Pat or Biddy for the last time, and raising a loud cry as the engine steamed out." "It was the time of the great emigration," Higgins observed, "that drew the life-blood out of Ireland. The cries were as clear, rising and falling, as the cries of 'keening' women who followed funerals."[7]

The first serious indication of the Higgins family considering emigration for themselves occurs in 1865 and focuses on Henry himself. Aged fourteen, he had been sent home from school suffering from inflammation of the lungs. Others in the family suffered from ill-health—younger brother Samuel, in particular, was plagued with bronchitis—but at this stage the condition of "delicate" Henry was of principal concern. According to Higgins's later recollection the doctor who treated him in 1865 recommended a warmer, drier climate, and the opportunity arose of his coming out to Australia in the care of a Methodist minister who was returning there. For some reason this project, seriously countenanced at first, was dropped: probably Anne would have been reluctant to part with the fourteen-year-old son to whom she was particularly attached. The ship on which the minister sailed was lost. It was by implication in Higgins's account, another instance of Providence watching over him.[8]

The next year, however, saw the actual emigration of eldest son, James, though for different reasons. James, like his Uncle Charley, was deemed a problem. Great had been the family shame when, after a record of troublesomeness at the Wesleyan Connexional School, he was virtually expelled. A place was found for him as a junior clerk in a timberyard at Newry, but it was for a pittance and the manager victimised him. Thus when he met a Mr Randolph MacCormack, a Methodist merchant from New York—presumably through chapel—and the merchant, taking a liking to him, advised him to try his luck in America, James, aged seventeen, was receptive to the idea. His parents quickly approved the scheme: MacCormack was a useful connexion, his Methodism something of a guarantee. Clearly they thought emigration, and the responsibility attaching to it, would be good for James; but it also seems that they were now considering the possible emigration of the entire family, for whom James might serve as the advance guard.

In October 1866 John accompanied James to Londonderry to see him off on the steamer to New York. James wrote home, full of resolve:

> My own darling Mother . . . I want to let you know that I am
> not going to fret at all, and I hope you will not either. I am
> assured that it is all for the best my going, and I hope very
> shortly to be able to send you good news about my situation
> in N.Y. I am determined to do everything right, and never
> for an instant to forget that I have the happiness of all I love

in my hands. You need not fear about me at all, for I intend to abide by the good advice I have received from you all my life.'

James was enthralled and exhilarated by the excitement and glamour of New York, which he attempted to convey to the family in his eager letters. Indeed, James's depiction of New York, from the knowing pertness of its children to the affluent comfort of its Methodist churches (not chapels), from the perspective of a wide-eyed Irish youth of sheltered upbringing, is a story in itself. However, James discouraged the idea of the family following him to the United States, pointing to the severity of the climate. South Africa, as well as Australia, was now considered.

All such plans were suddenly halted by the news of a collapse in James's health. The symptoms, first of all colds, neuralgia, and then a cough and loss of weight, were all too familiar. A doctor tactfully advised that a trip to the Old Country would do him the world of good. James returned, in consumption, rejected, as it were, by the New World. In one sense James's decline confirmed the Higgins family's resolve to emigrate, though America, of course, was now eliminated as a possibility; but in the short-term it meant the postponement of any such step while James was cared for. He took two years to die, two years during which a strategy for the migration of the entire family evolved.

When, in June 1869, James finally died, the strategy was quickly implemented. Australia, first considered for Henry four years earlier, was now the choice; a Dublin physician recommended Victoria for its climate. Anne financed the family's emigration, persuading an uncle to buy out her share of a charge which her father had given her over the Bournes family property. There seemed, after all the delays, a new urgency, so much so that it was resolved that Anne should sail for Australia with most of the family, leaving her husband to complete the current year on the Wexford circuit, whereupon he, with one remaining son, would followed them. So, in two contingents, the Higgins family arrived in Australia in 1870. The grim irony was that the trip itself dealt a further blow to the family, with the death at sea from diphtheria of the youngest child, Charley. So, nursing the twin tragedies of James, the eldest, and Charley the youngest, the Higginses began their new life in Australia. These tragedies made it all the more necessary that they should succeed in their endeavour.

It can be seen that emigration was always present as an option in the wider family circle—for one member if not for another—and that it was intermittently a matter for discussion. But it was the health factor which ultimately decided John and Anne to settle on distant Victoria. Fittingly, the climate was one of the first things Henry reported on to his father, still in Ireland. "The climate even exceeds our expectations," he assured him, adding that it would make a new man of him.[10]

Migration served neatly to divide Higgins's childhood years in Ireland from his adult life in Australia. From the day he entered Melbourne University (and a university education would have been impossible for him in Ireland), and thus embarked on his professional (and political) career, Higgins very deliberately set about integrating himself into colonial life. Yet it is remarkable how important the Irish, and more particularly, Anglo-Irish connexions, were to be for him. When the family arrived in February 1870 their first port of call was Wesley Church; then Wesley College, the latter having an Irish president, James Swanton Waugh, and an Irish headmaster, Corrigan. Through this help the Higginses found their first home, in a street not far from Wesley College. At Melbourne University there were two teachers, W.E. Hearn and C.H. Pearson, who were to influence Higgins, and Hearn was Irish. Hearn, son of a Church of Ireland clergyman, and educated at Trinity College, taught, at different times, history, literature, political economy, logic and classics. Hearn's great influence was to open Higgins's mind to religious doubt, and thus help to launch a process which was to see him abandon the warm but suffocating embrace of the family's Wesleyanism. This was hardly Hearn's intention— he himself remained a practising Anglican—but Hearn's lectures on the origins of religion (which contributed to his

book *The Aryan Household*)[11] raised questions which Higgins
had not considered before and gave him the intellectual
equipment to view religion from a sociological perspective.

Moreover in his legal and later political career Higgins
sought inspiration in colonial Victoria's most eminent states-
man and jurist, George Higinbotham, son of a Dublin
merchant, who had migrated to Victoria in 1854. Although
not widely known to contemporary Australians, Higinbotham
was a commanding intellectual presence in Victoria in the
second half of the nineteenth century, a figure who came to
symbolise, for younger men of the generation of Higgins,
Isaacs and Deakin, all that was bravest and best in colonial
liberalism. He was particularly identified with the struggle to
assert the colony's right to manage its own affairs, un-
trammelled by the interference of the Colonial Office.
Higinbotham was something of a hero to Higgins, and when
Higgins was called to the bar, his mother gained an
introduction to the great man, who consented to provide the
certificate of fitness which the nomination for the bar
required. Higinbotham did not take such a responsibility
lightly and questioned the aspiring young barrister closely.
Higgins's later account of this episode, written at a time
when he was acclaimed as Higinbotham's successor, gives it
the flavour of a ceremonial laying on of hands. In 1927,
when he attended the unveiling of a portrait of Higinbotham
at the Melbourne Trades Hall Council, Higgins was cheered
to the echo. There were, moreover, similarities in style
between the two. Gwynneth Dow describes Higinbotham as
"passionately religious and democratic," though his religious
outlook was unconventional and often anti-clerical. If
Higgins was more of an agnostic, he shared the concern for
things of the spirit; though his anti-clericalism was tempered
by the more particular social and political relationship he
developed with the Irish Catholic community. But Dow's
observation of Higinbotham that "his lack of snobbery . . .
mixed strangely with his courtly and elegant manners"[12] rings
almost exactly true of Higgins, and clearly could be seen as
reflecting their shared Irishness. Both Higinbotham and

Higgins would appear to have refused knighthoods. Higginbotham saw a knighthood as "a base contemptible distinction" that merely gave a man "a handle to his name." Higgins echoed the sentiment in describing titles as "devices for creating distinctions in name where there is no distinction in fact."[13]

Irishmen also figured prominently in Higgins's network of friends and colleagues. Perhaps his closest crony was John Henry MacFarland, born at Omagh, Tyrone in 1851 (the same year as Higgins) and educated at the Royal Academical Institution, Queen's University and Cambridge. He came to Australia to become master of Ormond College at Melbourne University. Both MacFarland and Higgins were on the university council for many years, MacFarland eventually becoming chancellor. MacFarland would have been unlikely to have shared some of Higgins's political views, such as support of Home Rule and opposition to the Boer War, yet there remained a very strong sense of a fellow feeling between the two. Higgins also retained relationships of particular respect with two politicians of Irish background, to whom he was usually opposed. Thus the conservative Sir William Irvine, born at Newry in 1858 (and Newry had figured in Higgins's youth) and a graduate of Trinity College Dublin, who, in implementing a policy of economy and retrenchment in 1902–4 in Victoria, gained the nickname "The Iceberg," remained a personal friend. (Irvine was later given an honorary doctorate by Trinity College Dublin; Higgins, of course, had never had the opportunity of going to Trinity in the first place.) Likewise, Higgins was on close terms with the New South Wales free-trader, Sir William McMillan. Apart from their Irishness they had something further in common—both were the sons of Wesleyan ministers.

The irony, perhaps, is that although from the days of the Redmonds' tour of 1883, Higgins was so identified with the cause of Home Rule in Australia, and although he mixed widely in the Irish community, often being called upon to attend St Patrick's Day functions and the like, he had few *personal* friends who were Catholics. The one obvious exception was Frank Gavan Duffy, son of Charles, who co-authored a legal textbook with Higgins, and who later sat with him on the High Court bench. But the Gavan Duffys were hardly a typical colonial Catholic family, insofar as they succeeded in integrating into Anglo-Protestant Melbourne society: they were the sort of Catholics whose religion could be accepted as an anomaly, the exception that proved the rule.

Higgins's dependence on this Irish—and more particularly Anglo-Irish—network is all the more interesting given the extent to which he adopted Australia. Quite apart from the contribution of his public career in law and politics to the making of the Australian nation (he has also a "father of federation," a member of the first federal parliament, and attorney-general in the short-lived first federal labour government of 1904), Higgins was also committed to Australia in a cultural sense, taking an interest, not only in education, but in the development of Australian literature, instigating one of the first moves towards providing a subsidy for the arts through the creation of the Commonwealth Literary Fund. His niece, Nettie Palmer, was a poet and critic, and married to the novelist Vance Palmer, who together became a focus for literary life in Melbourne. Higgins approved of and helped their work, and kept in touch with what was happening.

Yet in his later years the preoccupation with Ireland seemed to increase, not decline: I called the last chapter in my book "Irishman," because there was an important sense in which the last decade of his life raised questions about his Irishness. There was one special reason for this spiritual return to Ireland. Henry and his wife, Mary Alice, had had only one son, Mervyn, who, having dutifully enlisted in 1914, and having survived Gallipoli, was killed in Egypt in 1916. This was an immensely traumatic event, and for Higgins seemed to sever him from the Australian future. No matter how much interest he took in younger members of the wider Higgins family, particularly Nettie and her brother Esmonde, they could not replace his one and only son.

It seemed, too, that Ireland's crisis during the War synchronised with his own. The death of Mervyn encouraged a search for his own identity in the past, and in this he could draw sustenance from Ireland's parallel search for identity. In 1920, when A.E. Zimmern, professor at Aberystwyth, mentioned that he was studying Welsh, Higgins replied: "I should prefer to study Irish, if I had the time—not because I am an Irishman, but in Erse there is a buried literature of a most suggestive character."[14] It was in 1927 that he approached A.E. (George) Russell, whom he had met when he had made enquiries about the bequest to the Royal Dublin Society. Higgins wrote:

> My only child was killed in the Great War: and I intended to devote some £20,000 to the founding of a chair for Celtic literature in our Melbourne University. . . . I am not a Celtic scholar; but such glimpses as I have had into Celtic literature convince me that it has some unique value—spiritual value. I doubt, however, whether such a chair in Melbourne would be a success: who would be students, and for what purpose?[15]

Thus Higgins clearly relates the death of his son to the search for "spiritual value" in Ireland's Celtic past, and goes on to seek A.E.'s help in finding an appropriate home for the proposed bequest, which was to be the Royal Irish Academy.

In politics Higgins, who had moved the parliamentary resolution in 1905 for an Address to the King in favour of Home Rule, was naturally sympathetic to the old Irish nationalists. Nevertheless, he saw the dangers of the nationalists losing touch with the new republican forces. He blames the rise of Sinn Féin on British vacillation and weakness; the government's betrayal of the Irish people had tempted them to embrace the idea of an independent republic. But he pressed John Dillon not to close the door on Sinn Fein, and in 1919 urged him not to treat as enemies those who were likely to become friends. At home he did not find Mannix congenial, but was never to declare him beyond the pale. "I do not understand Dr Mannix," he told Dillon in 1922, "but he is able and plucky even if unwise."[16] Higgins wanted to see Ireland reconciled to itself, and to the Empire, but his Irishness did not hinge on such a solution.

But to what extent was Higgins perceived as being Irish? In 1900, T.W. Gregory, newly arrived in Melbourne to take

up a chair of geography, mentioned that he had been invited
to lunch with Higgins, and was warned that Higgins was
"one of those wild and irreconcilable Irishmen who are
always 'agin' the Government'."[17] This was the time of
Higgins's dual opposition to the Boer War and the proposed
Australian Constitution. While Higgins was stubborn enough
to be characterised as "irreconcilable"—it was said that he
"gloried in being in a minority of one"[18]—there was certainly
nothing "wild" about him. He distrusted emotion (an attitude
which was an inheritance of his stammer) and saw himself as
being guided by the light of pure reason. Those who knew
him well would more likely have seen his Irishness as residing
in his elaborate courtesy, his love of civilised discussion and
argument, and his humour. Higgins's young friend and admirer,
G.V. Portus, said of him:

> First let it be said that he was an Irishman through and
> through—with an Irishman's grace of hospitality, an Irish-
> man's twinkle of fun in his eyes, an irishman's passionate
> attachment to his country, and let it be added, with an
> Irishman's obstinacy in sticking to his own point of view.[19]

I am myself suspicious of generalisations about national
character, but there was certainly an Irish cultural milieu and
style to which Higgins related. He himself remarked on the
virtues of the Irish who had escaped "the harshness and
selfishness of the commercial age." He told his Australian-
born nephew, Esmonde, who was about to visit Ireland, that
the Irish "are more sympathetic, have more delicacy of
insight than English people. Your grandfather used to say
that he had never met people with such innate courtesy as
the Connaught people."[20] He made those observations in
1919: there was surely something Irish in remarking on such
qualities as "delicacy of insight" and "innate courtesy" at a
time when Ireland was sinking into chaos.

It is worth noting that at the time when Higgins was
making his will, and arranging the bequests to the Royal Irish
Academy and Royal Dublin Society, he was also, at his niece
Nettie's suggestion, writing a personal memoir.[21] Also at this
time he wrote to George Bernard Shaw, apparently enquiring

(the letter does not survive) whether Shaw had named the hero of *Pygmalion* after him. Shaw denied the connexion, but mischievously added: "There was a boy who came and went in my time whose name might have been Higgins, though I am not quite sure of it. But he was weakminded, or rather infantile. . . . He stayed only a very short time, and should never have been sent there. A most goodnatured creature, who may have turned out well after all. Your dates exclude the possibility of identifying you with him." Higgins had certainly "turned out well": it was only Higgins's "dates" which prevented the identification!

His childhood, characterised by his "delicacy" and the protection it required, and by the destructive relationship with his elder brother which in part stemmed from this condition, had raised a number of psychological problems, with which Higgins sought to come to terms. The enigma of Ireland was bound up with the enigma of his childhood. The very oddness of his Wesleyan Irish (but non-Ulster) background seemed to make his Irishness problematical. There is a sense in which one can see Higgins, in the course of his life, but particularly at the end of it, seeking to prove beyond doubt his Irishness. He had, in the course of his sixty years in Australia, become an Australian. Yet simultaneously—and through his Australian experience so to speak—he had been defining his relationship with Ireland, and, as a result, his Irish identity. Both Ireland and Australia can rightly claim Higgins as their son.

References

1. Most of the material in this paper is drawn from my biography, H.B. *Higgins: The Rebel as Judge* (Sydney, 1984). Appropriate page references are given in the notes below. The Higgins papers, which include a large Irish family correspondence, are in the National Library of Australia, Canberra.

2. "Memoir," Higgins Papers.

3. Leonie Kramer, Russel Ward et al. (eds.), *The Greats: The 50 Men and Women who Most Helped to Shape Modern Australia* (Sydney, 1986).

4. Nicholls did, however, earn a brief entry in the *Australian Dictionary of Biography*, vol. 5, p. 334.

5. Albert Métin, *Le Socialisme sans Doctrines* (Paris, 1901); there is an English translation by Russel Ward, *Socialism Without Doctrine* (Sydney, 1977).

6. James to John Higgins, 20 June 1854, 2/1084; "Robert" in Cardiff to John Higgins, 12 October 1854, 2/1118, Higgins Papers.

7. "Memoir," Higgins Papers.

8. The minister, Daniel Draper, is to be found in the *Australian Dictionary of Biography*, vol. 1, p. 321.

9. John Rickard, "'Poor James': An Incident in Irish/Australian History," *Victorian Historical Journal*, vol. 49, no. 4 (Nov. 1978), pp. 221–2.

10. H.B. *Higgins*, p. 42.

11. W.E. Hearn, *The Aryan Household, its Structure and its Development* (London, 1878).

12. *Australian Dictionary of Biography*, vol. 4, pp. 392, 395.

13. H.B. Higgins, p. 306.

14. ibid., pp. 301–2.

15. ibid., p. 300.

16. ibid., p. 294.

17. ibid., pp. 120–1.

18. ibid., p. 115.

19. ibid., p. 302.

20. ibid., p. 294.

21. ibid., p. 305.

9.

Mannix, de Valera and Irish nationalism

DERMOT KEOGH

Dr Daniel Mannix was in his last days as President of Maynooth when he wrote to Eamon de Valera on 2 October 1912 telling him that he had been given a part-time and temporary appointment as lecturer in mathematics and mathematical physics in the college.[1] Four days later, he was ordained titular Bishop of Pharsalus and Coadjutor Archbishop of Melbourne. For two men who were to become very close friends in later life, they shared very little in common at that stage in their respective careers.

Mannix was an academic with an established reputation in the environs of Maynooth. He was President of the National Seminary and a leading figure in Catholic life in Ireland. His major commitment was to the effective running of a college for the training of priests. In contrast, de Valera was a young academic, who failed to win a professorship at University College Cork in 1913. However, by that time he had already begun to neglect his academic career and concentrate his energies on politics. He was very active in cultural nationalist circles, and held advanced nationalist views which orientated him towards the separatist movement.

However, one of the things that both men had in common was that they had gone to school to the Christian Brothers in Charleville (Rath Luirc). They had not however been contemporaries. Mannix was born in 1864 and de Valera in 1882. At sixteen, de Valera won a scholarship to Blackrock College in Dublin which was run by the Holy Ghost fathers. He was only eight years old in 1890 when Mannix was ordained in Maynooth after a successful academic career as a student. The future Archbishop of Melbourne spent all his priestly life in the college on the teaching staff—and as President from 1903—until his departure for Australia in 1913.

But despite the common experience of education by the Christian Brothers in Charleville, there was much more than a generation gap separating both men in 1912. Mannix, who was to become as advanced a nationalist thinker as de Valera, had, as President of Maynooth, welcomed King George and Queen Mary to the college on 9 July 1911. The doorway was "appropriately decorated," according to the editor of the *Irish Catholic Directory*, for the occasion.[2] The Royal Standard, the Union Jack, the Irish flag with harp and shamrock and Papal colours decorated the doorway. "We join with all your faithful subjects," Mannix said in welcome, "in wishing your Majesties a long, happy, and a prosperous reign." These were not the words of a progressive nationalist. Yet less than eight years later the new Archbishop of Melbourne had become a spokesman for the cause of Sinn Féin and Irish separatism. His conversion to the cause of radical nationalism was all the more surprising to those familiar with the details of the Michael O'Hickey case, which resulted in the latter being dismissed from his professorship of Irish in 1909.[3] The robustness of the dispute is captured in an archival fragment in which Mannix accused O'Hickey of giving "the worst possible example to the students whom he was bound to train in obedience and respect for authority." The President summarised some of the accusations coming from the O'Hickey camp as follows:

West Britons who were in league with the British Government to destroy the Irish language; who had no concern for the faithful Irish speakers; for the administration of the sacraments; who pretended to support the Irish language but in reality through dispensation and other (ways) reduced it to worse level than it held in Trinity College.[4]

Mannix retaliated by taking the most severe action against the priests who had sided with O'Hickey, doing higher

studies under Professor Walter MacDonald in Dunboyne
House. They were ordered—and there were five Kerry priests
among the group—not to return to their studies in the new
academic year.[5] With the background of the O'Hickey case in
mind—a case that was not judged finally in Rome until April
1916—it may have been very difficult for many of Mannix's
peers at Maynooth either to comprehend or to accept his
conversion to radical nationalism. However, it is a little
unfair to juxtapose Mannix "the royalist" of 1911 with Mannix
"the rebel" of 1921. At the time of the second royal visit to
Maynooth, Mannix was President of the college. There is no
evidence that any of the Irish Catholic Bishops, including
William Walsh of Dublin, suffered any discomfort about
receiving the royal couple at the college. Indeed, Mannix's
political apotheosis may well have had much in common
with many other members of the Irish hierarchy. He was not
only the member of the hierarchy to shift political ground
between 1911 and 1921 on the "Irish question." It is, therefore, much more advisable to view the O'Hickey episode as a
major set-back to Mannix's career as President of Maynooth
than as an ideological clash between two men who shared
rival national outlooks. Although there is not the space to
elaborate on the matter here, it is probable that the turmoil
in Maynooth provoked by the President's austere managerial
style—particularly but not exclusively related to the O'Hickey
case—was a factor in the decision to terminate his presidency
and have him serve "on the missions."

After spending all his priestly time in Maynooth (1890–
1913), Mannix suddenly found himself at the age of fifty-
nine in a pastoral role in a foreign country. He was running
an archdiocese where many of the laity were Irish Catholic
emigrants and these were a religious minority in Victoria.
Mannix was only one of a number of very well-known Irishmen who had been given positions on the bench of Australian
bishops. Archbishops Michael Kelly of Sydney, James Duhig
of Brisbane and Patrick Clune of Perth were most prominent.
However, all three differed in political style from the more
confrontational Mannix.[6]

Perhaps it was the manner of his departure from Ireland, but Mannix does not appear to have kept up consistent contact with many of his fellow bishops at home. His Australian episcopal colleagues very often found him too much of an individual and somewhat trying.[6] This was particularly so on the "Irish question."[7] As President of Maynooth, Mannix had not had to take up a public position on the broader national question. In Australia, particularly in the wake of the 1916 Rising, Mannix expressed strong views. He is quoted by his biographer, Niall Brennan, as saying at the time that the events of Easter Week were:

> the natural regrettable sequence of events against the campaign of armed resistance which the Carsonites had been allowed to preach and get away with during the past few years. I am quite clear in my mind that the British Government, by its failure to deal with the treason of the Carsonites, by its shifty policy in regard to Home Rule, had unwittingly led up to the result that all must deplore.[8]

It is interesting that Mannix "deplored"—or so it would appear—the events of Easter Week and its aftermath. However, according to Patrick O'Farrell, "by 1921 Mannix's Irish republicanism was so far to the radical left of Irish Australian attitudes as to amount to an embarrassing abberation."[9] The outlook and attitudes of many Irish bishops in Australia was far from static, particularly during the years were 1919–1921. For example, James Duhig said on 28 June 1919:

> For centuries the laws of Ireland have been made in the parliament of another country, and the race has been governed not according to its own ideas but according to those laws. Hence arises the discontent and unrest of which we hear so much; hence today in Ireland you have an army of occupation and an armed peace.[10]

Mannix could have not been disappointed with such sentiments. There is little doubt that, from 1919 until the signing of the Truce in 1921, many Irish and Irish-Australian bishops were outraged by what was happening in Ireland and tended, as the violence escalated, to blame the British government more than the nationalists for the deterioration of the political situation. However, Mannix said in public what many bishops, out of prudence, were only prepared to say in private. He took sides while many bishops chose to use their good offices to mediate between the two warring factions. For example, Mannix was centre-stage during the Irish Race convention, held in Melbourne in November 1919, which adopted a resolution supporting "the right of the people to choose their own form of Government, and to govern their country without interference from any other nation."[11] He could not have hoped to bring many of his archiepiscopal colleagues along with him on that motion. Sensitive to their pastoral duties in Australia, the other bishops exhibited Christian concern for what was happening in Ireland. Mannix, on the other hand, supported a political programme.

1920 was a year designated for *ad limina* visits to the Vatican for the Australian hierarchy. This occurred every five years or so and many bishops who were Irish usually took the opportunity to combine the visit to see the Pope with a holiday at home. Mannix had not seen his mother since 1913 and he planned to visit Ireland on his way to Rome. Travelling via the United States, Mannix launched on a lecture tour organised by Dáil Eireann supporters. De Valera was among those Sinn Féin "envoys" in America at the time and both men met in St Columban's Missionary College, Omaha.[12] De Valera was no longer a young mathematician looking for a part-time job in Maynooth. He was the elected President of Dail Eireann and one of the best known Irish nationalist leaders abroad. The ideological gap, evident between the two men in 1912, had narrowed radically by 1920. Mannix had given a series of fiery speeches that had worried the British embassy in Washington. The Foreign Office were quite worried by the prospect of a "revolutionary" archbishop setting foot in Ireland at a time when the military fortunes of the British were somewhat strained. In the United States, Mannix had come into contact with many radical nationalists—lay and clerical—and his rhetoric had become quite extreme. The circumstances of the British refusal of permission for him to land at Cobh are very well known. However, that decision may have had greater political implications than if he had been allowed to travel home to see his mother.[13] From August 1920, Mannix was resident in London where he was a relatively free agent. He moved in Sinn Féin circles and was in a position to react publicly to the deteriorating events in Ireland. The 74-day hunger strike of Terence MacSwiney, who died on 24 October, was an event of international interest and Mannix provided support for a theology which defended the action. He visited MacSwiney three times. When the body was taken to Southwark cathedral, Mannix was among the prelates who received it.[14]

But if Mannix was unable to get back to Ireland for a visit in 1920, many of his Irish-Australian episcopal colleagues were in a position to do so. The conditions in the country and the draconian policies of the British government made many of the visiting bishops highly critical of what they saw. Irish bishops had undergone a similar process of radicalisation. Pope Benedict XV and the Secretary of State, Pietro Gasparri, were left in little doubt about the inadequacies of British policies in Ireland by the time most of the Irish-Australian bishops had been received in private audiences. Archbishop Patrick Clune of Perth is perhaps one of the best examples of my thesis. He went to Rome in February 1921 after he had been frustrated by the British in his efforts to bring about peace in Ireland. He was outraged at the actions of sections of the British forces in Ireland. Neither was he particularly impressed by Lloyd George's level of enthusiasm for peace. Clune blamed the British for the failure of his peace efforts.[15] The archbishop was not a political prelate, but his feelings on Irish nationalism had been strengthened by what he had witnessed in Ireland. As a former army chaplain in the First World War, the archbishop had been appalled by the lack of discipline among the British forces. He went to Rome via Paris where he dined with Séan T. O'Kelly, the republican envoy in the French capital. Clune had not, however, been converted to republicanism. O'Kelly was very much alive to the archbishop's moderate political views. But Clune—whose nephew had been shot in suspicious circumstances by the British—felt constrained to warn the Pope—from what he was able to witness in Ireland—not to be too swift to judge Sinn Féin and condemn Irish nationalism. According to his interpreter, Patrick Murray, the Superior General of the Redemptorists, the archbishop:

> told the Holy Father amongst other things that such a pronouncement would be a disaster for the church, not only in Ireland but in every country where there were descendants of the Irish race.

According to Murray, Clune's reasons seemed to make a great impression on His Holiness because he asked the archbishop

> to speak also to a certain Cardinal who, I presume, had the question in hand. I did not accompany him to this Cardinal. but he told me afterwards that the Cardinal in question after interview told him he saw the whole question of Ireland in a new light.[16]

Clune was not alone in his protest. The Irish hierarchy had written officially to the Vatican on the same subject. But what distinguished Clune and other members of the Australian and Irish hierarchies from Mannix was that they went much further in private than they were prepared to go in public. The Irish hierarchy tried to maintain a moral balance, condemning both Crown and nationalist violence. At the same time, in private correspondence, Irish bishops showed that they were very sympathetic to the objectives of moderate Irish nationalism. Mannix tended to allow himself to be swept along on a wave of emotion. That was very much the case when he followed Clune to Rome in 1921.

Mannix arrived in Rome on his *ad limina* visit in April 1921 where he was received at the railway station, according to a contemporary account, by "practically every Irishman in Rome as a mark of recognition of his services and sacrifices."[17] The archbishop stayed at the Irish College where, as a mark of the high esteem in which he was held, a reception and concert were held on Easter Sunday.[18] The room was "suitably decorated for the occasion"—according to another contemporary account—"the Irish national colours (tricolour) being prominently displayed." On the entrance of the archbishop, the assembly rose and enthusiastically joined in the singing of a number of musical items—including the "Soldiers' Song" in Irish. Dr Eric Fair DD, of Tuam, welcomed his grace in Irish in the name of the Gasra of the Fainne:

> Since that April day three hundred and thirteen years ago when the great Hugh O'Neill was welcomed like the prince that he was into this city, even though the hand of England lay heavily upon him, no more illustrious guest of Irish birth, and none to whom men of Irish birth and blood are glad to owe so deep a debt, has ever set foot on Roman soil.

Dr Fair also predicted that Mannix would be received with the same rapture:

> when the hour of trial is over and when our people will welcome you back to Erin and will strew the ground beneath your feet with the garments of their affection and will cry out to you in words once addressed to another great Crominal— (sic) Blessed is the womb that bore you and the breasts that nurtured your generous Irish heart.[19]

Decorated in the Sinn Féin colours, Mannix replied— according to a contemporary source—that although he was far from his country and further still from his country of adoption, never had he felt more at home than in the Irish College that evening. He had travelled round the world and met Irishmen in all parts. He could say that Ireland was indomitable and could not be extinguished. Ireland would live when other countries were remembered only in history. He had been branded as a disturber of the peace—as a stormy petrel—that he wished to level England to the dust. He never had such an ambition (laughter). He bore no ill to the British Empire, or to any Englishmen as such. He only wanted them to do justice to the land of his birth. He had been charged with saying hard things against the British Empire. He had said the hardest things but never as bad as they deserved.

According to the same source Mannix said that while he loved the land of his birth he had also learned to love the land of his adoption; and because he had put Ireland and

Australia before every other country he had been hounded by certain sections in Australia and was forbidden to set foot in Irish soil. He hoped to visit Ireland another day when the foot of the stranger should no longer be on the land and he might add that until that time he had no wish to visit Ireland, and if there were other domestic reasons which would draw him to Ireland he hoped they too would remain till he could go a free man into a free Ireland. But the end was coming, sooner or later, and there was only one end— that Ireland would achieve absolute and complete independence. Those who wanted to defame Ireland would have it believed that the British soldiers were up against a gang of murderers. There was no gang of murderers in Ireland but the gang sent over by the British government. Those in whose hands were the destinies of Ireland were not a gang of murderers. The British were not fighting a small gang of murderers but an infuriated and exasperated nation. All the people were in it—all worth counting, he said.

The contemporary account continues:

> While Mannix admitted that he could not speak from personal experience as he had not been to Ireland, he had met people from every part of the country and they testified that "if tomorrow Dáil Erin (sic) were to enter into any unworthy compromise with Mr Lloyd George and his government the men of Ireland would repudiate President de Valera and Dáil Erin (sic) and put other and better men in their places which was not likely (applause). If the men joined President de Valera in making an unworthy compromise the women of Ireland would repudiate the men (cheers) and if that were not enough—if the whole adult population from the Cardinal archbishop down to the Bishops, Priests and the men and women of Ireland were to hand in their guns, the boys and girls growing up in the schools would live to curse the fathers and mothers who made such an unworthy compromise and repudiate them to raise the flag and plant it where I hope it will never be supplanted.[20]

Mannix concluded his stirring address by

> praying that the ideals of President de Valera might be realised and that they might visit an Ireland both free and

prosperous and that Ireland might be one of the great if one of the small nations of the world.

Mannix was sure of that outcome because, echoing de Valera, he maintained that "God owes something to Ireland, to the Irish people if we might say so without irreverence and God is just and will some day stand by his own."[21]

Mannix was received in audience by Benedict XV on Easter Monday. Bonaventura Cerretti, who had been apostolic delegate in Australia, acted as his interpreter. The audience lasted for almost an hour and was, according to John Hagan, "of the most cordial nature," notwithstanding the fact that Mannix followed "his usual practice . . . and did not mince his words." According to Hagan, the Pope offered "to make diplomatic representations with a view to having the ban (on Mannix's travel to Ireland) removed." But Mannix demurred "on the ground that as he was not prepared to make a request of the kind himself he did not wish another to do it for him, nor would he accept it if granted in this way." Mannix was not anxious for a public protest by the Holy See on his behalf.

Mannix directed the majority of his remarks towards the "Irish situation," about which he was "most explicit." He spoke of the "propaganda of silence" which "aimed at suppressing the very mention of such things." He expressed his surprise that no official protest had come from the Vatican, "not even when attacks were made on Bishops, priests and nuns."

Mannix took full advantage of his position and the fact that his words were being helpfully translated by the friendly Cerretti:

> He pointed out that not only was there a general feeling of surprise that the common Father of Christendom who had words of sympathy for Belgium and Poland was silent with regard to worse things in Ireland, but there was also a widespread fear that the Vatican was allowing itself to be influenced by considerations of policy into an unfriendly attitude which might easily go so far as to issue in condemnations.

Mannix's ideas on Irish-Vatican relations appeared to coincide with those of de Valera and Hagan. The archbishop was expressing many of the fears which had been echoed in numerous letters from the pen of Hagan to prelates in Ireland and in the Irish diaspora.

Much to the satisfaction of Mannix, Benedict XV assured him that "there is not and has not been any idea of condemning the Sinn Féin movement." But that was not sufficient for Mannix who then laid stress on the fact that "even words of disapprobation for certain deeds connected with the policy of the movement would be interpreted by friend and foe as amounting to practically the same thing." The archbishop spoke frankly about the harm that would emerge from anything that could be open to such interpretation.

When the Pope turned to the alternatives for a settlement, he sought Mannix's opinion on the Dominion solution "which he understood had or would have the support of Lloyd George." Hagan noted:

> The Archbishop had no reason for forming any opinion as to what Lloyd George was inclined to do, but he had every reason to believe that even if that gentleman were ever so willing he could not bring the English people to accept that solution, which in their eyes would be just as bad as complete separation; while on the other hand the present temper of the Irish people, and the sacrifices they had already made, would render them slow to accept a settlement which when all was said and done left them at the mercy of England, just as in 1800.[22]

Benedict XV was—according to the memorandum—"clearly impressed by the Archbishop('s) statement regarding the fears of Vatican interference on the wrong side," and "asked if there was anything that could be done to eliminate such impressions." In reply, the archbishop suggested a contribution to the Irish White Cross, accompanied by a suitable letter. Benedict XV "eagerly grasped at" the suggestion and Mannix was instructed to see the Secretary of State the next day and arrange the publication. Mannix met Gasparri and the main outline of the letter was agreed upon after lengthy discussions. One of its chief features was to be "a hint as to the necessity of an independent and public enquiry into what has been happening in Ireland." Mannix was asked to submit a draft, which he did with the help of John Hagan and Peter Magennis. The draft was as strong as "could be hoped for" and it was delivered to the Secretary of State on 4 April. The same day the memorandum quoted above on the Mannix visit, prepared by Hagan, together with the draft letter were sent to the Coadjutor in Armagh, Patrick O'Donnell.[23]

It must be stressed that Hagan's memorandum is not an official account of the meetings between Mannix, the Pope and Gasparri. But in the absence of the availability of the official record, Hagan's version of events will have to suffice. But it was, however, a partisan account. Hagan concluded that Mannix's visit had "turned out to be a great personal and national triumph," which showed "the wisdom of uncompromising and plain language." The visit also demonstrated, from Hagan's point of view, "the desirability of frequent episcopal visits to this city by prelates who are prepared to speak out straight." Many years later, Mannix was to quip to an Irish bishop that the letter issued by the Pope on 27 April 1921 was the "only Papal encyclical I have ever written."[24]

It is doubtful, however, if Mannix could take all the credit for the publication of the Papal letter. It is much more likely that Mannix was one of the last on a line of Irish prelates who had impressed upon Benedict XV the need to make a statement about what was happening in Ireland. The Vatican may have wished to do so for a while but did not quite know what form the publication might take. Mannix provided the solution by suggesting a letter to the relief organisation, the Irish White Cross, with a suitable donation. The Vatican retained the central idea for the letter as discussed with Mannix. The Pope urged that the Irish question be referred to some body of men selected by the whole Irish Nation and when such a conference had published its findings, discussions could take place between both sides in a sincere spirit of peace and reconciliation.

How is it possible to evaluate the impact of this letter? It caused considerable irritation to the British government, and members of the Foreign Office pointed out in anger how the

Pope had been so even-handed in his description of the two sides—placing the British and Sinn Féin on an equal moral footing. The letter was deemed to be most unhelpful. London had been trying for many months to get the Vatican to condemn Sinn Féin violence and the outcome was such a letter.[25]

Sinn Féin envoys, like Seán T. O'Kelly, were quite upset by the outcome. They had had quite unrealistic expectations. However, very few members of Dáil Eireann knew about the background to the letter. Hagan was quite relieved by its contents. Other "republican" clerics in Rome were equally relieved. It was not an occasion for celebration, but, objectively speaking, it was a quiet achievement for Sinn Féin diplomacy. Hagan and de Valera had striven to prevent a Papal pronouncement on the Irish situation. When it had finally come it took the form of a letter enclosing a donation to the Irish White Cross. In the world of propaganda that might have been written-off as a failure. In the world of diplomacy, it was a significant success. Sinn Féin diplomacy had helped to discourage a Vatican pronouncement. It had chosen the right moment to make a request to the Vatican through Mannix as emissary. The tactic had met with success—perhaps much more so than Sinn Féin activists realised if Foreign Office reaction is to be used as a barometer.

Mannix arrived in Brisbane, without having gone back to Ireland to visit his mother, on 4 August 1921. He was given an enthusiastic reception in Melbourne where he revealed his admiration for de Valera: "I never met an Irishman for whom I had more admiration and in his hands the interests of Ireland are perfectly secure."[26] By early December 1921, many Irish bishops would not have agreed, although quite a number would have had considerable regard for him when Mannix made his remark. The role of Eamon de Valera in the Treaty negotiations has yet to be fully unravelled. But he certainly showed a lack of decision which contributed to the split following the signing of the Treaty on 6 December 1921. Irish bishops and their colleagues in Australia, with the exception of Mannix, took a very public stance in support of the Treaty from the very outset. There were no mental reservations. The outbreak of civil war in summer 1922 pushed de Valera down lower in the esteem of the Irish hierarchy.[27] When the Irish hierarchy issued a pastoral in October 1922 condemning the anti-Treatyites, de Valera wrote to Mannix complaining "never was charity of judgment so necessary, and apparently so disastrously absent. Ireland and the church will, I fear, suffer the consequences." De Valera, who had become President of a reconstructed "Republican Government" on 25 October 1922, told the archbishop of his conviction that the Free State agreement had to go:

It had brought nothing but disaster so far, and promised nothing but disorder and chaos, It gave no hope whatever of ordered or stable government. Human nature must be recast before those Irishmen and Irishwomen who believed in the national right and the national destiny as in a religion will consent to acquiesce in the selling of the national birthright for an ignoble mess of pottage, as they regard it.

According to de Valera the government had the prospect of existing only if the most unselfish patriotic citizens of the state were outlawed. De Valera believed that

the people everywhere, young and old, are beginning to realise that the only salvation for the nation now is a return to the old Sinn Féin principle of cleaving to their own institutions, whilst ignoring the authority and the institutions which the foreigner had tried to impose.[28]

It is not possible to state whether Mannix replied encouragingly to de Valera or not. The unopened de Valera papers will contain many answers to such historical problems. However, de Valera had displayed, by writing such an open and frank letter to Mannix, that the archbishop was indeed on his side. In fact, as early as August 1922, Mannix had taken up a position on Irish politics which had annoyed many Irish-Australian bishops. Following the sudden death of Arthur Griffith on 12 August 1922, Michael Kelly of Sydney had proposed sending a telegram of sympathy to Cardinal Michael

Logue. Alone among the Irish-Australian bishops, Mannix opposed the suggestion and wrote to Kelly on 29 August 1922:

> I am not ready, by sending his Eminence a message just now, to appear even in the least degree, to take any share in the views which he has so definitely expressed. If I were in Ireland during these dreadful days, rightly or wrongly, I should think it my duty to remain as nearly neutral as possible and to refrain from antagonising either party. My view may appear unwise: but it is my view . . . My recollection of the Parnell split is too vivid for me to wish to see the Irish Bishops again taking sides politically against any section of their own people.

Although that attitude infuriated Kelly and forced another Australian bishop to conclude "but reasoned argument is lost on Dr Mannix on the Irish question,"[29] the archbishop of Melbourne was pursuing a line of argument which was supported by John Hagan in Rome. The latter believed that the Irish bishops had polarised the political situation needlessly in Ireland by taking a political stance in support of the Treaty. That argument was further reinforced by the October pastoral, 1922, to which de Valera reacted so vehemently. Both Mannix and Hagan believed that the bishops should have remained more aloof. Instead, the statement of the Irish hierarchy provided moral justification for one side and drove the other further and further away from any possibility of securing an early end to hostilities. By remaining loyal to de Valera, Mannix and other churchmen may have served the interests of the Catholic Church in the long-term. De Valera was not alienated from the Catholic Church. He simply regarded the bishops as wrong in their political judgment, and he could say that on sound theological authority. De Valera, after all, had the services of a "parallel magisterium." Mannix was one of its central supports. The excesses of civil war underline the fact that Mannix may have had a point. However, the Irish hierarchy were not as closely aligned to the government as Mannix perceived from Australia.[30] It is ironic that Mannix, who saw himself as a reconciler even after the civil war, never appeared to realise just how unpopular he had become with W.T. Cosgrave and the government of the Free State. The utterances of the archbishop, both in public and in private, had "legitimised" de Valera's stance. They had provided the theological rationale for the anti-Treatyites to conduct an armed campaign. The intransigence of Mannix, who had no support for his position inside the Australian hierarchy, stood in contrast to the helpfulness of the Archbishop of Brisbane, James Duhig, who viewed the Free State Government with favour.[31] Correspondence between Cosgrave and Duhig in 1924 helps to convey the atmosphere of the time and depth of feeling that existed between the two sides in the civil war. The sense of betrayal which Cosgrave felt towards de Valera was not comprehended by Mannix.[32] Cosgrave wrote:

> ... we know from the opinions which we ourselves have heard from the lips of many of those who blindly followed de Valera in his orgy of destruction that close and enforced association with their leaders and with a number of the participants in the campaign has convinced the self-respecting among them that their cause has been a mistaken and a criminal one, and they are now determined to turn their energies to more profitable and more patriotic objects. They did not anticipate that their support of the malcontents of 1922 would have ended in the holocaust of blood and wholesale damage which ensued when the forces of disorder were unleashed. They did not believe that those who professed themselves concerned for the welfare of our people would ordain a "wading-through the blood of their fellow-countrymen" or a waste of their country's resources such as they unfortunately achieved.

Cosgrave felt that there was a change of heart among many of the anti-Treatyites. The country, he wrote, had a huge task before it: "We are fortunately possessed of a democratic constitution which will compare with that of any other nation. Our people are anxious to assist in the national development."[33]

Duhig and his fellow Irish ecclesiastics on the Australian bench—with the exception of Mannix—were hostile to any "republican" emissaries who arrived. In March 1923 Fr

Michael O'Flanagan and J.J. O'Kelly arrived in Melbourne where "they were enthusiastically received."[34] Archbishop Mannix introduced the two visitors to an audience in the town hall: "Father O'Flanagan and Mr O'Reilly will speak to the Irish people and to Irish sympathisers in Australia in de Valera's name.'[35] Archbishop Kelly, however, was concerned by the arrival of the two Sinn Féin representatives. They were a source of potential division in Irish-Australia. Accordingly, he circulated the Australian and New Zealand hierarchy setting out "a few principles of ecclesiastical discipline by which peace, order and respect for legitimate authorities in Church and State may be preserved in Australia.'"[36]

The bishops accepted the Kelly principles. But Mannix claimed that he was neutral and, taking de Valera's line in relation to the Irish hierarchy, told Kelly that the Australian hierarchy had abandoned its neutrality when messages were sent by the bishops to Ireland.[37]

However, there was support for O'Flanagan and O'Kelly among some of the clergy who were Irish-born and who identified with de Valera. Despite Kelly's best efforts, there were large meetings in Sydney. O'Flanagan was intemperate enough to criticise publicly his fellow Irishman, Archbishop Duhig, in Brisbane. The two "republicans" were arrested on a charge of sedition on 30 April 1923 and deported.[38]

Duhig on the other hand retained his great support for Cosgrave and wrote to him on 22 July 1924:

> What a tremendous struggle you have had. I am astonished that you did not break down under the terrific and lengthy strain of mind and body....Every one of our priests who has been home, has come back a convert to the Free State, and Australia is being slowly but surely permeated with a favourable impression regarding all of you who have stood out against the extremists.[39]

I am reliably informed that the de Valera archives contain similar letters of encouragement from Mannix to de Valera. Cosgrave and his arch-rival were being sustained by encouragement from two Irish archbishops ministering in Australia.

The bitterness of the civil war legacy has tended to impose a far too rigid bipolar division on Irish politics of 1923 and 1924. In the eyes of Mannix, Hagan and Magennis, de Valera was not a "gunman"; he was the political leader of the anti-Treatyites. What I have termed the "parallel magisterium" never deserted him. However, the complexities of Irish politics did not find any sympathy among members of the Irish hierarchy. After the Treaty, everything was seen in terms of "black" and "white." Mannix did not agree. He continued to view de Valera as a moderate who had attempted to exercise a restraining influence over the "gunmen."

However, Mannix was not a supporter of Sinn Féin and the anti-Treatyites in the way that Fr Michael O'Flanagan was. The archbishop was not a political activist. He had a good relationship with leading members of the anti-Treatyite elite—de Valera in particular—and he retained his confidence in these people notwithstanding the terrible events of the civil war. From that viewpoint, it was not de Valera who started the civil war. Knowing the internal politics of the anti-Treatyites very well, Hagan was quite well-aware of de Valera's limited room for manoeuvre in the area. I have developed this theory in my book, *The Vatican, the Bishops and Irish Politics, 1919–1939*. The complicated development of de Valera's political ideas has yet to be fully presented for the period of the civil war and the years immediately following. Future analyses may—as I have argued—be far less harsh on de Valera than earlier civil war historiography.

De Valera was arrested on 15 August 1923 in the midst of a general election campaign. Voting took place on 27 August and de Valera was returned at the top of the poll for Clare. He remained in gaol until July 1924. In the meantime, his party, Sinn Féin—which had done much better at the polls than commentators had predicted—pursued a policy of abstention. Deputies refused to enter the Dáil because they would have had to take an oath of allegiance. In Rome, Hagan doubted the wisdom of that policy. He kept in touch with Mannix and informed him of developments in Ireland. Returning home to Ireland on holidays each year, Hagan made a point of visiting the de Valera home and on one occasion wanted to leave some money to help support the family while the head of the household was in gaol. This generous offer was however declined by Mrs de Valera.

Where did Mannix stand on the question of abstention? I am reliably informed that the de Valera archive holds the answer to that question. It supports my theory that Mannix was a moderating influence on de Valera. He favoured a pragmatic approach to Irish politics. However, until de Valera was released from gaol in July 1924, there was little opportunity to make practical suggestions about the future of Sinn Féin.

In January 1925, Mannix's mother died. The archbishop was unable to return in time for the funeral, but de Valera was among the mourners. Given the friendship between the two men, it seems unlikely to me that de Valera was "exploiting" the occasion for political gain.[40] Both men had developed a close friendship and Mannix was among the very few prelates who had not wavered in support for him. They had a further opportunity to meet in 1925. Mannix had been chosen to lead an Australian pilgrimage to Rome. He again took up residence in the Irish College as a guest of Hagan. De Valera, using headed notepaper "Dáil Eireann, Government of the Republic," wrote to Hagan on 19 May 1925 using semi-coded language. He indicated that he was aware of the arrival of Mannix and hinted that "their action here will, when they come, have considerable influence."[41] This was a reference to the fact that Mannix intended to visit Ireland.

Hagan replied on 31 May 1925 to "My Dear President." The Rector of the Irish College outlined what Mannix intended to do when he arrived in Ireland. The archbishop was travelling as a pilgrim. He wanted to lead the Australians as a group into Dublin. However, it is possible to judge from the contents of the Hagan letter that he felt the archbishop did not fully comprehend the complexities of the political situation in Ireland. According to Hagan, he "understands the situation in most of its bearings." But that was really a polite way of stating to de Valera that there was a problem.

Mannix wanted a demonstration in Dublin to greet the pilgrims "without distinction of party." In post-civil war Ireland such a meeting was not possible to arrange. Mannix also wanted a Pontifical High Mass in the Pro-Cathedral, Dublin. Hagan was not, however, "sanguine as to the feasibility of this item of the programme." Mannix was not very realistic in his expectations. This letter supports in part de Valera's reminiscence in 1962—at a ceremony to mark the golden jubilee of Mannix's ordination—that he went to Rome to try to persuade the archbishop to come to Ireland as a private citizen. Even if the reminiscence is somewhat over-precise, de Valera certainly faced a serious problem with Mannix in 1925. If the archbishop was to help the anti-Treatyite side, he had to be tutored in the "realities" of Irish politics.

However, there were two other reasons why de Valera went to Rome in 1925. He had recently been released from gaol and badly needed a complete break from public life. But perhaps of greatest importance was the fact that Hagan had prepared a memorandum on certain dilemmas facing the anti-Treatyites and wanted to discuss the contents of the document with de Valera. Given the level of censorship in Ireland, Hagan was quite explicit in his letter to de Valera which indicates that it may have been hand-carried to Dublin. The rector wrote that, at the suggestion of "our tiny group in this city," he had drawn up a paper. Peter Magennis was among those who had asked him to do so. The latter described him as an "uncompromising man" and said that Magennis would not promote the taking of the oath of allegiance but he would not oppose it, provided a decision was taken unanimously on the subject. Hagan explained to de Valera his own position on the matter:

> I do not know how you regard the problem; but I tried to express my own mind as clearly as possible. I am greatly impressed by two aspects of the case: First there seems to be some, perhaps much, danger of cleavage or even of disintegration if the present trend is continued for long; and secondly it would seem well nigh impossible to hope to secure control of the army, or even to obtain a parliamentary

216

majority, until the oath has been either abolished or swallowed.

While our guest did not commit himself to any expression of opinion on the subject, I am inclined to gather that he would not be disposed to balk at the idea if it could be entertained without danger of a split. I should expect that his attitude would depend to a large extent on what you think best. At any rate I am safe in saying that he has an open mind and is prepared to discuss possibilities and give such assistance as will seem best calculated to serve the interests of the country, present and remote. As far as I am concerned I have only to add that in writing in this strain I am assuming that you will see no offence in the frank expression of opinion on the part of one who has tried to take an intelligent interest in the movement, and who has perhaps accomplished but little beyond making many enemies and rendering still more difficult a position which is never very easy at the best of times.[42]

It seems likely that Mannix was the "guest" referred to in the letter. Hagan, who was a good judge of his fellow clerical anti-Treatyites, was of the view that Mannix had "an open mind" on the question of the oath of allegiance. They were two very useful pieces of information for de Valera. Three of de Valera's most esteemed ecclesiastical backers were prepared to discuss the question of removing the major obstacle which stood between Sinn Féin members and taking their Dáil seats.

De Valera visited Blackrock College and borrowed the cassock and passport of his friend, Fr Patrick Walshe. Dressed as a priest, he left for Rome accompanied by Séan MacBride who acted as his secretary and interpreter.[43] It is possible that de Valera may have already left for Italy before Hagan's letter had arrived in Dublin. But that would not have meant that de Valera did not know about Mannix's unrealistic demands for his Irish trip. There was a regular flow of visitors between Dublin and Rome and de Valera was well-informed. On 2 June 1925, de Valera was in Florence. He sent a letter with MacBride to Hagan: "Mr Séan MacBride . . . will himself explain the object of his visit if you find it possible to accord him an interview."[44] De Valera was invited to Rome and stayed clandestinely in the rector's rooms in the Irish College. News of his presence in the college was not kept a secret from at least one observant seminarian who told me of having seen de Valera enter the rector's rooms.

Little is actually known about what transpired at the "republican summit" in Rome. Hagan was certainly present at the meetings. The Vice-Rector of the college, Michael Curran, was probably also present. The latter was a close friend of Séan T. O'Kelly and had hidden de Valera in the Gate Lodge of the Archbishop of Dublin's palace following his escape from Lincoln Jail in 1919. Peter Magennis and Mannix were certainly present. Séan MacBride was not in attendance at all the meetings.[45] The de Valera papers will cast more light on this episode in Irish history.

However, the Hagan memorandum is available. This document is an attempt to outline the various options before the anti-Treatyites. In it the rector rejected the notion that the majority in republican ranks were capable of struggling indefinitely. Only a minority, in his view, were capable of not deviating from the straight road, "as long as they are spurred on by hope of ultimate success or cheered on by an occasional victory." But denied the possibility of success, Hagan felt that fragmentation would follow:

> The extent to which some such tendency is manifesting itself in the Separatist ranks at the present hour is a matter for investigation, but not so the existence of some such feeling; nor is it going too far to hazard the forecast that if the days of waiting are too many a line of cleavage is bound to make its appearance in the ranks, if not among the members of the higher command.

The document then addresses itself to the best way of avoiding "the greatest of all possible Irish disasters—a split." That opened the broader issue as to how far the policy of protest and abstention was the wisest one calculated to accomplish its object within a measurable period of time. Hagan was very blunt in his assessment of the political realities in Ireland. The struggle had ceased to be a fight to destroy the armed forces of the British Crown. It now assumed the shape of an effort to destroy an English-made machine, manned, not by Englishmen, but by their own countrymen. Efforts to dislodge the Free State had failed; Hagan asked whether the time had not come to try and take the Free State from within by capturing and controlling the machinery of government, somewhat in the same way as the British government had set about destroying a more or less similar machine in 1800.

The problem was the taking of the oath. Hagan faced the problem:

> To cross the threshold of Leinster House, even in a hostile spirit, one must first take the oath of allegiance to the English Crown. Must all hope therefore be abandoned by those who enter here? Or can the oath be regarded as a mere empty formality which can be gone through without dishonour, without any lowering of the flag, without betrayal of the living and of the dead of Ireland?

Hagan then addressed the problem of the oath: "This oath, like every other oath, must be judged according to its antecedent and concomitant implications, and in particular must be interpreted in the light of the theoretical and practical value attached to it by theology and history". The rector then argued from personal experience, theology and history in favour of treating the oath as something other than an insuperable obstacle. Hagan pointed out that even if the republicans were to gain a majority outside parliament, the Free State army would remain loyal to the state. Republicans would be prevented from taking power indefinitely:

> As to the rest, may not the present situation be likened to a ship carrying Ireland and its fortunes but managed by a crew of madmen who are driving the vessel straight on to the rocks, while the doomed passengers refuse to step in and pitch the madmen overboard, on the plea that even that much contact with them would soil their hands?[46]

The minutes of these meetings are not available. It is doubtful if any official record of proceedings was kept. Séan MacBride, who was not privy to everything that went on, said that he argued against giving up to the policy of abstention. But he was in a minority. At this stage, the discussion remained at a theoretical level. But, according to Séan MacBride, there was general acceptance on the part of the others present at the meetings of the urgency to change direction in Irish politics before it was too late. Hagan's arguments had convinced Mannix, Magennis and Curran.[47] The question was whether it was possible to retain a united leadership in Sinn Féin and shift harmoniously away from a policy of abstention. It was up to de Valera to try to test the practicality of such a policy. After the Rome visit, he had, on what he would have regarded as the most reliable theological authority, support for the view that there were no religious obstacles to ditching the policy of abstentionism. I have argued elsewhere that de Valera was never very well-disposed towards that policy and wanted to enter the Dáil as early as autumn 1922 but was prevented from doing so by Liam Lynch. Between 1925 and 1927 Irish politics were transformed. De Valera broke from Sinn Féin, founded Fianna Fáil in 1926 and entered the Dáil in summer 1927. The de Valera papers will show that he was fully supported in those moves by Archbishop Mannix.

The Mannix visit to Ireland, which began with his arrival in Dublin on 29 June 1925, was a mixture of personal tragedy and high farce. He had insisted on coming in a semi-public capacity at the head of the Australian pilgrimage, against the advice of Hagan and de Valera. He was met by leading anti-Treatyites and put up in the Shelbourne Hotel after a brief visit to the Pro-Cathedral for prayers.

De Valera had succeeded in getting a few thousand people out to welcome Mannix at Westland Row station. He was not, however, invited to visit Archbishop Edward Byrne in Drumcondra. Mannix was in fact boycotted by all leading members of the Catholic hierarchy. William Cosgrave and the Irish government also ostracised him. When he arrived in his home-town of Charleville, he found the church locked and in darkness. He remained in Ireland until October spending most of his time with relatives. When he spoke in public on Irish politics, Mannix showed how completely out of touch he was with the realities of life in the country. He appeared never to be able to comprehend the bitterness of the civil war and that he was a partisan in that historical process. He left Ireland in 1925 never to return home. He died in 1963, aged 99.

Until the de Valera archives are fully open to researchers, it will not be possible to state authoritatively the nature of the relationship between the two men. However, there is oral evidence to support the hypothesis that Mannix remained a confidant of de Valera after the latter had come to power.[48] De Valera visited Mannix in Melbourne when he was in opposition in 1948. He was kept in constant touch with what was happening in Ireland and on one occasion an Irish Franciscan priest was asked to bring him out an advance copy of the draft 1937 constitution. De Valera knew the bitterness of post-civil war opposition politics in Ireland. He recognised the toll that imprisonment had taken on his own family. He also recognised the value of friendship and solidarity during those years. Mannix had displayed a personal loyalty to de Valera which helped him considerably from 1920. He acknowledged that debt in 1962 when he travelled to Charleville to attend jubilee celebrations in honour of the archbishop.

In summary, the relationship between de Valera and Mannix can only be understood within the historical context of the period. In pre-Treaty times, Mannix had emerged as a champion of Irish nationalism. He was a strong voice, perhaps a strident voice, in favour of Sinn Féin, and his denunciations of British misrule were clear and unequivocal. De Valera, a man very much his junior, was deferential to the prelate and respected his teaching authority. When the two men met in the United States in 1920, the relationship became less formal and more friendly. De Valera respected Mannix because of the office that he held. But he also respected him because he had proved his courage and independent-mindedness while under "house arrest" in England. The value of Mannix's support and friendship became all the more important to de Valera following the

Treaty split in 1922, when "the chief" was isolated by many of the Irish bishops who had moved closer to the position of Sinn Féin in the months leading up to the Truce. Mannix became part of what I have termed a "parallel magisterium"— a small group of senior clerics to whom de Valera could defer. The bond of friendship and respect between Mannix and de Valera developed in the post-civil war period.

Mannix was something of an episcopal maverick. He was a difficult colleague and many of his fellow bishops in Australia and Ireland would have preferred if he had chosen a quieter life away from politics. The fact that both Mannix and de Valera were two "outsiders" may have driven them closer together. Loyalty and friendship committed Mannix to remain a supporter of Eamon de Valera in the post-civil war period.[49] Hagan and Mannix, correctly as it turned out, believed that de Valera would again become leader of Ireland. That looked very unlikely in 1922. But by 1932 it was a reality. Paradoxically, as a consequence Irish Catholicism owed much to Mannix.

References

The research for this paper is based on archival research in Rome, London, Dublin and Armagh. I have been fortunate to gain access to the John Hagan Collection in the Irish College, Rome. Other personal collections have also proved very valuable, in particular, the William Walsh and Edward Byrne archives in Drumcondra, Dublin and the Michael Logue and Patrick O'Donnell collections in Armagh. I have also made use of Irish Cabinet Papers, State Paper Office, Dublin and Foreign Office Documents at the Public Record Office in London. I have been fortunate to interview a number of de Valera's colleagues—Frank Aiken, Séan MacEntee and Frederick Boland were very helpful. Mr Séan MacBride also gave me an interview and first drew to my attention the details of the 1925 meeting in Rome which I refer to extensively in this article. Unfortunately, I was not able to gain access to the Eamon de Valera papers on this topic. However, the existence of a relatively large correspondence between Mannix and de Valera has been confirmed for me. I would like to thank the editor of this volume, Dr John O'Brien, for his helpful comments on an earlier draft of the text.

Unfortunately, the John Hagan papers—one of the most important collections for the study of Irish ecclesiastical politics in the post–1916 period—have not been classified: They have been arranged in chronological order by Fr John Silke. Therefore, I have simply cited correspondence in references (Hagan papers). The researcher will simply have to go to the relevant year to find the documents.

1. T.P. O'Neill and Lord Longford, *Eamon de Valera* (London, 1970), pp. 14, 477.

2. *Irish Catholic Directory*, 1912, pp. 504–505.

3. See Michael O'Hickey file, St Patrick's College, Maynooth which was opened to me by the President, Fr Michael Ledwith and Professor Pádraig Ó Fiannachta. See article by León Ó Broin, "The Gaelic League and the Chair of Irish in Maynooth," *Studies*, Winter 1963, pp. 348–362; Walter A. MacDonald, *Reminiscences of a Maynooth Professor* (London, 1925), pp. 235–275; Ruth Dudley Edwards, *Patrick Pearse—The Triumph of Failure* (London, 1977), pp. 75–78.

4. This is an undated fragment of a speech made by Mannix to the Trustees of the college calling for the dismissal of O'Hickey. Father James Murtagh headed this "Rough Notes by Mannix on O'Hickey," O'Hickey archive, St Patrick's College, Maynooth. Partly quoted in Colm Kiernan, *Daniel Mannix and Ireland* (Dublin, 1984), pp. 47, 54.

5. The memory of Mannix's action still rankles with some of the older members of the Kerry diocese.

6. See Patrick O'Farrell, "Archbishop Kelly and the Irish Question," *Journal of Australian Catholic Historical Society*, Vol. 4 (Part 3), 1974, pp. 1–19 and Thomas Boland, *James Duhig, Archbishop of Brisbane 1917–1965* (Brisbane, 1986).

7. Mannix has been favoured with a number of biographies of varying quality: See B.A. Santamaria, *Daniel Mannix: A Biography* (Melbourne, 1984); Walter A. Ebsworth, *Archbishop Mannix* (Melbourne, 1977); Michael Gilchrist, *Daniel Mannix, Priest and Patriot* (Blackburn, 1982); Colm Kiernan, *Daniel Mannix and Ireland* (Dublin, 1984); Niall Brennan, *Dr Mannix* (London, 1965); Frank Murphy, *Daniel Mannix, Archbishop of Melbourne* (Advocate Press, 1948); For a somewhat polemical view of Mannix see James Griffin, "Daniel Mannix and the Cult of Personality" in Oliver MacDonagh and W.F. Mandle (eds), *Ireland and Irish-Australia* (London, 1986), pp. 95–118.

8. Brennan, *Mannix*, p. 125.

9. O'Farrell, "Archbishop Kelly," p. 1.

10. Boland, *Duhig*, p. 151.

11. ibid., p. 152.

12. Brennan, *Mannix*, p. 190.

13. See Dermot Keogh, *The Vatican, the Bishops and Irish Politics, 1919–1939* (Cambridge, 1986), chapter II; there was also a rumour that Mannix might replace the aged William Walsh as archbishop of Dublin. The British took this seriously enough to instruct their envoy at the Vatican to make representations against such an appointment. There was never any serious possibility of that happening but Mannix would not have been adverse to the idea himself.

14. Moirin Chavasse, *Terence MacSwiney* (Dublin, 1961), p. 174–175 and 185.

15. Keogh, *The Vatican* Chapter II.

16. Sean T. O'Kelly to Patrick Murray, 24 February, 1921 (John Hagan papers, Irish College, Rome).

17. Memorandum on visit prepared by John Hagan, rector of the Irish College, together with a hand-written account of Mannix's speech. (Hagan papers).

18. ibid. See also Griffin, "Daniel Mannix," pp. 100–101 (for account of his reception, by anonymous priest—Ballarat Diocese Historical Commission to MDHC).

19. Text of address of welcome by Dr Eric Fair (Hagan papers).

20. It is necessary to treat this source with caution. It is a contemporary account of the meeting found in the John Hagan papers. It is likely that the handwritten note was made by Fr Arthur Ryan of Belfast. However, I cannot be certain of that. It is not written in Hagan's hand. Furthermore, the note would either have to have been made from notes taken by the writer at the meeting or from the speaking notes prepared by Mannix. The nature of the speech does not lead me to support the view that it was scripted in advance.

21. It might be asked by the historian whether a speech delivered on such an emotionally charged occasion is an accurate reflection of Mannix's political philosophy. While the archbishop may have been moved by the sense of occasion to exaggerate, I accept that the content of the note reflects what Mannix had come to believe on the question of Irish nationalism. The content of the address was not very remarkable for the time. What made it unusual was that the sentiments were being expressed in public by an archbishop.

22. Hagan memorandum on Mannix visit (Hagan papers).

23. Cardinal Patrick O'Donnell Papers (Ara Coeli, Armagh) for copy of Mannix draft submitted to Benedict XV.

24. Dr Patrick Lennon, Bishop of Kildare and Leighlin, Diary entry of visit and interview with Archbishop Mannix in the 1960s.

25. For text of Benedict XV's letter see *Irish Catholic Directory*, 1921.

26. Kiernan, *Mannix*, p. 173.

27. Keogh, *The Vatican*, chapters II and III.

28. De Valera to Mannix, 6 Nov. 1922. Maurice Moynihan (ed.), *Speeches and Statements of Eamon de Valera 1917–1973* (Dublin, 1980), pp. 107–108.

29. Quoted in O'Farrell, loc. cit., pp. 12–13.

30. Keogh, *The Vatican*, Chapter III.

31. Duhig had a strong advantage over Mannix. He had been in Ireland in 1920, and again in 1922 where he saw at first hand the ravages of civil war. It took him considerable time to reach Broadford, Co. Limerick. He attended the funeral of Arthur Griffith. He was also present at the funeral of Michael Collins. According to his biographer, Fr Boland, Duhig regarded de Valera as "guilty of the murder of Michael Collins, friend of his friend, champion—however reluctant—of the Irish Free State within the empire. De Valera was that black figure of Ireland's historic curse, the man who betrays the chief. It was a long time before Duhig could forget." Boland, op. cit., p. 161.

32. Cosgrave telegram to Duhig, 27 January 1924, S 1369/21, SPO Dublin.

33. Cosgrave to Duhig, 4 January 1924, S 1369/21, SPO Dublin.

34. O'Farrell, "Archbishop Kelly," p. 13.

35. Kiernan, *Mannix*, p. 178.

36. O'Farrell, loc. cit., p. 13.

37. ibid.

38. ibid., and Kiernan, *Mannix*, pp. 178–179.

39. Duhig to Cosgrave, 22 July 1924, S 1369/21, SPO Dublin; Cosgrave replied on 14 November 1924 that it was gratifying to learn that our Australian friends "who have had an opportunity of visiting us and seeing for themselves the conditions here have carried back good impressions with them."

40. Colm Kiernan has argued that "De Valera did what he could to develop his friendship with Mannix and to exploit it." Kiernan, *Mannix.*, p. 187.

41. De Valera to Hagan, 19 May 1925 (Hagan papers).

42. Hagan to de Valera, 31 May 1925 (Hagan papers).

43. Interview Fr Séan P. Farragher. See his excellent book on Eamon de Valera's lifelong association with Blackrock, 1898–1975. (Dublin, 1984).

44. De Valera to Hagan, 2 June 1925 (Hagan papers).
45. Mr Séan MacBride first drew my attention to this meeting in an interview. Because the de Valera papers are still closed on this topic, his oral evidence is of considerable importance.
46. John Hagan Memorandum (Hagan papers)
47. Séan MacBride told me that he was in a minority when he held out against shifting policy on the oath. At the meetings Mannix is likely to have assumed the role of the theologian. He was asked for his opinion on the taking of the oath. Mannix supported the position adopted by Hagan. In other words, he favoured entry into the Dáil.
48. For example, de Valera travelled to Paris to meet Mannix in 1932. (Photograph in my possession).
49. I have not argued that Mannix was a political advisor to de Valera at any time. Mannix did not understand the details of Irish politics sufficiently to have been that. But he was a figure respected by de Valera who admired his singularity of mind and approved of his political indiscretions.

10.
Writing about the Irish in Australia

BOB REECE

One of the problems with the great burst of interest in the Ireland-Australian connection in recent years is its celebratory and somewhat indiscriminate nature. The Kilkenny conference for the Australian Bicentennial in 1983[1] marked a high point in the growth of popular enthusiasm in both countries and also served to maintain the momentum. And at one level there is no reason why the Ireland-Australia connection should not be celebrated, particularly in view of its long neglect and of the Anglophilia which has characterised Australian society. The Ireland-Australia industry will go on regardless of the comments made by individual academics, but I believe that it is important to look at what has been written and to ask some questions about the future direction of scholarly activity.

Writing about the Irish in Australia began as an act of filial piety or nationalist and religious affirmation on the part of Irish-born Australians. Historiographically, these efforts can be conveniently termed "contribution history" in so far as they attempt to demonstrate the way in which Irish people achieved material success and, more importantly, social respectability, in Australia. Hogan's *The Irish in Australia* (1887)[2] and Cleary's *Australia's Debt to The Irish Nation Builders* (1933)[3] bear witness to a continuing need for recognition, something which Patrick O'Farrell has called the "triumphalist 'me-too' principle."[4] Social acceptance in Australia was often at the cost of pride, but there were those like Cardinal Patrick Moran, Archbishop of Sydney, who preferred to eulogise and sanctify the historical experience of the (Catholic) Irish. In his *History of the Roman Catholic Church in Australasia* (1984),[5] he wrote of the Irish convicts: "... the great body... were genuine Martyrs. Hatred of the Faith was the motive of those who forced them into rebellion, and they freely died for their Faith."[6] In 1906 the Catholic journal *Austral Light* claimed that only the Irish-descended were untainted citizens since none of their convict ancestors were criminals.[7] The "me too" principle and the assertion of a higher virtue were twin responses to a society which offered economic opportunity but withheld full acceptance.

Other writers in the colonial era were as anxious to deny the Irish "contribution" as others were to assert it. The Protestant, colonial-born historians G.W. Rusden and H.G. Turner would have sympathised with journalistic retorts to Hogan that, while the Catholic Irish had advanced themselves, they had not advanced the common good, and that most of the notable Irishmen listed by Hogan were in fact Anglo-Irish.[8]

The traditional response of Australian academic historians to the Irish was to ignore them. Indeed, the first prominent writer to give them a mention was Manning Clark in the first volume of *A History of Australia* in 1962.[9] In his dramatic schema of how Western European civilization was established in the antipodes, Clark portrayed the three world views— Catholicism, Protestantism and the Enlightenment—vying for dominance. The Irish were useful to Clark in so far as they represented Catholic civilisation, but he made his own view of them more than clear:

> They were a people whose holy faith and family affections lent a charm to and softened the harshness of their lives in their wretched cabins and compensated them for their worldly privations. The wretchedness of their lives contributed to the extremes in their behaviour, to the creation of a type who one hour was dignified by every kind and noble sentiment only to be degraded the next by acts of the most brutal malevolence.[10]

The Irish were not as important for Clark as the "cultural baggage" they brought with them, although how they could be separated from their beliefs is difficult to comprehend. His treatment of them was within the "contribution" tradition, that contribution being seen in non-material terms.

While the contribution approach is still popular, the notion of what was being contributed *to* has changed in response to the altered ethnic make-up of Australian society in recent times and to the pseudo-ethic of multiculturalism which has been enthusiastically embraced with little regard for what it might actually mean. The high social and political profile of many of these ethnic groups, together with the general razzamatazz about multiculturalism, has suggested the absurd notion that "we are all ethnics now": that those of English and Scots birth or descent who comprised two-thirds of the "host society" by World War Two should also begin to behave as if they were minority groups. This is multiculturalism carried to its logical absurdity, doing less than justice to the Catholic Irish who constituted a classical social and political minority group during the first century of Australian history.

Multiculturalism has prompted a good deal of research into the history of ethnic group adaptation to the host society, assimilation and retention of ethnicity occupying the two opposing ends of the spectrum. The problem with this "model" is that it assumes the host society to be a homogeneous entity. This is convenient, but it ignores the fact that the Australian society which post-World War Two immigrants entered was itself the product of an earlier dialectic, or process, in which the Irish played an important rôle from the very outset.

The problem with "contribution history" is that it usually implies an aggregate or composite history which is the sum of its various parts. Pursuing this somewhat mechanical model, then, we study the different "contributions" of ethnic groups: Cornishmen, Welsh and Irish as well as the more recent arrivals such as Chinese, Germans, Italians, Greeks, Yugoslavs and so on. One of the obvious hazards here is that extravagant claims will at times be made for the contribution of one group or another. To make one early example: in 1954 C.H. Currey credited the Irish with the inspiration and leadership of the December 1854 revolt at Ballarat in Victoria against gold-digging licences.[11] It is true that Peter Lalor (the younger brother of James Fintan Lalor) played an important, if initially reluctant, rôle in events leading up to the Eureka incident. It is also true that Irish names figured significantly in the list of those who were shot and bayonetted to death by the troops during the dawn attack by government forces. However, the movement was a spontaneous one, reflecting the everyday frustrations of self-employed miners rather than any ideological principle of Irish origin.

Again, it is important to see Ned Kelly, that dominant hero-figure of Australian folklore, in the context of Irishness. "Game as Ned Kelly" is an aphorism now firmly embedded in the Australian tradition and there have been attempts to link the Kellys and their supporters with an Australian ethos which resists established authority. However, the Irish were probably as strongly represented in the Victorian Constabulary as they were in north-eastern Victoria where the Kellys lived. Constable Fitzpatrick, whose visit to the Kelly homestead in April 1878 triggered off the Kelly outbreak, was an Irishman. Constables Lonigan and Scanlon and Sergeant Kennedy, who were killed by the Kelly gang in October that year, were no less Irish than Ned Kelly. Indeed, since they were Irish-born and Ned was Australian-born their credentials were rather better. Again, Judge Redmond Barry, the Trinity College graduate who sentenced Kelly to be hanged, would also have called himself an Irishman. So might the man who betrayed the Kellys to the police.

In his famous Jerilderie letter which attempted to justify his actions, much of Kelly's rancour was directed towards the colonial Irish policeman,

> who, for a lazy, loafing, cowardly billit left the ash corner, deserted the shamrock, the emblem of true wit and beauty, to serve under a flag and nation that has destroyed, massacred and murdered their fore-fathers by the greatest of tortures...[12]

The Irish background which Kelly invoked was a simple one of Catholic tenant farmers versus Protestant landowners. The folklore of rebellion in Australia is predominantly Irish Catholic. The image of the rebel remains dear to the hearts of many Irish and other Australians in spite of (or perhaps because of) a remarkably conformist social reality. Perhaps the "Wild Colonial Boy" reflects part of the Australian psyche .

Although Patrick O'Farrell is an outspoken critic of filial pietism and multiculturalism as inspirations for historical writing about the Irish in Australia, he advances the radical and striking claim that until recently the Irish have been "the dynamic factor in Australian history . . . the galvanising force at the centre of the evolution of our national character."[13] Never in their wildest dreams would Hogan, Moran or Cleary have made such a breathtaking leap. So why should this be? Is O'Farrell an antipodean Irish supernationalist, determined to trump the claims of all those who have written about the "Irish contribution"? Not a bit of it, he tells us. He does not consider himself Irish and he was not even born and brought up in Australia. Then why has he, in his own words, "gone for broke"? The answer is that O'Farrell, the idealist historian, has chosen to fire a broadside at what he sees as the prevailing environmentalist, materialist interpretation of Australian history:

> What has ruled in Australian history hitherto [he writes] has been the unconscious and unfettered dictatorship of place, the unquestioned assumption that the Australian environment, this harsh, isolated land, has imperiously determined and contained from arrival, the concerns and horizons of its white inhabitants. More than influenced—it certainly did that—determined and contained. This historical orthodoxy is clearly revealed for the impersonal geographic and economic determinism that it is, by the practice of presenting Australia's population as best comprehended in categories relating to economic function, or occupation—convicts, farmers, trade unionists or whatever—that is, categories derived from what people did for a living. What about what they were as people, human beings of diverse backgrounds, beliefs, cultural

traditions? The traditional accounts deal with only one of the roles in which people in Australia acted, the economic facet of their lives, a very narrow conception of the boundaries of human existence—and one naturally contained by Australia's geographic confines. The whole truth is much wider, more human.[14]

So what is the "real history" of Australia, in his view? It is the "gradual growth and development, through confrontation and compromise, of a people of distinctive quality and character, derived from and produced by cultures—majority and minority—in conflict."[15] Needless to say, he credits the Irish with the responsibility for most of this conflict. Unlike other minorities such as the Germans and Italians who were happy to be tolerated within a British system, O'Farrell argues that "the Irish rejected or questioned the system, or at least demanded that it be adjusted to meet their requirements, with the effect of creating a new, modified system, a unique Australian blend and compromise which fitted the character of a mixed and interacting group of people, on the basis of equity."[16]

O'Farrell's main concern is to make Australians think about their history as a series of ideological conflicts rather than a material progression. In other words, apart from their intrinsic interest and importance, the Irish in Australia provide him with a heuristic device, a rhetorical club with which to beat the materialists. The important point is that the book's argument is not so much about what happened to the Irish in Australia—the Irish experience if you like—but what happened to produce a uniquely different Australian society.

"Why argue at all," O'Farrell asks.

Because [he goes on] the device of argument attracts attention, because the structure of argument compels rigid attention to evidence, because the historical ground of Australia's evolution and character is already occupied by other specious arguments about bushmen and Anzacs masquerading as received wisdom and obvious orthodoxy, and because this is a first-rate argument.[17]

O'Farrell is a national and perhaps even nationalist historian, whose concern is to explain why Australians are as they are. Impatient with the traditional explanations which stress the physical environment and the emergence of a rural-based social ethos—the "Australian Legend" articulated and explored by Russel Ward in the 1950s[18]—O'Farrell emphasises the spirit of compromise brought about by the conflict of imported ideas. The problem is that the new generation of Australian historians are impatient with traditional concepts of national identity, unique character and so on. Ward wrote at a time when it was possible to invoke a national consensus, when it was still respectable to talk about "nation-building." Vietnam, the alliance with the United States and the continuing tide of non-Anglo-Saxon and Celtic immigration have made it more difficult to be an Australian nationalist in the orthodox mould. Consequently, Australia's younger historians do not share the traditional interest in a national historiography based on unique identity. This is seen as a somewhat Whiggish and certainly conservative attitude, which cannot explain the diversity, contradictions and conflicts of Australian society.

In his book *Inventing Australia*, Richard White goes so far as to argue that "there is no point in asking whether one version of this essential Australia is truer than another because they are all intellectual constructs, neat, tidy and comprehensible—and necessarily false. . . . When we look at ideas about national identity, we need to ask, not whether they are true or false, but what their function is, whose creation they are, and whose interests they serve."[19] I would certainly not wish to suggest that O'Farrell represents the interests of any social group. But there is in his writing a preoccupation with the evolution of a distinctively Australian society which many would find old-fashioned. Revisionist Australian history has no need of a national pantheon of bushmen, Anzacs or Irishmen.

Although O'Farrell is also the historian of the Catholic Church in Australia,[20] and a Catholic himself, he is at some pains to play down the role of the Catholic Irish—possibly because this might appear partisan. But if we follow his argument about conflict, it was indeed the Catholic Irish who were at the forefront. Confrontations between Green and Orange certainly marked the history of most Australian colonies in the nineteenth century, but the worst sectarian excesses were not just a continuation of the old struggles that had scarred Ireland. Fears of Catholic numerical and political dominance marked the nonconformist anti-Irish Catholic rhetoric of the period, commencing in the 1840's when assisted immigration got under way.

One of the most useful points made by O'Farrell is that colonial society in Australia was pluralistic from the outset— that it is not appropriate to think simply in terms of the extent to which the Irish assimilated to or rejected a British ascendancy. There were certainly those, like the Revd Samuel Marsden and James MacArthur, who worked for that ascendancy—for the establishment of the Church of England's monopoly in spiritual and educational matters and for the enthronement of the big landowners as an hereditary aristocratic ruling class. But the realities of colonial life worked against this and one of these realities was that at all times the Irish, most of them Catholics, constituted at least a quarter and perhaps a third of the population of eastern Australia. And it was an Anglo-Irish liberal, Sir Richard Bourke, who, in the wake of the 1829 emancipation in Ireland, passed the New South Wales Church Act of 1836 which effectively disestablished the Church of England and laid the foundation for a pluralistic religious and educational system in Australia. The fact that an opportunistic political alliance between Catholics and nonconformists strengthened Bourke's hand only demonstrates that colonial society in Australia was not a matter of putting old wine into new bottles. The demographic, economic and political chemistry of the antipodes produced different results. Who would have thought, for example, that within ten years many of the 1798 men would be prosperous pillars of society in colonial New South Wales? Economic opportunity was a great force for change. The interesting question is how disposed, how equipped were the Irish to respond to opportunity?

In spite of the renewed interest in Irish-Australia, some of the most basic questions of Irish-Australian history have not been properly answered, possibly because they have been framed in a deceptively simple way. The question "who were the Irish convicts?", for example, involves making generalisations about no less than 50,000 men and women who went from Ireland and England to the Australian colonies between 1791 and 1868.

One response has been the genre of Irish convict hagiography suggested by Cardinal Moran. Ireland's first Ambassador to Australia, T.J. Kiernan, published his *Irish Exiles in Australia*[21] in 1954 and more recently Patsy Adam Smith has reworked the story of the Young Irelanders transported to Australia in *Heart of Exile*.[22] In the *The Fatal Shore*[23] Robert Hughes repeats the orthodoxy that no more than 20 per cent of the Irish convicts were political or social rebels, but he is not interested in writing about the other 80 per cent.

During those eighty years of transportation, the situation in Ireland and in the Australian colonies did not stand still. Indeed, there were dramatic economic, social and political changes which determined who was being transported and what for, at any particular time. Although the detailed work has not been done to demonstrate this, it is very likely that most of the Irish convicts sent out between 1791 and 1794 were urban petty criminals and that they were succeeded by people who had been involved to a greater or lesser extent in the 1798 rebellion. Petty criminals probably predominated again in the aftermath of the Napoleonic wars, but during the late 1820's and early 1830's there was a high representation of people from the rural areas where conditions were turbulent. Later the 1848 Young Ireland movement and the Fenians were responsible for another tide of political prisoners.

This periodisation of transportation is extremely important, but in their impatience to generalise, historians have produced largely impressionistic answers to simplistic questions. The actual empirical work on convict records has been surprisingly limited but despite (or because of) this, the generalisations made by Clark, Shaw, Waldersee and Robson[24] have assumed considerable authority. Of these, only Robson has made a methodical study of the records as a whole, but his one-in-twenty statistical sample over the entire eighty-year period produces a result which is so qualified and blurred at the edges as to be unsatisfactory.

In his statistically-based profile of the Irish convicts, Robson makes some interesting comparisons with English and Scots convicts: most of the Irish came from rural background and had been convicted in their county of origin; they included a greater proportion of women; a higher proportion of the men were married, and they were generally older than English prisoners. However, he believes that "a neat division between the two nationalities over-simplifies the case" and his concluding generalisation allows no distinction.[25]

The only historian who has resisted this new orthodoxy is George Rudé[26] and his writing is the most useful point of departure for future research in the area. While his work was initially directed towards political prisoners, the wider concept of social rebellion was usefully applied to the range of agrarian offences which Robson himself admits were more characteristically Irish. Again, however, more analysis needs to be done of social protest.

Although there are serious gaps in Irish convict records for the period up to 1836, they still await systematic study[27] in combination with other official records and of course the newspapers of the day. Records of the assizes for the early period have been lost, but the newspapers reported most of them, sometimes in detail. Furthermore, there is now a range of genealogical compilations available, such as those prepared by the Clare Heritage Centre, which are useful in relation to the question of convict origins. County-based studies need to be done for the entire transportation period in order to establish the broad context of offences. Work of this kind can provide a warp of the past, but we also need the weft in the form of year-by-year studies for the entire country, an approach which Brendan MacGiolla Choille[28] has usefully adopted in an unpublished compilation of all convict and other official records for 1836, the first year for which we have really comprehensive documentary evidence at the Irish end. Needless to say, this is a vast enterprise calculated to daunt the solitary historian, but in these times of co-operative scholarly endeavour (reflected in the collective authorship of *Australians*) it is surely possible to design and obtain support for a long-term project involving established academics and postgraduate students from Ireland and Australia. And it would be appropriate for the first fruits of such a project to appear in 1991, the bicentennial of the first transportation of Irish convicts from Cobh to New South Wales.

The other big question of Irish-Australian history, "who were the free immigrants?", is similarly misleading in its simplicity. Again, we have to periodise in order to make any real sense of it. Until the 1830s, most Irish free immigrants were the wives and children of convicts or ex-convicts brought out by government or at the cost of the men themselves. The period from the 1840s until the 1880s was the heyday of the assisted schemes, although the gold-rushes in eastern Australia in the 1850s accelerated the process by encouraging people who could pay their own way.

Generalisations about the pattern of Irish settlement in Australia, which was far more dispersed and agricultural than it was in the United States, have depended on a number of propositions put forward by Oliver MacDonagh[29] and David Fitzpatrick:[30] that immigration to Australia was better regulated; that Irish immigrants were mostly people whose economic and social status was threatened by change—principally the reduction of tillage; and that they possessed sufficient capital to enable some mobility and choice of employment in Australia.

The implications of the last two propositions are quite important but as yet they have not been quantified in any way and are as impressionistic as the statements made about the Irish convicts. If the pattern of wide geographical and occupational distribution is to be properly explained, we will need to know much more about free immigrant origins.

Migration statistics are available although they probably understate population movement. Nor do they tell us who the people were and we are still at the basic stage of making listings of those recorded as arriving in the Australian colonies. Richard Reid has made a computerised listing based on shipping records for New South Wales from 1848 to 1870, but this is just the tip of the iceberg. With those names, however, it may be possible to investigate the economic and social background of many individuals and thus to test the suggestions offered by McDonagh and Fitzpatrick.

We know that the Irish in Australia were not as confidently self-conscious and assertive as they were in the United States, perhaps reflecting the fact that they were almost invariably a thinly-spread minority. But can we conclude that they were, as Fitzpatrick puts it, merely "a soluble ingredient in some bland white sauce that became the Australian people"?[31] More knowledge of their economic and social background can help to answer this question.

I recognise that I have been saying more about the origins of the Australian-Irish than about their actual experience in the antipodes. But if we are to write confidently about them, we simply have to know as much as possible about their place in the society which formed their childhood and early adult experience. And we must recognise that that society over the course of a hundred years offered a wide diversity of experience which could legitimately come under the rubric of "Irishness."

Referring as we do to "emigrant experience," we can easily put on two sets of blinkers. The people who emigrated from Ireland to Australia came from the same socio-political system, but their experience of it varied from the career of General Joseph Holt,[32] exiled for his role in the 1798 rebellion, to that of George Fletcher Moore,[33] the Magee College and Trinity graduate who became Advocate-General and gentleman farmer at Swan River colony. Both were Irish Protestants, and yet their Irish backgrounds and their experiences in the Australian colonies were diverse in the extreme.

It is the subtle interplay between Irish *origins* and
Australian *experience* which offers the greatest challenge to
historians. To take one important example, the Irish in
Australia strongly supported the Home Rule movement but
proved luke-warm to republicanism and indifferent to the
movement for reunification after 1922. One explanation
could present this in terms of *origins*—that most of the Irish-
born in Australia in the late nineteenth century had left at a
time when Home Rule agitation was at its height. For them,
it might be argued, Ireland stood still. On the other hand,
their *experience* in isolated Australia whose economy and
security were so closely dependent on Britain may have
suggested to them that independence would be contrary to
Ireland's real interests. Irish nationalism may have given
Australian nationalism a nudge, but in the process it lost its
own momentum. Australia demonstrated very few signs of
republican sentiment and maintained a colonial attitude
towards Britain until relatively recent times. Australian
nationalism was reconcilable with Imperial loyalty, as Australia's enthusiastic entry into World War One demonstrated.
Much has been made of Archbishop Mannix's opposition to
the war and to conscription, but it would be interesting to
find out the Irish-descended component of those who volun-
teered for the first Australian Imperial Force. I suspect that it
was very high.

Denis O'Hearn has offered the alternative suggestion that
imperial sentiment remained strong in Australia largely as a
response to fears of Irish-Catholic dominance. "I see the
relationship of Australia to Britain and its persistent colonial
status," he writes, "as inextricably interwoven with a certain
fear of the presence and activities of the Irish Catholic
minority group. . . ."[34] He also believes that it was their
hatred of Australia's continued colonial stance this century
that led so many Irish Catholics to join the Communist Party
and to lead trade union movements. However, this has to be
reconciled with his more convincing claim that "for most of
this century Australia has been a shame culture and . . . the
Irish Catholic sub-group within Australia has most promi-

nently displayed the worst aspects of this shame culture."[35] Sectarian antagonism was revived for a time by the conscription crisis of 1916–17, but the pressure to conform and the desire for respectability by socially-mobile Irish-Australians were powerful forces for assimilation.

Apart from Stephen Alomes and Chris McConville,[36] no one has looked at the way in which class-consciousness and membership of the labour movement affected the Irishness of those Irish-Australians who were not so socially mobile. Irish ethnicity and the support of the Catholic Church were important cohesive factors within that movement, illustrating Max Weber's belief that ethnicity exists in direct relationship to its usefulness as a mechanism of group formation[37] and mobilisation.

Rather than the traditional focus on the "Irish contribution" to an Australian national or nationalist genealogy, future research might well follow the lead given by Waldersee, MacDonagh, Lyons[38] and McConville[39] at a regional or local level. It makes sense to examine the Irish in a particular context in the light of such questions as demographic distribution, economic rôle, social status and mobility, political consciousness and retention of ethnicity. The other obvious dimension, of course, is biography where we already have important works on Gavan Duffy,[40] Archbishop Mannix,[41] H.B. Higgins[42] and most recently Archbishop Duhig.[43] Perhaps we can look forward to reading about some of the lesser lights: those whose lack of conventional success can possibly tell us more about the emigrant experience. Patrick O'Farrell has opened a fascinating window on Protestant emigrants in his *Letters from Irish Australia* and it can only be hoped that more material of this kind will come to light.

O'Farrell's work has provided an enormous boost to the study of Irish-Australia and there are many who will be conscious of labouring in his workshop. They will find some interesting and significant things there without needing to claim that the Irish provide the philosopher's stone of Australian history. While the Irish in Australia were a force for change, they themselves changed in the process from being

Australian-Irish to Irish-Australians, a distinction which may sound equivocal or metaphysical, but which I believe expresses an important truth. Transplanted in a new environment in which their labour value and their social ambition largely triumphed over ancient prejudice, the Irish in Australia became something different. Economic success and social mobility were possible; political influence was within reach; the old preoccupations of Ireland were not so relevant. Irish nature was subjected to Australian nurture.

References

1. See Colm Kiernan (ed.), *Australia and Ireland 1788–1988: Bicentenary Essays* (Dublin, 1986).

2. J.F. Hogan, *The Irish in Australia* (Melbourne, 1887).

3. P.S. Cleary, *Australia's Debt to the Irish Nation Builders* (Sydney, 1933).

4. Patrick O'Farrell, "Writing the History of Irish-Australia," in Oliver MacDonagh and W.F. Mandle (ed.), *Ireland and Irish-Australia:* (London, 1986), p. 221.

5. P. Moran, *A History of the Roman Catholic Church in Australasia* (Sydney, 1894).

6. Cited by Patrick O'Farrell, *The Irish in Australia* (Sydney, 1987), p. 52.

7. ibid.

8. ibid., pp. 247–8.

9. C.M.H. Clark, *A History of Australia . . .*, vol. 1 (Melbourne, 1962).

10. Cited by G.C. Boltoan, "The Irish in Australian Historiography," in Kiernan, *Australia and Ireland.*, p. 17.

11. C.H. Currey, *The Irish at Eureka* (Sydney, 1954).

12. Cited by Max Brown, *Australian Son: A Life of Ned Kelly* (2nd ed. Melbourne, 1956) p. 281.

13. O'Farrell, *The Irish in Australia*, p. 10.

14. ibid.

15. ibid.

16. ibid., pp. 10–11.

17. O'Farrell, "Writing the History of Irish-Australia." p.222.

18. R. Ward, *The Australian Legend* (Sydney, 1958).

19. R. White, *Inventing Australia: Images and Identity 1788–1980* (Sydney, 1981)

20. P. O'Farrell, *The Catholic Church and Community: An Australian History* (Revised edition, Sydney, 1985).

21. I.J. Kiernan, *The Irish Exiles in Australia* (Melbourne, 1954)

22. P.A. Smith, *Heart of Exile* (Melbourne, 1986).

23. R. Hughes, *The Fatal Shore* (London, 1987).

24. L.L. Robson, *The Convict Settlers of Australia*. . . (Melbourne, 1965); J. Waldersee, *Catholic Society in New South Wales 1788–1860* (Sydney, 1974).

25. ibid., pp. 157–8.

26. George Rudé, *Protest and Punishment: The Story of the Social and Political Protesters transported to Australia 1788–1868* (Oxford, 1978).

27. The microfiche copying of these records by the Irish government as a Bicentennial gift to Australia will certainly encourage and facilitate this work.

28. Former Keeper of the Archives, Dublin Castle.

29. Oliver MacDonagh, "The Irish in Australia: A General View," in MacDonagh and Mandle, *Ireland and Irish Australia*, pp. 155–174.

30. David Fitzpatrick, "The Irish Immigrants in Australia: Patterns of Settlement and Paths of Mobility," in *Australia 1888*, Bulletin no. 2 (August 1979).

31. David Fitzpatrick, "Irish Immigration to Australia 1840–1914" (forthcoming in the *Encyclopedia of the Australian People*.

32. Clifton Croker (ed.), *Memoirs of Joseph Holt* (2 vols., London, 1838).

33. George Fletcher Moore, *Diary of Ten Years of an Early Settler in Western Australia* (London, 1884).

34. Denis O'Hearn, "Freedom from Mother Church: The Stephen Hero Image in Australian Literature," in Kiernan, *Australia and Ireland*, p.25.

35. ibid., p. 28.

36. Stephen Alomes, "Culture, Ethnicity and Class in Australia's Dominion Period, 1909–39," in Kiernan, *Australia and Ireland.*, pp. 182–193; Chris McConville, "Emigrant Irish and Suburban Catholic: Faith and Nation in Melbourne and Sydney, 1851–1933" (Ph.D. thesis, University of Melbourne, 1984).

37. Max Weber, *Economy and Society* . . . (2 vols., Berkeley, 1968), i, pp. 385–398.

38. Mark Lyons, "Aspects of Sectarianism in New South Wales, Circa 1865 to 1880" (Ph.D. thesis, Australian National University, 1972).

39. C. McConville, "Catholics and Mobility in Melbourne and Sydney, 1861–1891," in *Australia 1888*, bulletin no. 2 (August 1979).
40. Cyril Pearl, *The Three Lives of Gavan Duffy* (Sydney, 1979).
41. Niall Brennan, *Dr Mannix* (Adelaide, 1964).
42. John Rickard, *H.B. Higgins: The Rebel as Judge* (Sydney, 1984).
43. T.P. Boland, *James Duhig*, (Brisbane, 1986).

11.

A History of the Australian
Bi-Centennial History Project

OLIVER MACDONAGH

This article barely touches, I fear, the grand theme of the
present volume. True, it is, to some small degree, about an
emigrant—myself. But trying to set up an Australian national
history project is a rather rare, not to say rarified, form of the
immigrant experience.

There is, besides, an Irish-Australian connection in this
story. As we shall see, it was the *New History of Ireland* which
provided the original model for the Bicentennial History
project; and to a certain extent the lineaments of this model
still show through in the final Australian undertaking.

Australians: a historical library (as the Bicentennial History
Project came ultimately to be called) devotes much space
and consideration to the immigrant experience: otherwise,
why mark 1788, or how trace the history of the next two
centuries? In fact, perhaps the most important single theme
in the final volume, *Australians from 1939*, is the revolutionary impact of the multicultural post-war inflow upon an
almost uniformly Anglo-Celtic white settlement. Nonetheless,
immigration is rarely addressed specifically or directly in our
Project. It is the tapestry against which the studies are com-
posed rather than studied in its own right—or more precisely
perhaps, it is woven into the cloth rather than picked out as
its pattern. Let me try to illustrate this point by a single
instance. *The encyclopedia of the Australian people*, another
major, though much smaller, bi-centennial project, centred
in our Research School of Social Sciences in Canberra, is

primarily concerned with ethnic groupings and origins, and therefore with the disparate immigrations. Now whereas, for example, the *Encyclopedia* speaks in general terms of English craft unionism as part of the baggage of the English newcomer, the History Project would describe an individual English artisan transferring and transmuting his English industrial experience in an Australian environment, at a specific time and place, and with special palpable results.

I suppose I should ask indulgence for an article which is really little more than a story told, and which is rooted, in part, in my own involvement in the enterprise. But an elemental form of historiography—even, despite appearances, of the historiography in the project—is narration; and to ground an historical account in individual experience fits, after all, the basic pattern and guiding genius of *Australians: a historical library*.

To begin this account, then, with myself, I took over the Headship of the Department of History at the Research School of Social Sciences at the Australian National University in 1976. My first task seemed to be to find some major undertaking which our Department—as the only "national" Department in Australia, and the only Department primarily devoted to research—could promote and nurture. Our existing offspring, or at least stepchild, the *Australian Dictionary of Biography*, already well into its second decade of distinguished work, offered an encouraging precedent.

The 1970s as well as the 1980s were an epoch of centenaries in Australia, and I had come fresh from serving on the executive committee of the *New History of Ireland*. Indeed, throughout 1976 I was feverishly completing my own contributions to the *New History*. Given this combination of circumstances, it is not surprising that my first idea for the Department should have been an Australian equivalent to the *New History*, to be published in 1988 to mark the bicentenary of the European settlement of that continent.

Even my small experience of the New History of Ireland suggested to me, first, that even a decade's preparation would not be too long for any similar venture; secondly, that some mechanisms for eliminating laggard authors and replacing them in time would have to be devised and enforced; thirdly, that a considerable annual budget ($100,000 per annum for ten years was the figure plucked from the air) was indispensable; and fourthly, that the auxiliary volumes—the references section—would form a more important element in an Australian than in an Irish scheme, because of the relative paucity, then, of source work in Australian history, and the relatively short period of time which would be covered by the history proper. Specifically, the initial sketch plan was for eight volumes in all, four covering Australian history between 1788 and, say, 1970, with four auxiliaries, a chronology, an historical atlas, a bibliography and a collection of historical statistics. In form, this first back-of-an-envelope scribble came remarkably close to the final outcome. But in substance the Project was soon to change profoundly in several ways.

At this point I discovered that some sort of commemorative history for the bi-centenary had been mooted earlier at the A.N.U. by John Molony, but without evoking much response. None the less, we tried again and on 8 october 1976 half a dozen of the senior historians at the university met to consider the new proposal. The crucial happening of this meeting—for the absence of a decision to smother the infant at birth can scarcely be termed a happening—was Ken Inglis's proposal that, instead of four narrative volumes, the histories should be four "slices" of particular years, 1788, 1838, 1888 and 1938. The project was not to be an attempted summation of current scholarship but a revolutionary type of historiography. I have a lifetime of academic meetings to remember, but this was the only occasion that I can recall when a daring, original idea was accepted with excited acclamation within thirty seconds of its being set out.

The crucial problem, as it seemed at this initial meeting, was to prevent the Project being, or even being seen as, an exclusively A.N.U. undertaking. We wished to be truly national. We feared that the state universities might resent our taking so bold and universal an initiative. But in the end we bit the bullet, and decided that while the editorial work should be devolved and distributed as widely as possible among the states, and while we should try to entice contributions from every part of Australia, the Research School would have to remain the controller of, and headquarters for, the Project—"with," as the minutes of that first meeting ran, "all the odium but also all the advantages which this would involve." Perhaps I might add here the final item of those minutes (which I wrote myself): "It was accepted that the author of these notes was, in effect, the pin in the grenade, to be discarded shortly before explosion."[1] For good or ill, I failed to carry this point later, and became instead the Chairman of the Management Committee.

There followed some eighteen months of wooing the historical profession, stumping the country for support, attempting to appease opponents and counter critics, and lobbying the federal government for grants. To deal with the last first, despite years of soliciting and the painful preparation of an untold number of financial estimates and submissions, we never secured a penny from any state or federal department. The basic difficulty was not ill-will or scepticism about the value of the Project but simply that government ministers and bureaucrats think, at most, two or three years ahead, and our time-span fitted no official budget. Had we begun in 1984 or 1985 there is no doubt whatever—in my mind at least—that we would have received the government million which we had counted on originally. But if we had begun in 1984 or 1985 there would have been no Project ready in time for the bi-centenary, or perhaps even in the present century!

It also seemed at first as if we had been over-sanguine in expecting even substantial support and commitment from the Australian historical profession. True, our initial step— inviting, in February 1977, the head of every History Department in the country to Canberra in order to consider and (they and God willing!) endorse the Project—was smoothly taken. The atmosphere was genial; and at least one *bon mot* emerged. Someone asked what the feminine for Young Turk was and was answered "Turkish Delight." The scheme itself was warmly approved, as well as usefully elaborated, and the body turned itself into an Interim Management Committee.

But the appearance of enthusiastic unanimity was deceptive. One or two of the Departmental heads sang very different tunes when they returned to their constituents— not unlike nineteenth century Irish M.P.s when they had left behind the blandishments of London and Westminster and faced the public in Clare or Mayo. In one or two other cases, Departments soon made it clear that *they* by no means agreed with their respective heads. There were besides protests from particular interests, such as women's history, against their having no voice, and perhaps no sympathisers, in the Interim Management Committee. Marxist, Foucaultist and other radical historians considered the project vitiated by the likely predominance of liberal pragmatists—mindless empiricists was the phrase then in vogue. Again, how *could* the Project avoid being celebratory, and what was there to celebrate in the establishment of a penal settlement and the destruction of an indigenous culture?

There was, moreover, a powerful school of "senior" and conservative criticism. The very senior historians had already been excluded—not greatly to their satisfaction—by one of the very first decisions which we took, namely to recruit no one as contributor who had already passed the age of fifty-five. But even some less venerable seniors decried the Project as monopolistic—one deploring it as "the sole scholarly focus of an enormous investment, both of professional energy and government money." It was also decried as eccentric or idiosyncratic in concentrating on arbitrarily selected segments of time at the expense of the historian's proper procedures, which were, of course, according to the canon, the use of the narrative method and a linear time perspective. Finally, even some who wished us well thought the dream of harnessing teams of historians to work to the same end by absolutely immutable dates was madness.

Although very painful at the time, this gallimaufry of opposition, misunderstanding, wrong-headedness, right-head-ness, penetrating and obtuse criticism proved of the utmost value in the end. Late in 1977 Ken Inglis returned to Canberra from a tour of most of the state universities quite daunted, and even dismayed, by the various receptions which our scheme had met. But in fact several of the most doubting Thomases turned out to be crucial supporters of the Project later on. We were fortunate to have been baptised by fire. We were also fortunate to have been taught salutary lessons in time. More precisely, the scepticism, questioning and hostility focused our attention on points already mooted but in danger of being lost to sight in the multitude of early considerations.

First, the testing of the waters brought home to us the necessity—in Australia, at any rate—of a much more democratic structure and procedure than was customary in large-scale historical undertakings, up to that time. The volumes—and especially the slice volumes, now termed Section A—would have to grow from below rather than be imposed from above. This meant that, within the general, overarching principles of the operation, there might be considerable variety of emphasis and very different forms of teamwork.

Later on, I shall discuss this heterogeneity. But let me give a single example of unanticipated developments immediately. The 1838 volume of the *Australians* was in effect, bid for, some time on, by two young historians then in Perth, Alan Atkinson and Marian Aveling: their bid was eventually successful. They had been excited by the prospect which Ken Inglis had opened up when he took in Western Australia during his 1977 tour; they felt that it offered much hope for the sort of history which appealed to their generation. They were deeply interested in the possibilities of a new "history from below," fervently anti-authoritarian by instinct, and much attracted by collective forms of work. In fact, they set up an 1838 collective in 1980, open to everyone who contributed anything to the journal for 1838 studies which they had established, with the wryly pointed title, *Push from the Bush*. This ethos and this *modus operandi* were maintained throughout the composition of the 1838 book, with much consultation, exchange of drafts, conferences and co-operative writing. Most of the chapters ended up with several authors, one with no fewer than eight contributors, all loyal to the collective's initial resolution (I quote from the volume's introduction) "to present the minds of people living in Australia in 1838 as far as possible from inside, by recounting the language and behaviour of day-to-day situations . . . going *beyond* the records of the elite so as to recreate the minds of the inarticulate and powerless."[2] I think that all its readers will agree that Atkinson and Aveling have succeeded brilliantly in their purpose.

The second major benefit of the douches of cold and tepid water with which we were showered in 1977 was that they confirmed the importance of devolving as much of the Project as possible to other universities throughout the country. This was not—could not have been—as much a matter of strategic planning as of seizing opportunities as they rose. And in fact the requisite opportunities appeared. The obvious centre for the 1838 volume, in its early years, was Perth. The ideal editors for the 1888 volume emerged in Melbourne, and for the 1938 volume in Adelaide and Sydney. The most important devolution of all was the appointment of Frank Crowley as general editor of the whole series of auxiliary volumes, now termed Section B. Not only did this create another headquarters (or at least sub-quarters) in Sydney but also it meant that Crowley's university, New South Wales, would henceforth support the Project financially, on a very considerable scale. Of course, this successful dispersion of the undertaking owed much to luck; but I should like to think that the Founding Fathers of Canberra did something to help luck along, or at least that they recognised her when they met her in the street.

Thus we were democratised and judiciously scattered about the continent long before anyone had put pen to paper. But I should also make it clear that three centralising and controlling elements were retained: not for nothing had I served, however humbly, on the *New History of Ireland*. First, the ultimate authority, the Management Committee, remained substantially in the hands of our History Department in

Canberra: the Head of Department was chairman *ex officio*. Secondly, we set absolute deadlines, not only for completion but also for each major stage in the production: we were, in one sense (though only one!), fortunate in having a ready-made date by which, come hell or highwater, the books would have to appear before the public. And thirdly, we decided to use the various production stages as tests for the punctuality of our contributors and to eliminate all who failed to produce whatever was required by the specified time, and to search for replacements as soon as the malingerers (however eminent) were identified and disposed of. I cannot claim that we quite lived up to this stern resolution, but we certainly went a fair way down the audacious path.

On 28 March 1978 the Interim Committee wound itself up, and the Management Committee proper took its place. By now, general editors—Inglis and Crowley—had been appointed for sections A and B, respectively, as well as convenors (who were really proto-editors) for the 1788, 1838, 1888 and 1938 volumes. Besides, the A.N.U. had appointed a special Assistant General Editor for Section A, and the U.N.S.W. a similar officer for Section B: these were full-time appointments, essentially managerial and executive in design. In fact, the appointee for Section A, Stephen Foster, became such a vital component in the entire undertaking that he ended as Executive Editor for the whole series, as well as an Editor in his own right for two of the Section B volumes.

All these people, with some later additions, constituted a newly formed Editorial Board, which would govern the content, style and method of the books independently. Meanwhile between 1976 and 1978 a fifth volume (*Australians from 1939*) had been added to Section A, and that was still—and long to remain—in an indeterminate state; and although the Atlas and the Sources and Statistics volumes had been confirmed in Section B, its fourth volume (rather vaguely termed the *Handbook* for the time being) was also an uncertain venture. Final decisions on editors, contributors and all else were due to be made by 1981, but in the interim

the working parties for each volume would be laying the
foundations with an eye to completions by 1985 and 1986.

In short, we had hit ourselves over the head with a bottle
of champagne, glided down the slipway, and recruited many
of the artificers who would labour in the still-empty hull.

I suppose that historians are, almost by occupation, bad
prophets. We sit, so to speak, with our backs to the engine.
We certainly read the future wrongly, in several respects,
when we committed ourselves finally to the Project in 1978.
Let me select, and expand on, three major examples. First,
we believed that almost all our problems of composition
would arise in Section A, already a well-fought-over battle-
ground, and that Section B would prove comparatively plain
sailing. In fact, the opposite was the case, although in such
an inter-locked and complex undertaking, there could be no
plain sailing anywhere. In our innocence (or ignorance) we
assumed that the reference volumes would be straight-
forward—essentially comprehensive compilations by experts
dealing in their own area of expertise. Instead they provided
our chief difficulties. In this there were some accidental and
personal factors at play. But the major cause of trouble was
that we had grossly underestimated the costs, labours and
technical requirements of such books.

The *Atlas* was to illustrate this best—or rather, worst—of
all. There was no precedent for a work of this scale, ambition
or quality in Australia, perhaps no real counterpart anywhere
in the world. It was impossible to get the timing of the stages
right. With a final, final deadline of April 1986 for going to
press, the closing months of 1985 and opening months of
1986 constituted the Project's nightmare zone. At one stage
we had to employ fifteen cartographers to rush through the
last work on the maps, as well as call on many of the
contributors to the other volumes (Section A as well as
Section B) to make supreme sacrifices. It was they who had
to get the text, captioning and illustrations completed before
the guillotine—in the form of the printer's ultimatum—
descended, and all our heads rolled. This alone confirmed

the wisdom of still centring the Project, despite all the devolutions, in our own Research School. The necessary people were there to volunteer or be shanghaied—for weeks it was unsafe to walk along our corridor lest a hand stick out and haul one into a composing room—and the necessary credits could be wrung from our School's administration during those last horrific weeks when money just had to be spent like water.

Of course the needs of the *Atlas* created problems for the other volumes in Section B. Its crises were transferred successively to the next books on the line, and each of these, and particularly bibliographical and statistical works, had technical difficulties of its own. On the other hand, there were unconvenanted mercies. The Division of National Mapping, a federal government agency, was an enthusiastic supporter of the *Atlas* from the start. One of our editors has estimated that the agency provided about $1m. worth of assistance, free, over the seven years of production. $1m. was our original estimate for the entire Project, and we had not dreamt, at the outset, that any such help might be proferred. Again, the *Handbook* was eventually dismembered into an Historical Dictionary and a Chronology-cum-Gazetteer. The Gazetteer has proved a splendid, unanticipated ornament in the collection. I think that Section B has ended, in total, in a triumph. But it was certainly a triumph against endless adversities, most of them deriving from our own deplorable failure to comprehend initially what its production would mean—and cost.

Our second great failure of prediction was of course our counting upon public funding. At first, we lived from hand to mouth, for the day when the Australian Bicentennial authority would be constituted. When the Authority was at last set up in 1980, we lived for the day when it would receive federal monies for distribution. Then we lived for the day when the authority would determine its support policies and its criteria for patronage. Then we simply ran out of days. Meanwhile, the long suffering and nobly generous universities, in particular the A.N.U. and University of New South

Wales, kept us alive from year to year, diverting to us scraps of savings and pieces of unfilled posts until—and indeed long after—we received the cash transfusion from our publishers.

The publishers of the Project can be termed our third major misforecast. Publication had been discussed in a more or less desultory way even before the Management Committee was established. But it was not seen as an urgent matter to arrange. A minute of 28 March 1978 runs: "It was agreed that no decision need made yet about a publisher or publishers, but that the Management Committee would need to act by 1981." As this foolishly complacent note suggests, we did not envisage major difficulties in finding a victim or band of victims. But when in 1980 we invited tenders and received submissions, it became clear that the scale, technical sophistication, unknown market prospects and concentrated publication programme daunted most Australian publishers.

At this point, another of those strange, almost providential interventions which blessed the Project happened. Accidentally, Inglis encountered Kevin Weldon, an entrepreneur who published high quality books for the mass market. Weldon was immediately seized by the idea of our national scheme. Although much time was to elapse and many vicissitudes were still to be undergone, and though at least one regular publisher would probably have offered us a contract and the Australian university presses would probably have combined to publish the volumes in the last resort, Weldon's interest proved the turning-point. He was eventually to bring together a consortium consisting of his own publishing house, the Melbourne *Age* or Syme Group and the *Sydney Morning Herald* or Fairfax Group with the object of publishing *Australians: a historical library*. At that time the Syme and Fairfax Groups, between them, controlled some 70 per cent of all the media interests in Australia. We were about to enter the Big League, and certainly a very different league from that which we had originally contemplated.

I shall pass quickly over the protracted courtship and early lovers' quarrels between the Project and F.S.W., as the new conglomerate of Fairfax, Syme and Weldon came to be known. In 1982, the contract between us was finally signed and we were a married couple—at least in the sense in which Stevenson defined marriage, as a sort of friendship recognised by the police.

The Project had been originally expected to emerge as a sombre conventional type of multi-volume academic publication, such as the *Oxford History of England* or the *Cambridge History of Modern Europe*. It is true that we had hoped, from the beginning, to write for a more general public than such series were aimed at. It was also true that—partly for this reason and partly because the book of the future would (we thought) contain much more than the printed word—we intended that the volumes should be (I quote again from early minutes) "richly illustrated." But with F.S.W. as publishers each of these features was to explode outwards, alarmingly.

The publishers insisted upon direct selling of complete sets, at least initially, and spoke in terms of immense projected sales—20,000 sets was regarded as quite a conservative target. Heavy advertising, at selected stages of production, was implicit in such a strategy. Correspondingly, it became imperative that the volumes should be written in plain (which is far from meaning inelegant) English, and as free as practicable from the argot and jargon of the various disciplines which the Project would embrace. Later, Alan Gilbert, who joined Inglis as General Editor of Section A late in 1981, made this a special study. Drawing particularly upon American syntactical and grammatical research, he prepared a paper of great interest and importance for contributors, setting out principles and strategies of writing for a very wide and various audience. Effective presentation was another corollary of aiming at a mass market. It quickly became clear that F.S.W. contemplated illustration upon a scale, and of a degree of sophistication, far beyond what we had had originally in mind. Our volumes have ended up with some 3,000 illustrations, nearly half of them in colour: the ratio of illustration to text is roughly 1:3. Moreover, illustration was not treated as mere decoration. It was carefully interwoven with text wherever possible. These changes of emphasis added enormously to our load. In the case of illustrations, for example, a choice had to be made from many thousands of pictures and images; provenances had to be established; and the copyright of each item chosen had to be checked and cleared. The sum of man and woman hours involved in this alone was staggering.

A second unexpected consequence of choosing F.S.W. as our publishers—or should I say, of being chosen by them?—was financial and, to a lesser extent, technical salvation. As our crises succeeded one another, so did the lifelines which they threw to us in the form of advance royalties, until in the end these reached the immense total of some half a million dollars. Similarly, they set up editorial and design systems from the start, so that from 1982 on we were not working *in vacuo* but in continuous communication with our client or customer, so to speak. I must not give a Cheeryble Brothers impression of the relationship. Far from it—each additional advance of royalties had to be pleaded or struggled for, and no matter how much we received, we always needed more. Our files bulge with acrimonious exchanges on deadlines, word counts, each other's organisational methods, the quality of the reproductions, the design of pages, listings, layout—I could go on and on. None the less, without F.S.W's incessant badgering and editorial expertise, the project simply *could* not have been completed, at any rate in time. In one sense, we owe them not merely half a million dollars, but everything!

The other side of the coin was of course the absolute commitments which dealings with a commercial enterprise, dedicated to profit-making, necessarily entailed. In the contract, F.S.W. laid down a series of deadlines for the receipt of final copy, which was geared to the successive publication of the volumes, in pairs, between November 1986 and December 1987. This meant completion dates running from early to late 1985. The penalties for failure to meet a deadline were horrific. The project would have to repay £50,000 for each volume not submitted on time, and lose all control of that volume, into the bargain. F.S.W. could argue that they in turn had unbreakable contracts with the printers, as well as grave legal obligations, under state law in Victoria and elsewhere, to the advance purchasers. They claimed, moreover, that their eventual investment in the Project would fall little short of $20m., for which they would have to account, in due course, to their shareholders.

However in spite of such difficulties, theirs was the commanding position. We had no choice but to submit to F.S.W.'s requirements. Like the prospect of being hanged, the ever-present thought of impending ruin concentrated our minds wonderfully. For the publishers left us in no doubt that they meant what they said, and would foreclose if need be. It was all a far cry from the leisurely common-room conversations and easy speculations of the early days. We were now in what its inhabitants like to term "the real world." The consequent, totally unexpected, discipline may well be seen, in retrospect, as useful. Perhaps it was even necessary. What cannot be disputed, non any count, is that it was extremely painful and protracted.

But, having once committed themselves, the consortium needed us as much as we needed them. Their publicity depended largely on our furnishing them with material, and we early established, though often failed to enforce, our right to veto advertising and other matter put out by them or by their agents. Here was another field of dispute, but one in which we held at least the moral advantage. By the time that these issues became pressing, in 1984 and 1985, the Project had grown very considerably in scale, partly because of our *modus operandi*, but partly also because of our publishers' pressures. It now embraced some four hundred academics, most of them historians, but also numbers of geographers, economists, political scientists, anthropologists, sociologists and demographers, as well as such specialists as librarians and archivists.

The increase in woundable susceptibilities and zealously held principles was *at least* proportionate to the increase in the number of persons at work upon the Project, and the

Management Committee had to mediate continually between our producers and our consumers, between our authors and the consortium. Hard sell or garish presentation in publicity, and braggart claims as to finality or universality, had of course to be steadily resisted. But the resistance was rendered a great deal more effective by the vision of the legions whom we so to say—very much so to say!—commanded. Our contributors (all of whom were, of course, unpaid) became the equivalent of the Fairfax and Syme shareholders when it came to making menacing noises at the joint meetings of our respective Management Committees.

Moreover, one of the attractions of the Project for F.S.W. had been the possible spin-offs—into videocassettes, into school texts or school programmes, into the supply of materials for exhibitions, into—perhaps—an Australian equivalent of the BBC's new Domesday Book. The contract had carefully covered such developments. Now although none had yet come to fruition—thank God, for the production of *Australians: a historical library* was, and is, more than enough to cope with—the possibilities kept being canvassed. This too strengthened our hand *vis-à-vis* F.S.W. Any further venture depended more or less on our co-operation. At the very least, it would be very difficult to accomplish without our help; and in contract we had reserved the right to dissociate ourselves publicly from any derivative development with which we were dissatisfied. Again, all this did something to redress the balance in our relationship. Our fundamental aims were identical with those of F.S.W., and indeed in many instances we became warm friends. But in the crucial years, 1984–6, the sides were often, willy-nilly, in adversary positions, and it seemed important for our morale, and even at times our survival, that when we sat down at the table we should have some cards in our hands to play.

The very mention of the years 1984–6 recalls a host of desperate days, with which the publishers and our hoped-for public had nothing to do. For this was of course the time when the delinquents among our contributors and the gaps in our coverage, in Section A as well as Section B, were finally discovered or revealed, and successive rescue operations had to be mounted. Scarcely a week seemed to pass without some fresh emergency, and one emergency often triggered off another, as writers and research assistants had to be switched from one overdue task to another which was still farther behind. It is all much too recent and traumatic to detail now. Sufficient to say that, somehow or other, the project has managed to plug and patch, conscript and reinforce, more or less successfully, in the end. Not that it is all quite over yet. The processes and problems of production continue still. But at least we can begin a countdown on the number of crises still to come.

In the heady days in 1976 and 1977 we imagined that we would end in some immense thunderclap of achievement. Instead, we have seemed to dwindle gradually into annihilation. Exhaustion has overlaid and smothered jubilation.

> Too long a sacrifice
> Can make a stone of the heart.

In moments of lowness, one wonders, was it all worth while? Were those critics right who argued at the start that such a prodigious mustering and spending of intellectual resources was a mistaken, indeed a most wasteful strategy?

I can answer only for myself, and I may well be inclined to give a more favourable reply than most of the leading actors in the affair. My sufferings were unquestionably less than theirs. Money, contracts, disputes and decisions are bad enough. But writing and forcing others to write against the clock, year in year out, are agony. Doubtless, I lean too towards the Panglossian school of history. Who else but a Pangloss would have launched himself upon an unbounded venture?

But, seriously, there are, I think, many reasons for concluding that the game has after all been worth the candle; and I shall now offer you the five which seem to me most powerful.

First, in Section B, deep foundations have been laid for Australian historiography in general. In 1976 Australian history already possessed one fundamental resource of the highest quality, the *Australian Dictionary of Biography*. Perhaps no other national history is blessed with an aid comparable to the A.D.B. in either coverage or meticulous modern scholarship. But in no other respect could Australia then satisfactorily provide the infrastructure of historiography, so to speak. Virtually *de novo,* the Project has created a series of historical statistics, an historical gazetteer, a chronology, an atlas, a companion and a major guide to sources and bibliography. No one would pretend to perfection or finality for any of these volumes or part-volumes. But at least a solid basis has been laid over the entire range of reference works. Where else does such an array of tools lie ready—compact and interlocked—for the use of the historian, or indeed any other scholar or serious inquirer? Moreover, with the possible continuation of the bulletins first launched to facilitate the production of Section B of the project, systematic refinement, improvement and expansion may well be hoped for.

Secondly, the Project has, I believe, integrated Aboriginal with what we may loosely term European Australian history, as never before. The planned 1788 volume ended up as a *To 1788* volume, with four-fifths of its contents devoted to pre-European Australia. This brilliant survey of the Aboriginal era, itself a *tour de force,* is thoroughly knit into the doom of traditional Aboriginal life, as signalled by the arrival of the First Fleet in 1788. In addition—and of no less importance, I should say—each of the other volumes in Section A takes up other Aboriginal themes and interweaves them with the expansion of white Australia. Again, the historiographical map seems to have been changed significantly. Already, the old virtually automatic identification of Australian history with the settlements of the past two centuries looks *passé.* The Project itself has fiercely eschewed the celebratory note: 1988 is treated throughout as the anniversary of a revolutionary happening, not as the starting point of a neo-whig interpretation, or glorification, of a short stretch of time.

Thirdly, the Project has had a striking effect upon the historical profession in Australia. In fact, it is even arguable that it created this profession. During Inglis's tour of 1977, one shrewd historian observed that it was the Project which had brought it into existence. Never in his life before had he heard his colleagues speak of themselves as belonging to a corporate body.

Rather grandiloquently perhaps, we had at the outset described the series as the gift of the historical profession to the Australian nation. More deeply and seriously, however, the Project has, in fact, forced a multitude of Australian historians into collective activity and co-operative interaction upon a hitherto undreamt-of scale. There were working parties of up to thirty people on particular volumes and constant traffic between one volume and another: commonly, the interchanges proceeded for several years. Paradoxically, the inevitable—indeed desirable—differences in historical presuppositions and general philosophy had—all in all—a centripetal rather than a centrifugal effect upon the participants. The *esprit de corps* growing out of common commitment tended (if I may be permitted an Australian bull) to bring a corps itself into being, over time. Moreover, by a further paradox, the historians themselves have been not only enriched but also stung into a greater self-awareness, by all the close and constant work with people from other disciplines which the Project practically enjoined. Among these disciplines, I would stress particularly geography and anthropology, as well as our formerly separated brethren, prehistory and economic history. In short, it seems to me that history in Australia has emerged from the experience immensely strengthened, structurally and intellectually alike.

Fourthly, the Project dragged at least those of us who needed to be dragged into the late twentieth century. In saying this, I refer, in part, to our technical education. It need scarcely be said that without such *old* "new technology" as the word processor and the disk, our task would have been impossible. But even developments which post-dated our beginning have proved vital. The fax machine, for instance, enabled us to maintain near-instant communication between Canberra and Sydney (the publishers' headquarters) during the final stages of production. Again, our colour and design requirements called for the newest processes. All this experience of modern publishing has filtered downwards. Even if only at second or third hand, our academics should have received useful glimpses of the future.

This is perhaps also true of some much more fundamental matters. As we have seen the Project's objective has been to reach a very wide and varied public without the sacrifice of any principle of scholarship. This high ambition did not stop at windy rhetoric and exhortation. Gilbert's work on words reached and—we trust—exercised some degree of influence, small or great, upon our hundreds of contributions. Correspondingly, the systematic collection of non-literary forms of evidence, and the sedulous attempt to render text and illustration mutually supporting and cross-reflective, have surely made an enduring impression on our trade.

Few words have been more overworked by historians during the past twenty years than "modernisation." But rarely, if ever, do we think of it in relation to ourselves. Yet the mechanics of composition, the economics of publishing and the potentiality of readership—not to add, listenership and spectatorship—have been changing rapidly and profoundly. I do not want to exaggerate the importance of the *forms* of communication. The substance of what is to be communicated is, and always will be, absolutely paramount. None the less, we should know what we are about in the times in which we write; and the project has proved a technical school, or forcing-house, for many of the rising as well as the declining generation of Australian historians. As they say, none of us, not even the youngest, is infallible.

The fifth, final and (to my mind) most important reverberations of the Project will, I believe, follow from the slice approach adopted in Section A. The exclusive study of a single year is not of course without precedent. At least one distinguished book is based upon this method, and the *New History of Ireland* itself employs it. But never has it been attempted on such a scale, or by such large numbers of historians, or with such single-minded rigour. I think that one can fairly claim that, as deployed in *Australians: a historical library*, it is a truly revolutionary device. The traditional models of collaborative national history were deliberately rejected. As Ken Inglis explained his proposal in 1977:

> It seemed to us that to follow any of those models would be merely to elaborate our present understandings of the past. . . . Instead of inviting a team of writers to divide up history into chronological sectors and have each fill in a stage of it in his or her own way, we thought of having a series of groups each working together at a very short period; instead of the traditional relay-race along well worn tracks, a series of survey camps; instead of a continuous thread of narrative, we imagined drilling a number of bores or (to avoid the painful senses of that word) cutting a number of slices. [3]

Inglis's stress upon collective work should be noted carefully for this was probably the most distinctive characteristic of the particular slice approach selected for the project.

Each volume group interpreted its task, and dealt with its cross-sectional layer, in a different fashion. The final volume of Section A, *Australians from 1939*, was practically by definition barred from slicing its half-century assignment, although it was also to eschew conventional narrative structures. But all the other books took individual approaches. As one of the volume editors put it, "Gradually, each of the 'slice' groups developed a style and *esprit de corps* of its own." [4] The volume, *To 1788*, charged with 40,000 years of pre-white Australian history, could obviously not adhere to slicing proper. Even so, it was deeply influenced by the general method of Section A. In the final portion of the book, "Sydney in 1788" lent itself to and duly received an orthodox cross-sectional treatment. But what is really interesting is the manner in which much of the remainder of *To 1788* is shaped or coloured by the principle of slicing. Inglis, as General Editor of Section A, describes this development in these terms:

> The second section the editors thought of as a kind of slice, depicting Aboriginal life in an actual or metaphorical 1788, i.e. the eve of European settlement whenever that moment happened in different parts of the continent. This occupies

> the bulk of the book: 12 chapters, with authors using a variety of . . . devices to reconstruct Aboriginal societies as they were before the Europeans arrived.[5]

The 1838 volume was, as I have said, the most closely collaborative volume of all. Like coal mining, history from below lent itself to collective effort. The book has taken, as its introduction proclaims, "a critical stance towards the social values of the past," and tried to reconstruct the Australia of its particular year in terms of so-called ordinary events in the lives of so-called ordinary people, their weddings, church-going, funerals, groupings, legal and business dealings and the like. The very roll-call of titles of the middle chapters of 1838—Families, Work, Markets, Meetings, People Confined— is practically a manifesto of the history of the unsung and long-forgotten—men, women and children too.

The 1888 volume was *organised* upon more conventional lines, and subject to more authoritative editorial direction, than any of the others. The Chief Editors, Graeme Davison and John McCarty, both of Monash University in Melbourne, selected their own team of contributors and drove them systematically through exchanges of drafts and discussion meetings. Yet their interpretation of the slices was far from commonplace—at least, in the Anglo-Saxon or Anglo-Celtic tradition of historiography. Davison himself observes that the 1888 volume

> has been strongly influenced by the approach of the *Annales* school and insofar as we have a specific model it is perhaps the kind of fully-textured detailed portrait of environment, economy, society and politics that one finds in Fernand Braudel's *The Mediterranean and the Mediterranean World in the Age of Philip II*. We aim to portray, more fully than hitherto, the regional and social diversity of Australia in 1888 and the ways in which different environments and regional economies were mediated in family structures and class relations.[6]

Moreover, Davison and McCarty were bold in selecting chapter topics. These were often quite out of the ordinary; Distance, Death, Capitals and Energy are examples. In fact, the Energy chapter provides an excellent illustration of what the slice approach can yield. In conventional narrative historiography the emphasis would almost certainly be placed upon the extraordinary growth in the newer forms of energy, coal, oil and electricity, during the 1880s. This is the normal patterning of the narrative. But the slice view, across the entire spectrum and at a fixed point in time, shows that horsepower, in the ancient and literal sense, still easily predominated in the Australia of 1888; that the next most important source of energy was the oldest of all, human muscle; and that the rate of innovation varied widely from region to region and between the various sectors of the economy. Energy, in another sense, might well be taken as the emblem of this volume. One emerges—or at least I emerged—from reading it, dazzled by the new perspectives and tingling with intellectual excitement or liberation.

The 1938 volume took as its starting point the fact that the year itself was within the living memory of many Australians. One of the basic resources developed immediately by its editors was a collection of interviews with a sample of people who were growing up during the 1930s. In all, nearly 400 interviews were taped. In length they varied from forty-five minutes to nine hours; and they concentrated so far as practicable on the year to which the volume was dedicated. In a sense therefore it was *recollection* itself which was sliced in this particular exercise. The immediate value of the interviews in the composition of the book varied of course from topic to topic, and according to the author's inclination. But they have also a lasting value as a source, which quite transcends the specific purpose for which they were assembled. I suppose that the labours of the Irish Folklore Commission circa 1938 would provide an intriguing point of comparison. Our 1938 volume was also able to apply the slice precisely in its section entitled "Pioneers on Parade," which deals with the Australian sesquicentennial celebrations and anti-celebrations. In neither case did they constitute a dress rehearsal for 1988, but are rather two flies in amber fixed forever in their (please God) antique confrontation.

Even this lightning sketch should have made clear that the slice, as deployed in *Australians: a historical library*, is not a formula, not a new scholasticism, not an orthodoxy, not even a taking of sides in any great methodological debate. It does not assert that the slice is the only, or the best, or even an always practicable or an always desirable mode of composing history. It accepts that in Clio's, as well as a more transcendental, house, there are many mansions. It even refrains from throwing the occasional ideological brick—deliberately, at least—into any other dwelling. But, I would argue, the method has its own special value, which renders it the crown and glory of our Project. I know of no more eloquent or telling elaboration of this claim than that put forward by Graeme Davison in his paper, "Slicing Australian History." "In constructing his narrative," writes Davison,

> the historian has the immense advantage of hindsight: he selects those facts or events which appear to favour that known outcome and he ignores those which are irrelevant to it, whether or not they seemed important to contemporaries. By focussing upon an arbitrarily chosen moment of time the slice approach acts as a corrective to the inbuilt teleological bias of narrative history. It implies that we *temporarily* abstain from the search for "the most significant years, or the busiest or the epochal" and concentrate instead upon the routine, the ordinary and mundane. Instead of assigning significance to events in terms of a known outcome or *telos*, it gently subverts the "received notions of the rhythms or contours of Australian history." Instead of exalting the established heroes of Australian history, it aims to rescue the struggling selector, the suburban housewife, even perhaps the landboomer's clerk, from the "appalling condescension of posterity."[7]

But it would be quite out of kilter with the Project to end on too celebratory or even congratulatory a note. We have debts, and doubtless despair, delays and disputes in plenty, still to come. Moreover, even those of the contributors who would not despise Latin tags on principle would revolt against anything in the spirit of "*Exigent monumentum aere perennius*." Our authors tend to see the Project as a living thing, not a dead achievement, a seeding rather than a harvest cut and garnered. Nonetheless I, who have neither written nor edited a line in any of the volumes, may perhaps be allowed to boast on behalf of the many who spent years in this grinding work. Like it or not, they must suffer to point to *Australians: a historical library* and—like it or not, to apply to it another Latin tag, employing the same offensive term, "*Si monumentum queris, circumspice*'—which I most freely, and quite irresponsibly, translate as, "If you seek a testimony to the achievement of the Australian Bicentennial History Project of 1988, it is there."

References

1. "Bi-Centenary History aide-memoir, 8 October 1976," History Project Incorporated Archives, Australian National University.
2. Alan Atkinson and Marian Aveling (eds), *Australians: 1838* (Sydney, 1987), p.xvi.
3. K.S. Inglis, "Australia 1788–1988: a note on proposed approaches" in *Australian Historical Association Bulletin*, no.1 (1977), p.8.
4. Graeme Davison, "Slicing Australian history: reflections on the Bicentennial History Project" in *New Zealand Journal of History*, xvi, no. 1 (April 1982), p.8.
5. Seminar paper delivered in Canberra, 10 July 1986.
6. Davison, "Slicing," p.8.
7. ibid., pp 12–13.

Index